LOST PARADISES
AND THE
ETHICS OF RESEARCH
AND PUBLICATION

LOST PARADISES AND THE ETHICS OF RESEARCH AND PUBLICATION

Edited by
Francisco M. Salzano
A. Magdalena Hurtado

UNIVERSITY PRESS

2004

OXFORD
UNIVERSITY PRESS

Oxford   New York
Auckland   Bangkok   Buenos Aires   Cape Town   Chennai
Dar es Salaam   Delhi   Hong Kong   Istanbul   Karachi   Kolkata
Kuala Lumpur   Madrid   Melbourne   Mexico City   Mumbai   Nairobi
São Paulo   Shanghai   Taipei   Tokyo   Toronto

Library of Congress Cataloging-in-Publication Data
Lost paradises and the ethics of research and publication / edited by Francisco M. Salzano
and A. Magdalena Hurtado.
p.   cm.
Includes bibliographical references and index.
ISBN 0-19-515119-4
1. Anthropological ethics.   2. Yanomamo Indians—Crimes against.
3. Indians of South America—Health and hygiene—Brazil.   4. Neel, James V.
(James Van Gundia), 1915–2000.   5. Tierney, Patrick.   6. Chagnon, Napoleon A., 1938–
I. Salzano, Francisco M.   II. Hurtado, A. Magdalena.
GN33.6.L67 2003
174'.9309—dc21 2003043345

9 8 7 6 5 4 3 2 1

Printed in the United States of America
on acid-free paper

To the Amerindians, and their right for self-determination and biological and cultural survival

To those anthropologists and biomedical scientists who know the plight of indigenous peoples well, and who struggle to make a difference

PREFACE

"Bioethics," a term created by Van Rensselaer Potter in 1971, has been a source of increasing concern over the past three decades. The rights of the underprivileged or especially vulnerable persons, such as children, elders, ethnic minorities, or members of a specific gender, have been explicitly stated in a series of documents, issued by UNESCO and several other national and international agencies. An important aspect of this problem relates to the ethics of biomedical research in human populations, and particularly in those with distinct, preindustrial forms of subsistence. Biomedical investigators should strictly conform to these norms, therefore avoiding any harm to the groups they are going to study. But ethical principles are also applicable to other professionals, such as those who propose to describe the scientific findings to the lay public, as well as those responsible for the dissemination of these evaluations in the media.

These considerations, which may be perfectly obvious to most biological scientists, became the subject of scrutiny beginning in August of 2000, when an announcement was sent to a large number of scholars via the Internet describing Patrick Tierney's book *Darkness in El Dorado: How Scientists and Journalists Devastated the Amazon* (Norton, New York, 2000). The announcement included terrifying revelations about unethical behavior conducted by anthropologists and geneticists among the Yanomamö.

As the discussions both in favor of and against the charges made in the book became especially intense, we decided at the end of 2000 to organize this book. It is a joint effort by one Venezuelan, three Brazilian, and six U.S. authors to evaluate both general aspects of bioethics and the charges leveled by Tierney. The book is divided into four parts, totaling eleven chapters. We regret that its appearance is a consequence of this unfortunate event, but it was important for us to present our firm convictions about many of the questions under discussion.

In a work of this magnitude, it is almost impossible to perform the task without the help of many colleagues and friends. A special acknowledgment should be made to Inés Hurtado (who happens to be Magdalena's mother) for her insistence that a book considering Tierney's charges should be produced, since otherwise reactions to it would remain scattered in journals, on the Internet, and so forth. In addition, many people helped the authors with the elaboration of the individual chapters. A. M. Hurtado (chapters 1, 9, and 11) is especially thankful to Kim Hill for his generous contribution to lengthy discussions on the ethical implications of our numerous field research projects. A. M. Hurtado and F. M. Salzano are indebted to Kim Hill, Thomas Headland, Tony Oliver-Smith, and Stuart Plattner for their critical comments and edits of chapters 1 and 11. M. S. Lindee (chapter 2) thanks the editors, as well as Robert S. Cox, Robert Kohler, and Kenneth M. Weiss, for assistance and suggestions. F. M. Salzano (chapter 3) is grateful to Norio Takahashi and Nori Nakamura for information about the present status of the Radiation Effects Research Foundation of Hiroshima, Japan; they are, however, not responsible for any of the views he presented in this chapter. C. E. A. Coimbra Jr. and R. V. Santos (chapter 6) thank Nancy M. Flowers (Hunter College, CUNY) for translating their text from Portuguese. She also provided important comments that helped them to clarify some ideas. R. Hames and J. Kuzara (chapter 7) thank the editors for their useful comments and suggestions for revisions. A. M. Hurtado, I. Hurtado, and K. Hill (chapter 11) are greatly indebted to the Aché, Hiwi, Machiguenga, and Yora natives for sharing their feelings about how outsiders affect their communities and their suggestions about how relationships with outsiders could improved in the future. They are also grateful to Louise Lamphere for encouraging them to write about the ethics of anthropological research based on their experiences in native communities. Laci Krupahtz skillfully prepared the final manuscript.

We are also grateful to Kirk Jensen for helping us meet the objectives of our original book proposal, and to Jack Baker for putting together a very thorough index under considerable time pressure and under difficult field conditions.

Permission to reproduce previously published material was granted by *The New Criterion* (chapter 4), and by Kluwer Plenum (figure 9.1), Oxford University Press (figure 9.2), and Garland Press (figure 11.1).

Many agencies supported the work published in this book. They include the Programa de Apoio a Núcleos de Excelência (PRONEX, Brazil); Financiadora de Estudos e Projetos (FINEP, Brazil); Conselho Nacional de Desenvolvimento Científico e Tecnológico (CNPq, Brazil); Fundação de Amparo à Pesquisa do Estado do Rio Grande do Sul (FAPERGS, Brazil); Pró-Reitoria de Pesquisa, Universidade Federal do Rio Grande do Sul (PROPESQ, Brazil); Conselho Nacional de Desenvolvimento Científico e Tecnológico (CNPq, Brazil); Coordenação de Aperfeiçoamento de Pessoal de Nível Superior (CAPES, Brazil); Programa de Apoio à Pesquisa Estratégica em Saúde; Fundação Oswaldo Cruz (PAPES/FIOCRUZ, Brazil); MacArthur Foundation (USA); National Science Foundation (USA) (BNS576-11859; BSR910-1571; OPP-990590); Public Health Service Research Career Development Award (PHS, USA) K04DE028-05; National Institutes of Health (DE04115-02, 1R01TW005627-01; 5R01TW005627-02); National Science Foundation (BCS–0118016, BCS-8613186, BCS-9717692); the AVINA Foundation; the Fundación Moisés Bertoni; Wenner-Gren Foundation for Anthropological Research (USA); National Geographic Society (USA); General Research Fund, University of Kansas (USA) 3507, 4932; Biomedical Sciences Research Grants 4349, 4309, 4932.

CONTENTS

Part III Epidemiological Contexts

Part IV The Future

CONTRIBUTORS

Carlos E. A. Coimbra Jr.
Departamento de Endemias
  Samuel Pessoa
Escola Nacional de Saúde Pública
Fundação Oswaldo Cruz
Rua Leopoldo Bulhões 1480
Rio de Janeiro, RJ 21041-210,
  Brazil
carlos_coimbrajr@gbl.com.br

Paul R. Gross
University of Virginia
Charlottesville, VA, 22904
PRGHOME@aol.com

Raymond Hames
Department of Anthropology
University of Nebraska
Lincoln, NE 68588
rhames@unlserve.unl.edu

Kim Hill
Department of Anthropology
University of New Mexico
Albuquerque, NM 87131
kimhill@unm.edu

A. Magdalena Hurtado
Department of Anthropology
University of New Mexico
Albuquerque, NM 87131
amhurtad@unm.edu

Inés Hurtado
Department of Anthropology
University of New Mexico
Albuquerque, NM 87131
ihurtado@tampabay.rr.com

Jennifer Kuzara
Department of Anthropology
Emory University
Atlanta, GA 30322
jkuzuz@yahoo.com

M. Susan Lindee
Department of History and
  Sociology of Science
University of Pennsylvania
Suite 303 Logan Hall
Philadelphia, PA 19104
mlindee@sas.upenn.edu

Francisco M. Salzano
Departamento de Genética
Instituto de Biociências
Universidade Federal do Rio
  Grande do Sul
Caixa Postal 15053
91501-970 Porto Alegre, RS, Brazil
francisco.salzano@ufrgs.br

Ricardo Ventura Santos
Departamento de Antropologia
Museu Nacional
Universidade Federal do Rio de
  Janeiro
Quinta da Boa Vista s/n
Rio de Janeiro, RJ 20940-040,
  Brazil
santos@ensp.fiocruz.br

Part I

Lost Paradises

1

INTRODUCTION

A. Magdalena Hurtado & Francisco M. Salzano

On Trial

In August of 2000, two anthropology professors, Terence Turner (Cornell University) and Leslie Sponsel (University of Hawaii), sent an e-mail to Louise Lamphere, then the president of the American Anthropological Association, to warn anthropologists that a book by Patrick Tierney would soon cause an international scandal. The book, *Darkness in El Dorado: How Scientists and Journalists Devastated the Amazon* (Tierney 2000), examined, among other things, how anthropological and biomedical research by James V. Neel (University of Michigan), Napoleon Chagnon (University of California at Santa Barbara), and others recklessly contributed to the spread of infectious diseases and violence in Yanomamö villages from the 1960s to the 1990s. Turner and Sponsel had seen the galley proofs of the book and concluded correctly that "this nightmarish story—a dark anthropological heart of darkness. . .—will be seen by the public, as well as most anthropologists, as putting the whole discipline on trial."

With *Darkness in El Dorado*, anthropology lost its academic paradise. The book has indeed put the discipline on trial with its descriptions of preventable deaths in Yanomamö villages many years after the conquest of the Americas in 1492. These descriptions tell audiences throughout the world that outsiders have not done enough to ensure the protection of

3

native rights to health, particularly those outsiders who work most intensively with natives. Although anthropologists are well aware of the spread of infectious diseases and their effects on native peoples, they have failed to turn this knowledge into a collective good that can be used to improve health in native communities. This may be one of the reasons that natives throughout the Americas have become increasingly less willing to participate in anthropological research projects.

However, Tierney's objective was not to consider the institutional shortcomings that might be responsible for this outcome. Instead, his goal was to claim through scandalous assertions, rather than through careful epidemiological research, that anthropologists and biomedical scientists had caused deaths and suffering in Yanomamö communities. Excerpts on the front and back flaps of the book describe his intentions well: "[Patrick Tierney] demonstrates how . . . researchers, as well as journalists . . . echoed the trails of the Spanish and English explorers of five centuries ago as they sought the illusory city of El Dorado. . . . In painstaking detail, Tierney explores the hypocrisy, distortions, and humanitarian crimes committed in the name of research. . . ."

The debate over the veracity of *Darkness in El Dorado* is important to anthropology, to science, and to the accused (Bosh et al. 2001; Dalton 2000; Mann 2000, 2001; McCarthy 2000; Morton 2001; Olsson 2000). However, it should not be used to gloss over the message in the book that is most important to the Yanomamö and other natives. While we write and argue, the Yanomamö and many natives throughout South America continue to die from preventable causes and to suffer from very high disease loads: tuberculosis, malaria, measles, cholera, influenza, pneumonia, intestinal parasitic infection, ectoparasitic infection, syphilis, gonorrhea, human T-cell lymphotropic virus (HTLV) infection, hepatitis, leishmaniasis, Chagas' disease, onchocerciasis, dengue, leprosy, and trachoma. Natives are aware of their tendency to be more affected by illness and to be less likely to recover from bouts of infectious diseases than are neighboring mestizos (United Nations 1996c). While science has managed to reverse many ills for their neighbors, and the rest of humanity, morbidity and/or mortality rates among South American natives are among the highest in the world and continue to increase through time.

According to a survey carried out by the Institute of Tropical Medicine of Manaus, Brazil, in the forty-seven National Indian Foundation (FUNAI) administrative units in one year (1993–1994), the average life expectancy of natives dropped from 48.2 years to 45.6 years. Among natives in Mato Grosso do Sul, it was only 37.7 years in 1994 (United Nations 1996c).

Similarly, among the Aché of eastern Paraguay, the life expectancy at birth between 1978 and 1993 was 45.6 and 50.4, respectively, among males and females (Hill and Hurtado 1996). Natives in other continents fare even worse. The life expectancy at birth among the Agta of the Philippines is only 24.9 years (Early and Headland 1998). These figures are close to those reported for Sierra Leone, which has the lowest national life expectancy in the world (48.5 years). They are also substantially lower than the Brazilian average life expectancy of 59.1 years (Murray 2000).

Declines in life expectancy are likely to be tracked by other health indicators such as height and weight for age. A recent study of trends in height among Central and South American natives over a period of 8,250 years shows that after the conquest of the Americas, mean adult stature declined until the late 1930s and then progressively increased. However, since 1979, in at least some populations, the height of ten- and eleven-year-old children has significantly decreased (Bogin and Keep 1999).

The discipline of anthropology is on trial. Even if Neel, Chagnon, and others did not intentionally deprive the Yanomamö of a basic human right—the right to "the health and well-being of himself and of his family, including . . . medical care, and the right to security in the event of . . . sickness" (Article 25, Universal Declaration of Human Rights of 1948)—the fact still remains that many Yanomamö have died of preventable causes in spite of the continued presence of anthropologists, missionaries, and government officials in their communities. And these people have all made their careers from the cooperation they received from native populations. Anthropology is on trial to explain why, after amassing an abundance of information on topics related to the extinction of natives (Hurtado 2003), presented in thousands of scientific articles, books, films, magazines, and photographs, it has not done more to improve health in native populations worldwide (Cohen 1998).

Anthropologists do not cause the bulk of native disease, as Tierney incorrectly suggests (see Hurtado et al. 2001), but they have not done enough to help prevent disease, despite their expertise on the problems that natives face. Field-workers learn about illnesses and premature deaths through demographic and other interviews, or simply as participant observers. They are also likely to be informed about possible causes (e.g., exposure to outsiders, government neglect, environmental exposures), to know native languages, to know who are the most influential members of communities, and to have insights into what types of interventions are likely to work. Therefore, anthropologists are, and always have been, the most knowledgeable, but often the least able to help, because they seldom have had the institutional support, the resources, or the networks with public health agencies that would make it possible for them to act on this knowledge.

Why Neel Could Not Do More

Throughout the controversy, individuals from all professions who have taken a stand have either promoted or disapproved of *Darkness in El Dorado*. For most, the plight of natives has not been the focus of either side. Anthropologists Leslie Sponsel and Terence Turner praise the book as a "candid" and amply documented treatise on the "ethics of anthropologists" and the "scandalous involvement of prominent" scholars (Tierney 2000: book cover). Such indiscriminate endorsement ignores reports showing that most accusations in Tierney's book are incorrect. They rely on misleading interpretations of published data and on the testimonies of individuals who are unqualified, biased, or uninformed (Alberts 2000; Romano 2000; International Genetic Epidemiology Society 2001; Hagen et al. 2001; Hames 2001; Ramos 2001; American Society of Human Genetics 2002; Hume 2002; University of Michigan 2002).

Several investigations (Alberts 2000; American Society of Human Genetics 2002; International Genetic Epidemiology Society 2001; Headland 2001) focused specifically on accusations made against Neel and amply documented their lack of truth (tables 1.1, 1.2; see also chapter 8, this volume). As a medical doctor, Neel was the most qualified to intervene in medical crises that afflicted the Yanomamö, and yet he was accused of causing an acute measles epidemic and callously ignoring the sick. If anything could be done, someone with Neel's background (table 1.3) and contacts in the international medical community could do it. He obtained M.D. and Ph.D. degrees early in his career and had worked in Africa and in South America, among the Xavante and the Yanomamö. He was a member of the National Academy of Sciences of the United States of America, had been president of the American Society of Human Genetics, and held a faculty position at the University of Michigan, one of the most prestigious American universities.

In 1968, Neel ventured into one of the most inaccessible and unforgiving regions of South America, the Amazonas tropical forests of Venezuela. At that time, very few Venezuelan professionals dared to accompany Neel on his expedition into Yanomamö territory. The most sophisticated biomedical research facility of the country, the Instituto Venezolano de Investigaciones Científicas (IVIC), where Neel had the title of visiting

TABLE 1.1 Main Charges Made by Patrick Tierney against James V. Neel

1. That he deliberately caused a measles epidemic among the Yanomamö through the use of a contraindicated vaccine (Edmonston B), causing "hundreds, if not thousands," of deaths
2. That he failed to provide medical care to the Yanomamö during the measles epidemic
3. That he was an eugenicist, believing that civilization violated natural selection, and was looking for a "leadership gene" among the Yanomamö
4. That deceitful ways were used to obtain pedigree data among the Yanomamö
5. That proper informed consent from the individuals and community leaders was not obtained
6. That the research provided no potential benefit to the Yanomamö
7. That the Yanomamö studies were also devised as a control for work performed among Japanese atomic bomb survivors
8. That human radiation experiments had been conducted among the Yanomamö
9. That he was somehow involved with the administration of plutonium injections in the Rochester hospital where he was a medical house officer in the 1940s
10. That he discounted the risks of atomic radiation

Sources: Tierney (2000); International Genetic Epidemiology Society (2001); American Society of Human Genetics (2002).

scientist, had only recently come into existence. At the time, there were only a few anthropologists on staff (Romano 2000). Dr. Inés Hurtado, a contributor to the present volume, was one of several physicians who were actively engaged in biomedical research in IVIC at that time. She is one of our authors and Magdalena's mother.

To save lives, Neel did what Venezuelan government officials should have done. He obtained large quantities of vaccines and medications to prevent new cases of measles and to treat existing ones. However, he was attempting to do so in a country that cared little for its native population. The professional elite and growing urban masses were uninformed about the size and diversity of native communities and had little interest in their rights. Thus, it is not surprising that in 1968 only 1 out of 153 Venezuelan native communities had a land title (Hurtado 1986). Nor is it surprising that, when the epidemic among the Yanomamö was reported to Venezuelan officials, very few joined Neel in his efforts or followed the trajectory of the epidemic after he left. Instead, he had to rely mainly on foreign medical supplies, on missionaries, and on his own time and efforts. He worked long hours under very difficult, hot, humid, remote, insect-ridden field conditions without access to medical facilities, roads, telephones, or running water. To Neel's family, friends, and colleagues

TABLE 1.2   Answers to the Charges Made by Patrick Tierney against
James V. Neel

---

1. The measles epidemic started before Neel's visit in 1968. The daughter of a
   missionary who had come down with the illness in August 1967 appears to
   have been the index case, or the first case diagnosed with measles in
   Yanomamö territory within a few months of the massive epidemic that Neel
   witnessed. In addition, the decision to use the Edmonston B vaccine was made
   after considerable review of the literature and discussion with several experts.
   This vaccine was widely used in the United States at that time (more than
   1 million children were vaccinated with it in 1968) and also worldwide; and
   the vaccination was approved by Venezuelan authorities. The vaccinal virus is
   not transmissible. There is no evidence that members of Neel's team
   contributed to the dissemination of the epidemic. On the contrary, there is
   strong evidence that the epidemic was disseminated by contact between the
   natives themselves, and missionaries and their families with them.
2. In all expeditions in which Neel participated, he was always very much
   concerned with supplying plentiful medical aid to the visited populations. The
   sound recordings for a motion picture that was being made at the time in one
   of Yanomamö villages were clearly misinterpreted by Tierney and contested by
   the field notes elaborated by Neel at that time.
3. There is no evidence, in all the voluminous scientific literature produced by
   Neel, of adhesion to eugenic theories. On the contrary, he openly expressed
   strong reservations and opposition to such ideas. Moreover, as one of the
   most important authorities in genetics at the time, he would not look for a
   nonsensical "leadership gene."
4. The Yanomamö had, at least at the time of the expeditions, a cultural taboo
   against naming both living and deceased individuals. Therefore, indirect
   methods of obtaining genealogical information had to be devised.
5. Informed consent is a difficult matter in illiterate, isolated communities.
   Preliminary meetings with the native leaders were always scheduled, where
   they were informed as clearly as possible of the objectives of the investigation.
   Afterward, any person who did not want to participate was free to decline.
6. Medical treatment was always provided during the stays in the field. The
   criticized vaccination program saved many lives. At the end of the fieldwork,
   detailed reports and recommendations were submitted to the appropriate
   authorities in Brazil and Venezuela. The biomedical studies helped to establish
   the sanitary conditions of these populations and could serve as a baseline for
   any intervention program. In addition, much was learned and widely
   communicated about Yanomamö history, an aspect of obvious cultural interest
   to both the Yanomamö and humankind in general.
7. The Yanomamö, clearly, could not have been chosen as controls for irradiated
   Japanese. Actually, the original studies of the atomic bomb survivors were
   designed to incorporate internal *Japanese* controls. Initially the city of Kure,
   located about eighteen miles from Hiroshima, was chosen. However, with the
   development of the study it was clear that a considerable proportion of the
   inhabitants of Hiroshima and Nagasaki during the years 1948–1953 had not
   been there at the time of the atomic bomb explosions. They therefore were
   chosen as internal controls, and the studies were discontinued in Kure.
8. The only study that involved radioactive isotopes developed among the
   Yanomamö was carried out by Marcel Roche, from Venezuela, to investigate
   the unexpected finding that members of tribal groups living in iodine-

TABLE 1.2   (*continued*)

deficient areas exhibited increased levels of iodine uptake without showing clinical signs of goiter. To verify this finding (which was confirmed), Roche performed diagnostic tests in some Yanomamö individuals. The radioactive test used is widely employed even today in the evaluation of thyroid function and is therefore entirely safe. Neel was not directly involved in this study.

9. Neel had no background or special expertise in the investigation of radionuclide metabolism, and there is no evidence whatsoever that he participated in the Rochester toxicologic experiment. One of his collaborators, William Valentine, who had been accused by Tierney of taking part in it, denies the charge.

10. Neel examined on different occasions and with abundant details the results of the Japanese studies, extensively considering also other types of evidence. The reasons for the risk estimates obtained were clearly presented. Therefore, any criticism in this regard has to be performed in scientific terms, taking into consideration that humans cannot be subjected to experiments and that observational data can lead to different interpretations.

Sources: Headland 2001; Neel and Schull (1991); Neel (1994); Tierney (2000); International Genetic Epidemiology Society (2001); American Society of Human Genetics (2002).

who knew this well, Tierney's accusations were ruthlessly devoid of common sense or human emphathy (Koivu 2000; Neel 2001).

While Neel did what he could to help the Yanomamö over the short term, he did not have the funding or the institutional support to set up long-term public health programs, nor was he expected to develop and implement them (see chapter 2, this volume). This is because, then and to this day, 500 years after the conquest of the Americas, many institutions with an interest in native rights to health—the World Health Organization, the Pan American Health Organization, the United Nations, the World Bank, the Interamerican Development Bank, the American Anthropological Association, university academic departments, and many others (United Nations 1996a)—have not carried out concrete plans to improve native health worldwide. Instead, representatives of these agencies feel impotent. On the one hand, they expect governments to provide health care to native populations, yet they know that this rarely happens. As one official of the Paraguayan government spontaneously commented to one of us (Hurtado) in July 2002, "There is no reason for the state to invest in natives as long as they represent only 2 percent of the total Paraguayan population." On the other hand, representatives of international agencies are aware that their own institutions will do little, if anything, to intervene. Can anthropologists do something to correct this situation? If so, perhaps in the future, individuals with backgrounds like Neel's will

TABLE 1.3   Main Events Related to the Life of James V. Neel

Year	Main Event
1915	Born on March 22 in Hamilton, Ohio.
1925	Father died of pneumonia, and life thereafter was not easy financially; move from Detroit to Wooster, Ohio.
1931–1935	Undergraduate studies at the College of Wooster; decision to work in genetics (*Drosophila*) under Warren Spencer's influence.
1935–1939	Ph.D. studies (also with *Drosophila*) at the University of Rochester, New York, under Curt Stern's guidance.
1939–1940	First academic position at Dartmouth College, Hanover, N.H.
1941–1942	National Research Council fellowship at Columbia University; work with *Drosophila*, in association with Theodosius Dobzhansky.
1942–1944	Studies at the University of Rochester Medical School; acquisition of an M.D.
1943	Married Priscilla Baxter on May 6.
1944–1948	Military service at Waltham General Hospital, Murphy General Hospital, and Japan. The full program related to the survivors of the atomic bombing began in February 1948, in Hiroshima.
1948	Start of work in March at the University of Michigan, especially its Heredity Clinic, one of the first in the United States (it is not clear whether it antedated a similar clinic established at the University of Minnesota by Sheldon C. Reed).
1953–1954	President, American Society of Human Genetics.
1955	Trip to Africa, related to his interests in the hemoglobinopathies.
1956	Chairman of the newly created Department of Human Genetics, the first of its kind in the United States.
1960–1961	Farewell as attending physician at the University of Michigan Hospitals.
1961	End of main involvement with the hemoglobinopathies.
1962	First fieldwork among the Xavante of Central Brazil.
1963	Elected as a Member of the U.S. National Academy of Sciences.
1965	Allan Award, American Society of Human Genetics.
1966	First fieldwork among the Yanomamö of Venezuela.
1975	National Medal of Science.
1981	President, Sixth International Congress of Human Genetics, Israel. End of chairmanship at the Department of Human Genetics of the University of Michigan.
1985	Formal compulsory retirement, at age seventy. He continued his studies, as emeritus professor, until his death.
1997	Ibero-American Society of Human Genetics Annual Award.
2000	Died of cancer on February 1.

Source: Salzano (2000). See also Schull (2000) and Weiss and Ward (2000).

be able to provide medical relief, as well as to help build and maintain public health infrastructures.

Thus, in spite of its inaccuracies and ethical shortcomings, *Darkness in El Dorado* puts anthropology on trial by pointing to the absence of institutional plans of action that anthropologists can create to help ensure the protection of native rights to health. With this wake-up call, anthropology has lost its academic innocence. Anthropologists can no longer fall back on antiquated arguments suggesting that in order to do good research in native communities, researchers only need to be good participant observers. Instead, good researchers need to be as well educated in the ethical implications of research at the individual and societal levels as they are in theory and methodology. By the time the trial ends, anthropologists should have well-developed guidelines and a vision for the types of infrastructures and networks needed to implement them (see chapter 11, this volume).

Some might find this wake-up call to be extreme, arguing that even when better guidelines are implemented, anthropologists would never be able to substitute for the duties of government officials, international organizations, or communities. The goal is not to take the place of these institutions but to work with them more effectively on well-funded projects that ensure native rights to health.

Would anthropologists in Western countries be willing to have members of non-Western cultures become intrusive observers in their homes and communities so that the observers may build their own careers at home? They might, but they would certainly demand just compensation much greater than what natives have traditionally hoped to receive in return for their collaboration. *Darkness in El Dorado* sent out the message that the price of collaboration that the Yanomamö and other natives hope to be offered is *the protection of their long-term welfare*. This is a reasonable request that anthropologists have often inadvertently or consciously ignored by claiming that anthropological research must remain "scientifically objective."

Roots of Complacency

Viewed in this way, the lack of health improvements through time in Yanomamö communities serves as an indicator of a larger problem. It reflects the priorities of funding agencies, publishers, and academia. Fields like anthropology promote the careers of individuals who do outstanding basic research and who publish their findings. Disciplines outside of anthropology are expected to review the published findings and to work out and implement the humanistic potential of these findings at some unspecified point in time, but they rarely do so. For the most part, the few indigenous health programs that exist in South America are not based on reviews of the anthropological or biomedical literature.

Neel and others were funded only to extract information from the Yanomamö that the Western world wanted (chapter 2, this volume). They were not funded to give the Yanomamö what they wanted, nor to provide medical assistance, to pay well-trained local doctors for their time, transport, and local medications, to train health care workers, or to sustain these interventions over time. If Neel and others had been funded accordingly, Tierney would never have written his book. Clearly, a few individuals cannot be blamed for a lack of humanitarian foresight by funding agencies and academic institutions that restricted their activities.

Although international declarations and conventions that call for ethical conduct of research date back to the nineteenth century (table 1.4), anthropologists have done relatively little to translate its most basic principles into research. Principles set forth by the World Health Organization as early as 1964, by the National Commission for the Protection of Human Subjects of Biomedical and Behavioral Research, the International Labor Organization, and many other agencies suggest that scientists and humanists need to play a greater role in the protection of native rights to health (table 1.4). Several guidelines or conventions focus on native rights. For example, the ILO Convention on Indigenous and Tribal Peoples in

TABLE 1.4   Documents Issued by International Organizations Involving Ethical Problems[1]

Document	Date
1. Issued by the United Nations (UN)	
1.1. Convention on Prevention and Punishment of the Crime of Genocide	December 9, 1948
1.2. Universal Declaration of Human Rights	December 10, 1948
1.3. Convention on the Elimination of All Forms of Racial Discrimination	December 21, 1965
1.4. International Convenants on Economic, Social, and Cultural Rights, and on Civil and Political Rights	December 16, 1966
1.5. Convention on the Prohibition of the Development, Production, and Stockpiling of Bacteriological (Biological) and Toxin Weapons, and on their Destruction	December 16, 1971

TABLE 1.4.   (*continued*)

1.6.	Declaration on the Rights of Mentally Retarded Persons	December 20, 1971
1.7.	Declaration on the Rights of Disabled Persons	December 9, 1975
1.8.	Convention on the Elimination of All Forms of Discrimination against Women	December 18, 1979
1.9.	Declaration of Basic Principles of Justice for Victims of Crime and Abuse of Power	November 29, 1985
1.10.	Convention on the Rights of the Child	November 20, 1989
1.11.	Standard Rules on the Equalization of Opportunities for Persons with Disabilities	December 20, 1993
1.12.	Convention on Biological Diversity	June 5, 1992
2.	**Issued by the United Nations Educational, Scientific and Cultural Organization (UNESCO)**	
2.1.	Universal Copyright Convention	September 6, 1952
2.2.	Convention against Discrimination in Education	December 14, 1960
2.3.	Declaration of the Principles of International Cultural Co-operation	November 4, 1966
2.4.	Recommendation on the Status of Scientific Researchers	November 20, 1974
2.5.	Declaration on Race and Racial Prejudice	November 27, 1978
2.6.	Universal Declaration of the Human Genome and Human Rights	November 11, 1997
3.	**Issued by the International Labor Organization (ILO)**	
3.1.	Convention on Discrimination in Respect of Employment and Occupation	June 25, 1958
3.2.	Convention on Indigenous and Tribal Peoples in Independent Countries	June 7, 1989
4.	**Issued by Other Institutions**	
4.1.	Paris Convention for the Protection of Industrial Property	March 20, 1883
4.2.	Budapest Treaty on International Recognition of the Deposit of Micro-organisms for the Purposes of Patent Procedures	April 28, 1977
4.3.	Trade Related Aspects of Intellectual Property Rights Agreement (TRIPS)	January 1, 1995
4.4.	Guidelines on Ethical Matters in Aboriginal and Torres Strait Islander Research	March 12, 1991
4.5.	Code of Conduct for Research Involving Human Subjects, Canadian Tri-Council Working Group on Ethics	June 15, 1996

[1]Other documents that could be consulted are the Nuremberg Code (*United States vs. Karl Brandt*, 1948–1949); the Declaration of Helsinki (1964); the International Ethical Norms for Biomedical Research Involving Human Beings (CIOMS and World Health Organization 1993); and the Guidelines on Ethical Issues in Medical Genetics and the Provision of Genetic Services (World Health Organization 1995).

Independent Countries states that natives worldwide have the right to direct their own economic, social, and cultural development; it urges states to facilitate and support these measures, but to date only thirteen countries have ratified it (Cohen 1998).

World Health Organization documents (1964, 1968) clearly outline what constitutes ethical research. These documents include statements that call for (1) respect for privacy of the individuals under study, as well as their comfort and well-being; (2) access to medical, dental, and related services; (3) clear explanations of possible rewards related to the research; (4) congenial relationships between researchers and participants; (5) consultation with local experts about cultural preferences and traditions; and (6) utmost regard for the cultural integrity of the group.

Principles outlined by the National Commission for the Protection of Human Subjects include autonomy, nonmaleficence, beneficence, and justice (table 1.5). By failing to put more effort into the control of infectious diseases, the institutions that fund and support those who work among natives have failed to "remove the causes of harm altogether" (nonmaleficence), "to secure the well-being of persons by acting positively on their behalf," for example, "improvement of public health infrastructure" (beneficence), and to balance "individual rights and societal welfare," for example, the "right of all to affordable medical care" (justice).

TABLE 1.5   The Basic Ethical Principles

1. **Autonomy.** The duty to respect the self-determination and choices of autonomous people, as well as to protect persons with diminished autonomy, e.g., young children, mentally retarded subjects, and those with other mental impairment. Examples are right to decide, right not to know, respect concerning confidential matters.
2. **Nonmaleficence.** The obligation to minimize harm to persons and wherever possible to remove the causes of harm altogether. Examples: truth-telling as a source of harm, prevention of guilt or anxiety, preservation of the family unit.
3. **Beneficence.** The duty to secure the well-being of persons by acting positively on their behalf and, moreover, to maximize the benefits that can be attained. Involves a positive inclination to do good, as opposed to the mere avoidance of harm. Examples: improvement of public health infrastructure, truth-telling as a way of maximizing good.
4. **Justice.** The obligation to distribute benefits and burdens fairly, to treat equals equally, and to give reasons for differential treatment based upon widely accepted criteria for just ways to distribute benefits and burdens. Involves balancing individual rights and societal welfare. Examples: right of all to affordable medical care, public health, employment opportunities taking into consideration merit only, proper resource allocations.

Sources: Belmont Report (1979); Wertz and Fletcher (1989).

The "right" balance between protection of individual rights and societal welfare is hard to find in anthropology. In contrast to other disciplines, anthropological research often takes place in well-defined communities that are peripheral to the services of nation-states. In most observational sciences, internal review boards (IRBs) primarily require the protection of individual rights. In anthropology, however, most research practices involve careful consideration of societal rights (chapter 10, this volume). Observational studies of infectious diseases provide good examples.

Researchers who study human immunodeficiency virus (HIV) infection in New York City generally work with departments of health that are funded to track and treat all cases and to implement programs to prevent new ones. In contrast, researchers who measure the incidence of HIV in native communities of South America generally work alone, and if public health officials are involved, they often lack funds for basic laboratory analyses and other interventions. Researchers in New York City only need to worry about protecting individual rights—that is, the right to treatment, education, and other benefits that the team can offer either directly through grants or through local departments of health. In contrast, researchers working with a South American native community need enough funds to protect the rights of individuals, as well as the community as a whole. For them, the detection of a few cases of HIV without follow-up community prevention and intervention programs could result in the loss of economic well-being, vitality, and lives, eventually leading to extinction.

But most anthropological research grants are likely to have insufficient funds to handle such crises because major HIV research funds are spent on large populations, not on small native populations. In addition, local departments of health and international public health agencies like the World Health Organization and Pan American Health Organization (PAHO) are not prepared or willing to handle such crises. These agencies would refer our hypothetical researchers to the local ministry of health, and ministry officials would probably respond, as they often do, that their funds are limited and inadequate to provide assistance in rural settings. This is what happened to Hurtado during an acute tuberculosis epidemic in native communities of eastern Paraguay in 1994. Hurtado requested logistical support and medications from PAHO to contain the epidemic. The response of these officials was to refer Hurtado to the head of the National Tuberculosis Commission of Paraguay, a commission that was seriously underfunded at the time. PAHO officials did not offer to intervene in the event that the commission could not, which is exactly what happened. Funds from the Avina Foundation and logistical support from the Fundación Moisés Bertoni allowed Hurtado and native health care workers to contain the epidemic. Without this private support, the tuberculosis medications stored at the National Tuberculosis Commission would have never been delivered, treatment would not have been monitored, and a serious tuberculosis epidemic would not have been contained in native communities of eastern Paraguay.

The realization that the entire field of anthropology, not just specific individuals, may be guilty of complacency calls for substantial changes in how we train students and how research awards are allocated by granting agencies. For native populations at high risk of elevated, preventable mortality, some of the most important benefits that can come from participating in research are medical and public health assistance. Nevertheless, in spite of extensive knowledge about diseases and native extinction, the American Anthropological Association (AAA) Code of Ethics (American Anthropological Association 1998) does not include clauses requiring that researchers protect the right to health in native communities. This is not one of the charges of anthropology. The field requires only that anthropologists behave "ethically":

> As the principal organization representing the breadth of anthropology, the American Anthropological Association (AAA) starts from the position that generating and appropriately utilizing knowledge (i.e., publishing, teaching, developing programs, and informing policy) of the peoples of the world, past and present is a worthy goal; that the generation of anthropological knowledge is a dynamic process using many different and ever-evolving approaches; and that for moral and practical reasons, *the generation and utilization of knowledge should be achieved in an ethical manner.* (American Anthropological Association 2002)

Ethical conduct is not defined according to the principles specified by the National Commission for the Protection of Human Subjects and the World Health Organization. The AAA Code of Ethics simply states that ethical obligations include the following:

- To avoid harm or wrong, understanding that the development of knowledge can lead to change which may be positive or negative for the people . . . worked with or studied.
- To respect the well-being of humans. . . .

- To work for the long-term conservation of the archeological, fossil, and historical records.
- To consult actively with the affected individuals or group(s), with the goal of establishing a working relationship that can be beneficial to all parties involved.

Anthropology can learn from other disciplines. Several National Institutes of Health grant programs require that researchers invest funds in capacity building, training, and activities that help to promote partnerships between researchers and communities (i.e., societal welfare). In addition, researchers are expected to use funds to provide health care to participants who become ill (i.e., individual rights).

In contrast, the National Science Foundation anthropology grants programs and most other anthropological foundations and granting agencies do not provide funding for activities of this nature. Instead, researchers are expected to call upon government agencies to intervene. In most cases, this is equivalent to ignoring emerging health problems or other crises. Moreover, anthropology students are not required to take basic medical courses and are not taught how to build research teams that include medical doctors or nurses. Finally, anthropologists do not have access to international support networks that can help them respond more effectively when faced with health-related human rights abuses or governmental neglect.

A call for medical training in anthropology graduate programs raises concerns about what types of training will be appropriate for the situations that anthropologists are likely to encounter. Such decisions must be made in close collaboration with departments of family and community medicine. Anthropologists should be taught how to distinguish between conditions that require treatment in the community or at local health care posts versus conditions that require better-equipped facilities. Students should be trained in ways similar to those used to teach health care workers in many parts of the developing world (Werner 1980; Werner and Bower 1982).

Anthropology can also learn from individuals within the discipline who have found ways to incorporate societal and individual welfare into fieldwork. Forster et al. (1998), based on their experience with the Apache of Oklahoma, have suggested general guidelines for anthropological genetics that include an eleven-step process (table 1.6).

Such initiatives are useful starting points, but they must include clear guidelines for health interventions, and they must be supported by improvements in training, funding, and multidisciplinary networks through-

TABLE 1.6   The Eleven-Step General Model Suggested by Forster et al. (1998) That Could Be Followed in Population-Specific Genetic Studies

Steps	Action to Be Performed
1.	Conduct survey of individual health-care decision making
2.	Identify culturally appropriate decision-making units (public and private)
3.	Consult community members about inclusion of representative units
4.	Assist in formation of community review board
5.	Initiate dialogue between researchers and community in public meetings
6.	Interval discourse in public and private social units
7.	Negotiations between researchers and the community review board
8.	Community consensus and agreement
9.	Researchers' institutional review board evaluates documentation of communal discourse
10.	Recruitment of subjects from community
11.	Standard informed consent for individuals

out anthropology. Otherwise, anthropologists will include in their proposals vacuous plans of action for the purposes of getting funded, rather than to do the work. They will continue to be forced to rely on governments to provide assistance when they face medical emergencies or crises in the field, such as the ones described in *Darkness in El Dorado*. However, we know that in most developing countries with large ethnic aboriginal minorities, governments are unresponsive (see chapters 6, 7, and 9, this volume). This creates a vacuum that puts anthropologists at risk of being accused of neglectful, if not genocidal, behavior. This vulnerability will not go away when the *El Dorado* controversy is over. Anthropologists will continue to be at the mercy of attacks for "complacently" allowing native peoples to suffer from preventable diseases. Instead of waiting to be put on trial again, anthropology must address disciplinary deficiencies through cooperative efforts across its subfields.

Is such cooperation possible? Our colleagues are well known for their fondness for employing battles for justice as vehicles to promote the superiority of their respective subfields, theories, methodological preferences, or political ideologies (chapter 4, this volume; Gregor and Gross 2002). The rhetoric divides the field into scientists and humanists, complacent academics and extremists. Sentences like "Science . . . tends to dehumanize its subjects . . . and to turn human communities into experimental laboratories in the field" (Scheper-Hughes 2001) denigrate the profession and thwart any hope for multidisciplinary work. Because some of the best solutions for communities come from a combination of excellent qualitative (humanistic and scientific) and quantitative (scientific) research (Wolstenholme 1999; Murray and Graham 1995; Hohmann and Shear 2002), anthropologists of diverse backgrounds must find ways to seek justice for natives through collaborative teams.

Thus, we conclude that *Darkness in El Dorado* raised a fundamental question in anthropology: What rules of ethical conduct should anthropologists and other outsiders (journalists, missionaries, government officials) follow when they work with populations that are denied the most basic human right to health? Changes in training, funding programs, and multidisciplinary and international networks must back any new guidelines. The field of anthropology faces a problem that goes beyond what researchers may have done in Yanomamö villages at some point in time. The problem involves the institutions that fund and promote anthropological research that natives never wanted or no longer want, and that agencies and universities should no longer support.

The purpose of this book is threefold. In part II, the authors provide analyses of the contexts that gave rise to Neel's research agenda (chapters 2 and 3), to Neel's field research objectives (chapter 2), and the antiscience forces that emerged in academia over the same period (chapter 4). Antiscience tendencies helped fuel Tierney's book and have greatly affected the future of genetic studies among South American natives (chapter 5). In part III, the authors delve into the epidemiology of infectious diseases among Lowland South American natives (chapter 9), Brazilian natives (chapter 6), and the Yanomamö (chapter 7) and elaborate on immunological, environmental, and genetic aspects of native health (chapters 8 and 9). In part IV, we close with a discussion of the main ethical frailties of anthropological research guidelines, the institutional constraints that have kept anthropologists from investing more in native health, and the ways in which we may overcome them.

REFERENCES

Alberts, B. 2000. Setting the Record Straight Regarding Darkness in El Dorado. National Academy of Sciences. Washington, D.C. Available at http://www 4.nationalacademies.org/nas/nashome.nsf.
American Anthropological Association. 1998. Code of Ethics of the American Anthropological Association. American Anthropological Association, Washington, D.C. Available at http://www.aaanet.org/edtf/index.htm.

————. 2002. Final Report of the American Anthropological Association El Dorado Task Force. American Anthropological Association. Washington, D.C. Available at http://www.aaanet.org/edtf/index.htm.

American Society of Human Genetics. 2002. Response to allegations against James V. Neel in *Darkness in El Dorado*, by Patrick Tierney. *American Journal of Human Genetics* 70: 1–10.

Belmont Report. 1979. *Ethical Principles and Guidelines for the Protection of Human Subjects of Research.* National Commission for the Protection of Human Subjects of Biomedical and Behavioral Research, Department of Health, Education and Welfare, Washington, D.C.

Bogin, B., and R. Keep. 1999. Eight thousand years of economic and political history in Latin America revealed by anthropometry. *Annual Review of Human Biology* 26: 333–351.

Bosh, V., L. Carbonell, E. Coll, G. Chuchani, M. Laufer, M. Layrisse, J. Vera, G. Villegas, and R. Villegas. 2001. Venezuelan response to Yanomamo book. *Science* 291: 417–418.

CIOMS and World Health Organization. 1993. *International Ethics Guidelines for Biomedical Research Involving Human Subjects.* Council for International Organizations of Medical Sciences and World Health Organization, Geneva.

Cohen, C. P. 1998. *The Human Rights of Indigenous Peoples.* Ardsley, New York.

Dalton, R. 2000. Anthropologists in turmoil over allegations of misconduct. *Nature* 408: 391.

Declaration of Helsinki. 1964. Recommendations guiding medical doctors in biomedical research involving human subjects. *New England Journal of Medicine* 271: 473.

Early, J. D., and T. N. Headland. 1998. *Population Dynamics of a Philippine Rain Forest People: The San Ildefonso Agta.* University Press of Florida, Gainesville.

Forster, M. W., D. Bernsten, and T. H. Carter. 1998. A model agreement for genetic research in socially identifiable populations. *American Journal of Human Genetics* 63: 696–702.

Gregor, T. A., and D. R. Gross. 2002. Anthropology and the search for the enemy within. *Chronicle of Higher Education*, July 17.

Hagen, E. H., M. E. Price, and J. Tooby. 2001. The major allegations against Napoleon Chagnon and James Neel presented in *Darkness in El Dorado* by Patrick Tierney appear to be deliberately fraudulent. University of California, Department of Anthropology, Santa Barbara. Available at http://www.anth.ucsb.edu/ucsbpreliminaryreport.pdf.

Hames, R. 2001. Perspectives on Tierney's *Darkness in El Dorado. Current Anthropology* 42: 271–274.

Headland, T. 2001. When did the measles epidemic begin among the Yanomami? *Anthropology News* 42(1): 5–6.

Hill, K., and A. M. Hurtado. 1996. *Aché Life History: The Ecology and Demography of a Foraging People.* Aldine de Gruyter, New York.

Hohmann, A. A., and M. K. Shear. 2002. Community-based intervention research: Coping with the "noise" of real life in study design. *American Journal of Psychiatry* 159: 201–207.

Hume, D. 2002. Information on Darkness in El Dorado. University of Connecticut, Storrs, Conn. Available at http://www.anth.uconn.edu/gradstudents/dhume/darkness_in_el_dorado/index.htm.

Hurtado, A. M. 1986. Research report for cultural survival: The Cuiva land problem in Venezuela—April 1986. Manuscript. University of Utah: Salt Lake City.

———. 2003. The epidemiology of South American native health. *Annual Review of Anthropology*, January.

Hurtado, A. M., K. R. Hill, H. Kaplan, and J. Lancaster. 2001. The epidemiology of infectious diseases among South American Indians: A call for ethical research guidelines. *Current Anthropology*, 42: 425–432.

International Genetic Epidemiology Society. 2001. Commentary on *Darkness in El Dorado* by Patrick Tierney. *Genetic Epidemiology* 21: 81–104.

Koivu, L. 2000. Colleagues continue to defend "U" researcher. *Michigan Daily*, November 13.

Mann, C. C. 2000. Anthropology: Misconduct alleged in Yanomamo studies. *Science* 289: 2251–2253.

———. 2001. Scientific community: Preemptive strike sought to discredit book before it is published. *Science* 291: 417–418.

McCarthy, M. 2000. Did US scientists kill Amazon Indians with vaccine? *Lancet* 56: 1247.

Morton, N. E. 2001. *Darkness in El Doradao*: Human genetics on trial. *Journal of Genetics* 80: 45–52.

Murray, C. 2000. World Health Organization issues new healthy life expectancy rankings: Japan Number One in New "Healthy Life" System. Press Release. Available at http://www.who/int/inf-pr-2000/en/pr2000–life.html.

Murray, S. A., and L. J. C. Graham. 1995. Practice-based health needs assessment: Use of 4 methods in a small neighborhood. *British Medical Journal* 310: 1443–1448.

Neel, J. V. 1994. *Physician to the Gene Pool: Genetic Lessons and Other Stories.* Wiley, New York.

Neel, J. V., Jr. 2001. The Yanomamö and the 1960s measles epidemic. *Science* 291: 416–421.

Neel, J. V., and W. J. Schull. 1991. *The Children of Atomic Bomb Survivors: A Genetic Study*. National Academy Press, Washington, D.C.

Olsson, K. 2000. An ethics firestorm in the Amazon. *US News & World Report*, October 2, p. 51.

Ramos, A. R. 2001. Perspectives on Tierney's *Darkness in El Dorado*. *Current Anthropology* 42: 274–276.

Romano, E. 2000. Comments on the book Darkness in El Dorado. Instituto Venezolano de Investigaciones Cientificas. Available at http:/hokaido. ivic.ve/ivicspan/darknese.html.

Salzano, F. M. 2000. James V. Neel and Latin America—or how scientific collaboration should be conducted. *Genetics and Molecular Biology* 23: 557–561.

Scheper-Hughes, N. 2001. Neo-cannibalism: Anthropologists in the Amazon. *Anthropology Today* 17 (1): 19–20.

Schull, W. J. 2000. James Van Gundia Neel. *Genetic Epidemiology* 18: 289–291.

Tierney, P. 2000. *Darkness in El Dorado: How Scientists and Journalists Devastated the Amazon*. W.W. Norton, New York.

United Nations. 1996a. Discrimination against indigenous peoples. Report of the Working Group on Indigenous Populations on its fourteenth session (Geneva, 29 July–2 August 1996). Report 14.TXT. Available at http://cwis.org/fwdp/International/report14.txt.

———. 1996b. Review of developments pertaining to the promotion and protection of human rights and fundamental freedoms of indigenous people: Health and indigenous peoples. Information received from indigenous peoples' organizations. Addendum. Indigenous Missionary Council. Economic and Social Council, Document IMC-96.TXT. Available at http://www.cwis.org/fwdp/Americas/imc-96.txt.

———. 1996c. Review of developments pertaining to the promotion and protection of human rights and fundamental freedoms of indigenous people: Health and indigenous peoples. Note by the Secretariat. Addendum. Information received from indigenous peoples and nongovernmental organizations. Economic and Social Council, Document 96-16746.TXT. Available at http://www.cwis.org/fwdp/Americas/96-16746.txt.

United States versus Karl Brandt. 1948–49. *Trials of War Criminals before the Nuremberg Military Tribunals under Control Council Law*. No. 10. Vols. 1 and 2, "The Medical Case" (Military Tribunal 1, 1947). U.S. Government Printing Office, Washington, D.C.

University of Michigan. 2002. Resources Regarding *Darkness in El Dorado*. University of Michigan, Ann Arbor, Michigan. Available at http://www.umich.edu/~urel/Darkness/darkmenu.html.

Weiss, K., and R. K. Ward. 2000. James V. Neel, M.D., Ph.D. (March 22, 1915–January 31, 2000): Founder effect. *American Journal of Human Genetics* 66: 755–760.

Werner, D. 1980. *Where There Is No Doctor.* Hesperian Foundation, Palo Alto, Calif.

Werner, D., and B. Bower. 1982. *Helping Health Care Workers Learn.* Hesperian Foundation, Palo Alto, Calif.

Wertz, D. C., and J. C. Fletcher. 1989. *Ethics and Human Genetics.* Springer-Verlag, Berlin.

Wolstenholme, E. F. 1999 Qualitative vs. quantitative modelling: The evolving balance. *Journal of the Operational Research Society* 50: 422–428.

World Health Organization. 1964. *Research in Population Genetics of Primitive Groups.* World Health Organization, Geneva.

———. 1968. *Research on Human Population Genetics.* World Health Organization, Geneva.

———. 1995. *Guidelines on Ethical Issues in Medical Genetics and the Provision of Genetics Services.* World Health Organization, Geneva.

Part II

Historical Contexts

2

VOICES OF THE DEAD: JAMES NEEL'S AMERINDIAN STUDIES

M. Susan Lindee

Spokesmen for the investigating commission and expert psychiatrists established that the members of the criminal gang were hypnotists of extraordinary power. . . . They were able to remove from the field of vision things or people who were in fact within that field of vision. . . . And so almost everything was explained, and the investigation came to an end, as everything in life comes to an end.

—Mikhail Bulgakov, *The Master and the Margarita*

During his 1967 fieldwork, James V. Neel, professor of human genetics at the University of Michigan, spent a good deal of time collecting chicken dung. He scraped up dirt and chicken waste from the ground around the Yanomamö villages. He sought out dirt from the floors of the Yanomamö houses, where parrots were kept as free-roaming pets. He crawled under chicken coops, filling seventy-five labeled plastic bags with samples, using a fresh plastic spoon for each sample, and he worried about getting this soil and bird waste safely back to Atlanta, Georgia, for testing at the Centers for Disease Control (CDC).[1]

Chicken dung was only one of many things extracted from the Yanomamö and their environment during Neel's field research in the 1960s and 1970s. Blood, stool samples, saliva, urine, viruses, parasites, dental casts, human milk, tissue samples, and texts describing physical examinations and family relationships moved from the villages along the Orinoco River to the CDC in Atlanta, to the University of Michigan, and eventually to other laboratories and universities and tissue banks.

Neel's decision to continue to collect these objects and materials in early 1968—despite a major medical crisis in the form of a measles epidemic— is one of the aspects of his fieldwork that may be particularly jarring to twenty-first-century sensibilities: the blood samples remained a very high priority for Neel, even as those around him were dying. Indeed, throughout his field research in Central and South America in the 1960s and 1970s, he measured his success by the number of blood samples he sent back to Ann Arbor or to Atlanta. He celebrated when his group collected more samples than expected, and he was distressed when the yield was lower.[2] Furthermore, he built a network of South and Central American agents— anthropologists, missionaries, physicians, government officials—who could collect blood samples and other materials by proxy for his research program. The vacutainers would be shipped from Ann Arbor ready to fill. The return flights would be announced by cable so that someone from Neel's lab could be ready to track and collect the samples when they arrived. Neel engineered a system of social and bodily resources that brought blood and many other field materials into his laboratory for analysis and interpretation.

These things were signs, clues, evidence. But signs of what? In 1966, Neel told a mycologist at the CDC, "I believe I can assure you that from your standpoint, these specimens come from people who have had absolutely minimal contacts with the Western world; i.e., they come about as close to reflecting the disease pattern of the primitive Indian as we are going to be able to find."[3] The extracted materials were signs of the "primitive," of the original state of man, and of the conditions under which human evolution had occurred, when "man" became "man." And they were the primary justification for the field research: "Although we collect much information in the field through genealogies and physical examinations, the real medical pay dirt comes from the careful and intensive study of blood, saliva, urine, and stool specimens which we collect in the field."[4]

In his collecting, his analysis, and especially his theorizing, I would suggest, Neel was engaged in a resurrection project, in which the bodily and environmental traces drawn from the populations living around the Orinoco could be used to reconstruct the experiences of people who had been long dead, the people who had experienced the forces that shaped human evolution 10,000 or more years ago. In chicken dung, which might contain the fungus that caused the respiratory illness histoplasmosis, he saw the human gene pool and, by extension, the human future. Stools, urine, hair samples, and saliva were prosaic and cosmic, waste and evidence, contemporary and ancient.

In this chapter, I explore how and why Neel and his collaborators gathered the diverse objects they extracted from tropical field sites. I notice particularly what Neel and his diverse collaborators sought to learn from the many things that came from the field. I assess why Neel chose to work in Brazil and Venezuela, what he thought he was looking at when he looked at the Xavante and Yanomamö, and what his field practices and the material legacy of those practices (the blood samples stored in State College, Pennsylvania) suggest about changing human subjects research protocols over the last forty years. I propose that the bodily traces taken from Amerindian groups constituted a form of testimony that could be used to reconstruct the experiences—with some literary license, "the voices"—of the dead. The Yanomamö, Xavante, Cayapo, Seminole, Cuna, Creek, Bokota, Caddo, Machusi, Wapishana, Guaymi, and other groups tracked by Neel and his colleagues spoke of disease and survival directly through their blood. But the dead who wandered through these scientific texts also included all the humans and protohumans who had experienced "human evolution," people who had been dead so long they spoke only through the bodies and antibodies of living "primitives," through the titers compiled in Atlanta laboratories, or the fecal parasite counts prepared by a New Orleans specialist in tropical medicine.[5] The dead in my text also include James Neel, who died in February 2000, eight months before the Tierney controversy, and who left behind a remarkable textual record, both published and unpublished, of his life and his work.

Beginnings

Neel may have been interested in isolated South American populations before 1955, but it is clear that his professional relationship with Francisco Salzano played a critical role in the initiation of actual field research in Brazil, which then led to other studies in Panama, Costa Rica, and Venezuela.[6]

Salzano first contacted Neel in December 1955, with a request to spend a year in Neel's laboratory. He had been reading the *American Journal of*

Human Genetics, he said, and had found the work coming out of Neel's lab particularly relevant to his own interests. He had tentative Rockefeller Foundation funding and hoped that the year at the Heredity Clinic in Ann Arbor would prepare him to develop a program in human genetics at the University of Rio Grande do Sul, where he was on the faculty of genetics. A young *Drosophila* geneticist, Salzano had published several papers on chromosomal polymorphism in South American *Drosophila* and on a new species of *Drosophila*.[7] Neel replied almost immediately that he was happy to hear about Salzano's plans, but that certain points needed to be considered. First, he wondered if Salzano had sufficient mathematical training. Second, he said a year was not long enough to carry out a research project in human genetics. "When you shift your attention from *Drosophila* to man (as I have also done), you must adopt a different time scale. Problems in human genetics move much more slowly than those utilizing fruit flies."[8] Meanwhile, Neel wrote to a contact at the Rockefeller Foundation to ask his opinion about Salzano. "I rather prefer to have a candidate sell himself to the investigator with whom he wishes to have a fellowship experience," this contact said, "but can tell you that Salzano has a very nice personality and would, I am confident, fall in 100 percent with any program you might lay down for him."[9]

Salzano arrived in Ann Arbor in early September 1956. One of his projects that year was to prepare a survey or summary paper on studies of Amerindian groups, and this paper suggested some of the inadequacies of earlier studies (Salzano 1957). He noted that at the time there were already ninety-five published scientific papers dealing with blood groups in South American Indians. Beginning in the 1930s, investigators had tracked down isolated groups, convinced individuals to submit to a blood test, labeled the blood to be sent in to the laboratory for processing, and aggregated the findings to reach conclusions about human history. The Carib, Guajiro, Piaroa, Guahibo, Arawak, and Caramanta had all been bled and tested—439 Pijao Indians in Colombia subjected to blood testing for a paper published in 1944, and almost 3,000 Andean Indians of various groups in Ecuador in 1952. The Quechua of Peru, Tucano of Brazil, Alkuyana of Surinam, Mataco of Argentina, Macá of Paraguay, and Panzaleo of Ecuador—all bled and thereby physically brought into technical explorations of race, migration, mutation, and "white admixture," their blood providing signs, clues, evidence. The blood samples analyzed in the laboratory revealed the presence of the Diego factor, different proportions of the ABO groups, the MN groups, S antisera, and Rh factor, and presumably historical relationships between Amazonian and Andean groups.

But Salzano was dissatisfied with these data and research programs, observing that simply collecting blood samples did not provide enough information for the results to be analyzed in a meaningful way. Blood sampling and laboratory results left out too much about culture, about health, and about known historical relationships that sometimes contradicted what might be assumed based solely on blood tests. "It would be highly desirable that future surveys would include data on the mating system of the tribes under study, the degree of consanguinity of the individuals studied, and the effective population number of these populations. This of course, would require much more time and energy than is now devoted to these surveys, but would greatly increase their value" (Salzano 1957: 575). His acknowledgment in this paper thanked both Neel and James N. Spuhler, a University of Michigan biological anthropologist interested in blood groups, human behavior, and human biology.

Why did Neel himself begin to work with isolated populations in Brazil and Venezuela? There are several possible explanations. Neel was certainly attracted to the romanticism of the "vanishing world" of the Amerindian, at least partly because he seems to have interpreted fieldwork as a test of character and masculinity (Neel 1994). As Oreskes (1996) suggested in her exploration of scientific heroism, the field was seen by many scientists as a particularly masculinized research site, a place where heroic efforts might be required and physical strength was necessary. Rossiter (1995) has documented the systematic exclusion of women scientists from many kinds of fieldwork, in some domains as late as the 1980s. The field was a place where a male scientist might test himself and demonstrate masculine resolve. In one particularly revealing letter from 1965, Neel told one of his administrative assistants:

Our man in Venezuela [a reference to Napoleon Chagnon, then on his first field trip with the Yanomamö] is in a situation guaranteed to test the strongest. It's difficult to describe to one who has not experienced it, the strange mixture of exhilaration and foreboding which quickly develops when suddenly all those familiar props you grew up with are gone and you are very much alone, or virtually alone, in a completely strange culture which doesn't regard your life or interests as much concern of theirs. Many men can't take it. These include even professed anthropologists, which explains why PhD theses in that field often do not get the follow-up they should.[10]

Thirty years later, in his autobiography, he made a similar point, evoking the "elaborate rationalizations as to why we do this or that" and suggesting that his Amerindian work was an opportunity to test himself, and his character. "Mine had thus far been a rather safe life . . . in a setting where help in case of miscalculation was close at hand. This would be different" (Neel 1994). A historian interested in psychological motivations could therefore propose that the Amerindian work began because Neel reached middle age. Like many others before and since, he felt compelled to prove himself, in this case through a highly masculinized notion of physical trial in the field and in contact with "natural" man.

From a different perspective, a historian could propose that the Amerindian work began because of Neel's sense of history and his concerns about the long-term impact of science and technology on human health. For someone deeply committed to the legitimacy of the technoscientific worldview, Neel could be quite skeptical about the impact of "progress." He commonly invoked the threat of "civilization" as an urgent justification for his Amerindian studies: "The relatively few remaining primitive populations of the world were so rapidly being disrupted that ours was almost surely the last generation to encounter any of them in relatively undisturbed condition," he wrote in his autobiography (Neel 1994).

Neel's first major field research, of course, had focused on a population as devastated and temporally limited as any group of isolated forest dwellers—and one directly damaged by technoscientific progress. These were the Japanese survivors of the atomic bombings at Hiroshima and Nagasaki, where Neel began work in the spring of 1947. In Japan, aided by local physicians, nurses, midwives, and scientists, and working with his long-term collaborator William J. Schull, he developed an elaborate and complicated genetic study of the survivors' offspring, in whom germ-line mutations resulting from atomic radiation might be presumed to be expressed and visible. His subjects were uniquely vulnerable products of history and of science, the focus of worldwide sympathy and outrage, at the center of vituperative unfolding debates over nuclear weapons in the 1940s to the 1960s, and they were victims of what was arguably a technology that changed "what it means to be human."[11] A young M.D. and Ph.D., with a strong grounding in *Drosophila* genetics, Neel was suited not only by training but also by temperament and political skills to take over the genetics project. He handled field research well, could manage the cultural tensions of working in occupied Japan, and tolerated the ambiguity of much of the data analysis, at times almost reveling in the complexity of the problems before him (Lindee 1994).

Like the atomic bomb survivors, Amerindian groups were a limited resource, a human database that was available only for a brief historical moment, the moment Neel interpreted as the period between first contact and assimilation. Neel believed that the 1960s constituted this moment. He said there was a great need for parallel studies of selection in both "advanced and primitive societies," and that such work could be important in "our efforts to understand man's past and predict his future" (Neel 1958: 59). Neel then presented a research justification that could be applied to his later work with the Xavante and the Yanomamö:

> Over the world, primitive people are being projected in a few generations from a Stone Age to an Atomic Age culture. In making this transition, they will be called upon to telescope into a few generations biological and cultural adaptations which have extended over a period of thousands of years in Europe. To the extent that these adaptations involve genetic systems, here is a priceless opportunity to study biological selection. One of the most exciting opportunities today is that of collaborative studies along these lines between anthropologists, geneticists and physicians all over the world. (Neel 1958: 59)[12]

Neel's first visit to Brazil was, appropriately enough, in his guise as radiation expert. In 1961 he attended a World Health Organization meeting in Rio de Janeiro, where the group considered the feasibility of biomedical studies in areas of high natural radiation in Brazil. But on that same visit he met with his former post-doctoral fellow, Salzano, to discuss possible studies of Brazilian Indians,[13] and Salzano provides my third explanation for Neel's Amerindian studies: his relationship with a culture broker. While there do seem to have been both psychological and temporal factors shaping Neel's interest in indigenous groups in South America, a historian more interested in social networking might propose that Neel began to work with Amerindian groups because he began to work with someone who could be a translator, a local contact. Salzano led him directly to the Mato Grosso and the Xavante, and from there to the massive research agenda he constructed around this first fieldwork in Brazil.

It is clear that in the early years Neel and his American collaborators depended heavily on Salzano's judgment. They deferred to him on the question of which groups should be studied, and they often seemed to assume that he could and should direct their selection of field sites. For example, less than four weeks before the departure date for the second field trip to Brazil in 1964, Neel still did not know which tribe he would be studying. He expected to be in Brazil with a large interdisciplinary team by April 4, and on March 10 he wrote to Salzano saying, "Please drop us a quick note as soon as a tribe has been selected, so we can read what is available here. [Terry] Turner has just spent a day with us—the Gorotire and Kuben Kran Keng still look good, but the Xavante and the Xingu tribes perhaps even better."[14] Salzano helped Neel make the necessary contacts to start field work in Brazil, which in turn prepared him to expand into Venezuela and other locations.

Research with Amerindian groups suited Neel. It suited his intellectual interests, his concerns about modern culture, his personal sense of what it meant to be male and masculine, and his social networks. Brazil and Venezuela were close and convenient, easily accessible from Ann Arbor. Neel later wrote that one of the advantages of working with Brazilian groups was "their relative proximity to the laboratory facilities of the Department of Human Genetics in Ann Arbor. This was important, because in conjunction with the field work we would be sending a stream of biological samples back to Ann Arbor for analysis."[15]

The Total Population Concept

If the question were posed in this way—What exactly was James Neel *doing* in South America?—one perfectly reasonable answer would be "collecting blood and other human bodily materials and fluids, and shipping them back to Ann Arbor." His letters and notes are filled with details about specimen handling, identification, storage, shipment, and assessment. His field notes, particularly, constantly refer to the numbers of blood, saliva, urine, or stool samples collected that day and to the frustrating uncertainties of getting those materials out of the forest and back to Ann Arbor. Some examples, of no particular note, taken from his 1968 field trip: "Up early, organized and here in village today get pedigrees, 87 ACD, 76 clots, and 82 salivas, and Chas teeth and Arends special studies. Work until 2:00. Pack the specimens, get Boris off" (23 January 1968); "Up at dawn and draw 44 bloods by 10:15" (25 January 1968); "Spent the AM finishing obtaining blood and saliva spec. the Maks here at Santa Maria 64 specimens" (27 January 1968); "We are in our first real bind, with a fridge full of blood but no transportation" (27 January 1968); "A good day—73 bloods and salivas" (28 January 1968); "Full day at the Dojo—33+ physical exams, anthro's, salivas, bloods, 9 urines, BCGs. Busy, busy" (30 January 1968).[16]

Neel was looking for invisible things, for *Streptococcus mutans* (dental caries) and *Histoplasma capsulatum* (histoplasmosis), and for copper, lead, cadmium, and mercury, for antibodies against salmonella, streptococci, the enteroviruses and arboviruses, for hepatitis B, diphtheria, malaria, and for roundworm, hookworm, pinworm, and amebic dysentery. These invisible things, detectable in the laboratory, covert in the field, would provide clues to the disease pressures that might be shaping reproductive success in the Yanomamö. The individual life story—the medical history—was written in antibody response. "Medical histories [in these groups] are almost worthless," he told a specialist in infectious disease who was helping him track down relevant sources relating to the streptococcal viruses. "There is of course no qualified observer in there continuously and, further, the moment you begin to introduce qualified observers the change in living habits is such that your observations from then on may not reflect the past. In other words, we are pretty well driven to a careful study of the antibodies to get a true bill of goods on what has gone on."[17] The "true bill of goods" was not in whatever the Yanomamö or the Xavante might say about their health but in the evidence that their bodies had been exposed to diseases.

The antibodies revealed not only events that had occurred within living memory, however, but also events that had occurred during "the long period of human evolution." "Basically what we are attempting to do is to obtain a picture of the Indian in pre-Columbian times," Neel told a missionary at Manaus in September 1966.[18] Disease pressures, manifest in blood and stool samples and tracked through immune response tests at the CDC, could, he proposed, "make an extremely important contribution to our knowledge of the disease pressures operating on primitive man during the long period of human evolution."[19] The Yanomamö and other Amerindians, he wrote later, presented "an imperfect mirror of the later stages of human evolution, the mirror cracked and dusty, but as accurate as any we have" (Neel 1994: 139). They were, in some fundamental way, like the Indian in pre-Columbian times. They could stand in for the dead. Blood was a sign of the medical experiences of people both dead and living. In its responses, human history was revealed.

The framework guiding Neel's fieldwork and analysis of bodily materials was the "total population" concept, the idea that studies should include attention to the biological, biochemical, anthropological, linguistic, historical, and sociological characteristics of a population. This multidisciplinary approach was needed in order to understand human evolution, which Neel believed had occurred primarily in hunting-and-gathering groups that were very much like twentieth-century "primitives." "If we would understand modern man, we must study such primitive groups as still remain in a way in which they have rarely if ever been investigated to date" (Neel et al. 1964).

The first trial of this concept in the field occurred in the summer of 1962, when Neel, Salzano, the anthropologist David Maybury-Lewis, and several others visited a Xavante Indian village near the Rio das Mortes in the state of Mato Grosso, Brazil. Maybury-Lewis had worked with the Xavante in 1958 and knew the language and social structure. Salzano provided the local expertise. Neel considered the Xavante an ideal group, not because it was isolated and untouched—to the contrary, the Xavante had been interacting, often through warfare, with Europeans and outsiders since at least the eighteenth century—but because it was "at that critical point in its relations with the outside world when it is approachable but yet culturally intact." The Xavante were neither so remote and untouched that working with them would be difficult nor so acclimatized to the outside world that they could no longer provide a model of the "primitive." Furthermore, there was "a small airstrip near the post, providing the means for rapid transportation of blood samples to a base laboratory at Rio de Janeiro" (Neel et al. 1964: 53). Airstrips and pilots mapped onto research plans, and the "stream of biological materials" bound the research group to the islands of the Mato Grosso that were embedded in flight technology and Indian Protective Service programs.

On this field trip Neel and his colleagues set up their examination room at the post of the Indian Protective Service, which was one kilometer from the village and had better facilities for examinations. "For the first several days in the field all Xavantes looked alike, by virtue of their broad faces, their large noses, and their striking uniformity in skin, eye and hair color and style. But as familiarity grew, so did the ability to recognize differences, an ability increased by later study of the photographs obtained in the field" (Neel et al. 1964: 68). Ninety-one individual tribe members came to the post to be examined and interviewed about their families (for pedigrees) and bled. They were measured, and their skin, eye, and hair color codified on the Kruse scale and the Fischer-Saller table. Five standardized photographs were taken of each subject. The breadth of the inner zone of the iris was estimated. The thickness of the lips was measured. Fingerprints and palm prints were taken from some of these participants. The bodies of these ninety-one Xavante, ranging in age from newborn to approximately sixty, were thus packed into numbers and transformed into charts. The charts compared Xavante and residents of Hamburg, Germany, for a range of parameters, including the presence of the "Mongolian fold," general form of head and face, dermatoglyphics, and intrapopulation variability. The Xavante were also compared to other speakers of related languages, though as the authors pointed out in their 1964 paper, "We are aware that language is acquired rather than inherited, ie that these are not necessarily biologically related peoples" (Neel et al. 1964: 66).

In this anthropometric phase, the Xavante were constructed as a genetic whole, a breeding population that could be compared to "Europeans" or other groups in Brazil for phenotypic qualities of face, body, hair, and eyes. At the next level of analysis, the level of the blood, the Xavante were genetically diverse, differing in the MNSs, RH, Duffy, Kidd, and Diego traits. Neel saw blood as a way to get around the "problems inherent in eliciting accurate pedigree and demographic data from a short-lived, illiterate people where marriage occurs at an early age and the resulting clan affiliation is regarded as more meaningful than biological descent" (Neel et al. 1964: 89). Blood typing could reveal nonpaternity or inbreeding; analysis of blood antibody response could reveal disease exposure through time; tracking parasites (treponema, malaria) could reveal biological vulnerability or environmental variation.

After their second field trip in 1964, Neel and his collaborators began preparing an elaborate set of papers to be published together. Neel felt overwhelmed by the enterprise in the summer of 1966.[20] Each aspect of the multidisciplinary study seemed to need its own paper, and finally, in November 1966, Neel submitted ten papers about the Xavante—a linked series of texts laying out a vast empirical and theoretical frame for studies of the genetics of "primitive peoples"—to the editor of the *American Journal of Human Genetics*. These 153 pages of text could disturb any editor, and Neel expected H. Eldon Sutton to be taken aback (though Sutton had been warned some time before that this was coming). "Before you throw up your hands in horror, let me make several points," Neel told Sutton. He then mapped out a grand agenda:

I suspect these papers are going to help initiate a whole-scale reevaluation of many aspects of human population genetics. The field must move beyond the aimless accumulation of gene frequencies which now occupies so much space in the journals. . . . As I indicated in our earlier conversation, there are two papers here which are largely non-genetic, namely number VIII and IX, although even these have some interesting implications for population problems. I very much hope it will be possible to accept them also (assuming acceptance of the others) since they illustrate our concept of the need of the total study of selected populations if we are ever going to understand the interplay between the genetic and the environmental."[21]

Eight of these papers finally appeared in the journal under the joint title "Further Studies on the Xavante Indians" (*American Journal of Human Genetics* 16 (1967): 463–574). Two others went to the *American Journal of Tropical Medicine and Hygiene*, apparently because Sutton concluded they were not relevant to a journal of genetics (Neel et al. 1968a,b). It was still a huge publication package, and an ambitious presentation of a research agenda that Neel and Salzano expected to have broader applications in human population genetics.

In their final summary paper, they proposed that it seemed "self-evident that much about contemporary man can be truly understood only in the light of his past." Some critics of population studies of this kind had questioned whether any of the surviving primitive groups were truly typical—given that all had been to some extent influenced by "contacts with higher cultures." Neel and Salzano countered that

> to denigrate these studies simply because the Garden of Eden is no longer pristine is surely not the scientific approach. There is a clear challenge to the geneticist to join in the study of these cultures in the greatest depth possible while the opportunity still persists, mindful of the presence of cultural contamination, striving (in the case of the American Indian) to detect post-Columbian influences, and searching among groups for common denominators which by their constancy suggest their primordial nature. (Neel and Salzano 1967: 555)

The theme of this final paper, which was intended to bring home the central point of the entire enterprise, was that "primitive" man in some ways surpassed "civilized" man. Here, Neel's romantic ideas about balance, simplicity, and social order were fully expressed. Regarding Xavante controls on reproduction (including abstention, abortion, and infanticide), the paper noted that "at a time when the world is increasingly concerned with fitting its numbers to its resources, it is cause for contemplation that these 'primitive' people have met the issue of reconciling numbers to

resources and way of life." Regarding Xavante resistance to disease and parasites, they said "primitive man was in better equilibrium with his environment than is civilized man" (Neel and Salzano 1967: 567). They hoped that
population genetics could help man "develop the society most consistent
with both his present genetic endowment and his continuing evolution"
(569). Neel had used the word "primitive" without articulating any reservations in his earliest papers, but by 1967 he seems to have begun to recognize some of its political implications. In his paper with Salzano they said
the word was employed "as a convenient synonym for a nonmaterial culture whose economy is based on hunting and gathering with or without
simple agriculture or pastoralism" (Neel and Salzano 1967: 555).

After the Xavante studies, Neel and his colleagues went on to study
the Yanomamö, in a series of field trips to both Brazil and Venezuela, from
1967 to 1975. They also collected blood and materials from Native American groups,[22] and from other isolated populations identified and sampled
by their network of contacts.[23] Some of this blood yielded the "rogue cells"
with heavy chromosome breakage that became the subject of his later
research (Neel et al. 1996).

Conclusion

Neel spent much of his professional life collecting blood and other materials from groups that were uniquely victimized by history—those isolated
by culture or environment, those devastated by nuclear weapons. Sometimes he wondered if he himself were a technical extension of that vic-
timization: "As we examined the Indians and collected our samples, all
this the basis of learned papers that would ultimately contribute to our
professional reputations, were we only the latest of the exploiters, now
for scientific reasons? Students have on several occasions raised this point
when I have lectured on these studies" (Neel 1994: 171). In another context, he wrestled with the possible conflict between the needs of the
Yanomamö and the needs of technical knowledge systems.[24]

As early as 1969—perhaps even earlier—both Neel's prodigious collecting of human bodily materials and Chagnon's field practices had attracted
some negative attention. Chagnon wrote to the head of the New Tribes
Mission in October 1969 that he had been accused of "coming like a thief
into the country" to study tribal groups without giving all his information to local scientists. He had also heard "from reliable sources that there
are now people in the country [Venezuela] who are trying to make it dif-

ficult for 'certain foreign medical people' to perform their harmful craft and drain the blood out of all of the Indians in the country, taking it, again like thieves, back to the United States."[25] In 1970 the missionary Jim Bou told Neel and Chagnon that the Guaicas and Makiritare "still talk about the people who came to take their blood in order to do witchcraft on them"![26] Neel had been attacked much earlier, during his field research in Japan, in ways that echoed the criticisms in Brazil and Venezuela. Some of the atomic bomb survivors studied by the Atomic Bomb Casualty Commission had expressed a sense of violation when autopsy materials were sent to Washington, D.C., to the Armed Forces Institute of Pathology, for storage. The same commission had been criticized by Japanese activists for its failure to provide medical care to the survivors who were the subject of study (Lindee 1994).

In a climate of shifting attitudes among indigenous groups and growing awareness of possible exploitation, Neel, like many others who collected human bodily materials from the field, had to accommodate and adapt to these concerns. After changes in human subjects practices and rules in the 1970s and 1980s, field researchers stopped collecting the huge numbers of blood samples—6,000 to 10,000 in many studies—that had characterized an earlier era. It was difficult and complicated to acquire large numbers of informed consent agreements, and some indigenous groups had become uncooperative, "commercialized and resistant to being studied." Appealing to a Costa Rican colleague in 1983 to collect blood, samples from the Cuna, Neel noted, "I think we would have to be prepared to reimburse them for blood samples; we need your suggestion as to how much this should be per individual."[27]

At the same time, some population geneticists believed that collecting thousands of blood samples was both too expensive and unnecessary, and that samples of twenty-five to forty from any population would be sufficient to assess biological and historical relationships.[28] Neel favored expansive blood collection, but his style of field research was not the model for the proposed (but not realized) Human Genome Diversity Project.

In Neel's papers in the archives of the American Philosophical Society in Philadelphia, there are some bodily traces of the Xavante: thick, dark clumps of hair folded into a file, wrapped in plastic and numbered.[29] The blood samples are not in Philadelphia but a few hours' drive away at the Pennsylvania State University laboratories in State College, Pennsylvania. Neel's sometime collaborator Ken Weiss, a biological anthropologist, stores them there. They could in theory be used in research, embedded as they are in a paper trail of origins and pedigrees, and relevant to explorations of migration and population shift in the Americas. In practice, however, they are not currently being used by researchers. They are stored, frozen, indefinitely.

They are not the only blood samples thus stored. Thousands of others, collected by many investigators in the 1950s, 1960s, and 1970s, are now sitting in laboratory freezers in many institutions, often uncataloged and unused. These materials are physical manifestations of a lost world of biomedical research: they are dramatic evidence of the changing social relations and theoretical perspectives of researchers and human subjects over the last forty years. In a paper promoting what he called "freezer anthropology," D. Andrew Merriweather, a biologist at the University of Michigan (at Neel's home institution in Ann Arbor) has proposed that scientists should exploit these blood samples, collected in the heyday of large-scale anthropological fieldwork. He proposed that they might contain DNA that could allow investigators to "look back in time at a unique snapshot in the history of human populations" (Merriweather 1999). Merriweather himself has used such samples to conclude that there were four founding lineages in the peopling of the New World across the Bering Strait, and that the Pacific Islanders migrated out of Southeast Asia through Indonesia, New Guinea, Melanesia, and out into the Pacific. Human blood tells many stories and contains many voices.

Another voice appears in this chapter, quoted in the epigraph. Mikhail Bulgakov was a Russian writer whose novel *The Master and Margarita* James Neel was reading in the airport when he left for the 1968 field trip to the Orinoco. The novel tells several interwoven stories—of the Crucifixion of Christ, seen through the eyes of Pontius Pilate; of the decapitation by tram of the editor of an important literary journal (who then wires his relatives to inform them of his own death); of a large black cat that drinks vodka; and of Satan, a visitor to the modern Soviet Union, who wears a gray beret and passes for a "foreigner." The master is a troubled writer; Margarita is his muse and married lover, who sacrifices everything for him. The devil causes much trouble, and in the end all the rumors and hysteria are dispelled by a formal investigation, which concludes that none of the events chronicled in the novel happened at all. They were the products of mass hysteria, of hypnotists, magicians, and tricksters.

Bulgakov was a skilled social critic with a wry sense of humor, attuned to the ways that public outrage can be manipulated to suit the needs of power and sensitive to the ubiquitous and mundane presence of evil. He is perhaps a proper commentator on the Yanomamö controversy—posthumously, of course, and entirely unintentionally. Neel, reading Bulgakov's novel, thought it "at once a work of colossal arrogance and conceit and ego, but tempered by the integrity that would permit him to polish and polish even believing it would never be published, as well as the superb craftsmanship and in places penetrating insight. Tonight, if we get to it, we start Yanomamö language lessons."[30] Thus begin the field notes for what has become one of the most famous or infamous field trips in the history of genetics and anthropology.

In May 1968, as the measles epidemic continued in Yanomamö populations, the missionary Robert Shaylor told Neel that his work fighting the measles outbreak earlier in the year had been inspired by God: "We thank God through Jesus Christ our Saviour for supplying all this vaccine and the medicine you helped with while you were here. You are the man God used to meet real needs at a very important time."[31] The man God used had been dead for seven months by the fall of 2000, when the controversy over his work with the Yanomamö began, but he had preserved and left behind a vast collection of papers and correspondence. The Amerindians he studied say very little in these texts, except by virtue of their parasites and antibodies. Because of the structure of knowledge-making (in history, science, journalism), some people's voices come through their bodies, their chicken coops, their diseases. Some people's voices appear in scholarly papers like this one. And some people's voices are conjured by the hypnotists, who can "remove from the field of vision things or people who were in fact within that field of vision" (Bulgakov 1967).

In his book *Darkness in El Dorado*, Patrick Tierney conjured up a story of the heart of darkness. In this chapter, I have done some conjuring myself, not of hearts but of urine, blood, chicken dung, and Yanomamö hair, of the material culture that brought "primitive man" into evolutionary time and that resurrected the experiences of the dead. I propose that Neel's romanticism about the Xavante and Yanomamö could be read as a stark technoscientific rejection of twentieth-century technology and culture and a deployment of the tools of quantitative and laboratory analysis to show that "man" was making devastating biological and social choices, and that "culture" (as in the culture of Western civilization) was not particularly good for the gene pool. Neel clearly and passionately believed that modern society had set in motion forces that were damaging to the genetic health of the human species. And he believed that groups living in a primitive or natural state were exemplars of what was genetically natural. Neel's scientific project with Amerindian groups was thus informed by an impassioned critique of progress and a deep skepticism about modern culture: he drew on all the standards of the scientific method to call into question the evolutionary benefits of science and technology.

NOTES

1. "I am obviously disappointed that no histoplasma turned up in these soil samples, since I personally spent considerable time scraping around in chicken coops, not to mention a number of miscellaneous places"; Neel to Libero Ajello, chief of the mycology section at the National Communicable Diseases Center (later Centers for Disease Control), 4 December 1968. The reference was to a fungus with worldwide distribution that causes histoplasmosis when inhaled. The infection can lead to chronic progressive lung disease or acute fatal disease, and the disease may mimic tuberculosis. Earlier serological studies of the Yanomamö had suggested that they had been exposed to this fungus. See also Ajello to Neel, 21 December 1966 ("I am sending you 75 plastic bags and spoons for the collection and shipment of the 'soil' specimens. The specimens should be collected in bat and bird habitats, where guano accumulated and enriched the soil. The upper layer of the guano-soil mixture should be collected at a depth not to exceed one inch. The bags are numbered V1–V75. They should be filled completely to ensure enough material to carry out the intended tests. A fresh spoon should be used for each bag." And see Ajello to Neel, 12 January 1967; Neel to Ajello, 6 March 1967. All in Papers of James V. Neel, American Philosophical Society, Philadelphia (hereafter Papers of JVN, APS).

2. The number of specimens collected was linked to the expense of the trip—more specimens cost more, fewer could not justify the cost of the field research. See, for example, Neel to Moacyr A. Mestriner, Department of Genetics, University of São Paulo, Ribeirão Preto, Brazil, 1 September 1976. Indians: Macushi and Wapishana (Alpha Helix trip), Papers of JVN, APS.

3. Neel to Leo Kaufman, of the Mycology-Parasitology Section of the Communicable Disease Center in Atlanta, 1 December 1966, Papers of JVN, APS.

4. Neel to Wayne Miller of the Servicio Geodésico Interamericano, Caracas, Venezuela, 2 November 1965, Papers of JVN, APS.

5. Neel corresponded with and sent samples to Stanley H. Abadie, assistant professor of medical parasitology at the School of Medicine of Louisiana State University Medical Center, Papers of JVN, APS.

6. Salzano has himself reconstructed this long-term collaboration in a commemorative essay, Salzano (2000).

7. Salzano to Neel, 17 December 1955, Papers of JVN, APS.

8. "Accordingly I think it might be to your advantage if you did not come with the idea of carrying on any specific line of investigation, but rather with the idea of devoting your time to learning the techniques which would be of most benefit to you when you return to Brazil"; Neel to Salzano, 28 December 1955, Papers of JVN, APS. Salzano wrote back that he had statistical training but would be willing to train more before he came, and Neel said he should do so. Neel also said he could not give Salzano an office: "We here are working under quite crowded conditions, and I am unable to promise you the luxury of an office of your own. Rather it seems quite probable that it will be necessary to share space either with some other visiting Fellow, or one of our graduate students. I hope you will not regard this as too much of an inconvenience"; Neel to Salzano, 10 January 1956, Papers of JVN, APS.

9. Harry M. Miller, Associate Director, Biological and Medical Research, Rockefeller Foundation, to Neel, 3 January 1956, Papers of JVN, APS.

10. Neel to Frankie Davidson, 17 February 1965, Papers of JVN, APS.

11. The massive literature on the cultural and social impact of the development and use of nuclear weapons includes Smith (1965), Sherwin (1977), Easlea (1983), Boyer (1985), and many, many others. The use of nuclear weapons has been commonly construed as a fundamental break, a turning point in human history, by many commentators.

12. In this paper, Neel focused on differential fertility studies (a few carried out in various locations around the world) and on sickle-cell anemia in Africa, which provided a compelling story demonstrating the power of the environment (or of environmental disease pressures) to shape human heredity. "For the time being, this is probably the clearest example in all human genetics of the effect of an environmental change on the future evolution of man" (Neel 1958: 66).

13. "This would be a very different sort of undertaking from the traditional fieldwork of the single cultural or physical anthropologist, or the dash of a geneticist to a remote area to obtain blood samples," Neel wrote in his autobiography (1994: 121). For a useful comparison on Neel's research in South America—particularly his involvement with the International Biological Program—and the Human Genome Diversity Project, see Santos (2002).

14. 10 March 1964, Neel to Salzano, Papers of JVN, APS.

15. Neel 1994: 121. Also: "How often have I envied the members of expeditions whose collectibles—plants, insects, artifacts—could be preserved indefinitely permitting a much less driven schedule. Each time—no

matter how often we had done it—that we got a shipment out in good shape, it was an occasion for a small celebration, albeit, since I ran a dry camp, nonalcoholic. The alcoholic celebration came later, when we returned to Ann Arbor, and learned the specimens had not only gone out in good shape but arrived in good shape. In all, we only lost one shipment" (Neel 1994: 147).

16. All quotations are from Neel's field diary for the 1968 trip, which is in his papers at APS.

17. Neel to Gene H. Stollerman at the Northwestern University Medical School, 24 July 1963. Neel told Pentti Kokko at the CDC three years later, in September 1966, almost the same thing, that antibody titers were the only way to get medical histories in these populations: "Since there are no trained medical observers stationed in these areas, and since it is impossible to get meaningful medical histories, we have come to rely heavily on antibody titers in defining disease pressures." Kokko was chief of the laboratory branch of the Communicable Disease Center, Atlanta. Neel was seeking his collaboration on their very large samples; Neel to Kokko, 23 September 1966, Papers of JVN, APS.

18. Letter, JVN to Macon C. Hare, missionary at Manaus, 20 September 1966, Papers of JVN, APS.

19. "However, they also tell us to what extent the diseases of civilization have already reached these Indians, with a possible modification of the primordial disease and reproductive patterns. Since we are doing our best to get good morbidity-mortality data, from which we are attempting to build population models for primitive man, it is of the utmost importance for us to have the best possible insight into whether these mortality-morbidity patterns might have been altered already by their fleeting contacts with our culture"; letter, 30 August 1967, to Joseph Schubert, Bacterial Serology Unit, CDC, Atlanta, asking if he could spend a day at CDC that fall discussing his work among the Yanomamö, Papers of JVN, APS.

20. His correspondence with Salzano and others in this period contains many references to his anxieties about getting the papers out and getting all the details straight—the results of blood tests, the identities of individuals, the credits; Papers of JVN, APS.

21. Neel went on to suggest reviewers—Jim Crow, because he expected Crow would be critical of some aspects of the study, and René Dubos, because he viewed Dubos as "the most knowledgeable person of whom I know in this 'total population' concept"; Neel to Sutton, 9 November 1966, Papers of JVN, APS.

22. For example, in May 1966, William S. Politzer of the Department of Anatomy of the School of Medicine, University of North Carolina at Chapel Hill, sent James Neel 264 blood samples collected from Seminole and Creek

Indians at Wewoka, Oklahoma, including that of three-year-old Bill Davis Jr., and eighty-five-year-old Ida Factor. Each person was listed with race (Seminole, ½ or Seminole, Creek or Seminole Caddo, Choctaw, Chick. Navajo, Chickasaw). "The great majority of the people appear to be full blooded Indians, or close to it"; Politzer to Neel, 28 May 1966, Papers of JVN, APS.

23. "This laboratory would indeed be interested in typing blood specimens from representatives of any of the *pure*-blooded Indian tribes left in Paraguay. While there may be no such thing as a completely pure tribe, we are reluctant to spend very much effort on tribes with the admixture estimated at greater than 5 percent, because then it becomes difficult to make many of the kinds of inferences in which we are interested." Neel to Ricardo Moreno, 22 February 1974, Papers of JVN, APS. Moreno was a professor of Genetics in the School of Medicine at National University, Asunción.

24. "These people pose a special challenge to our conscience," he told a Pan American Health Organization group in 1974, "and as symbols of past violations of the brotherhood of man call for a particular effort on our part. Their treatment should of course be dictated by humane considerations, but the investigator in me can't resist commenting on the unique research resource they constitute—our last chance to revisit ourselves evolving"; Neel, "Control of Disease in Amerindians in Cultural Transition," p. 7, presented at the thirteenth annual meeting of the Pan American Health Organization Advisory Committee on Medical Research, 24 June 1974, Papers of JVN, APS.

25. Chagnon to Paul Dye, Field Director, New Tribes Mission, Puerto Ayacucho, Venezuela. 1 October 1969, Papers of JVN, APS.

26. Jim Bou, New Tribes Mission, to Neel and Chagnon, 27 April 1970, Papers of JVN, APS.

27. Neel to Ramiro Barrantes, Escuela de Biologia, Universidad de Costa Rica, San José, Costa Rica, 19 December 1983: "We would like to raise at this time the possibility that you might be able to go to Panama, and obtain samples from the Cuna as well as repeat samples from the Bokota (from a different area). I realize that this may be very difficult and perhaps impossible given the various political problems of Central America at the present time. If, on the other hand, you thought it was a feasible undertaking, we would try to supply the funding from here in Ann Arbor. We are thinking in terms of perhaps 100 samples from the Cuna and another 100 from the Bokota"; Papers of JVN, APS.

28. This was the perspective of Luca Cavalli-Sforza, and it was accepted by many population geneticists.

29. In one file are records of physical examinations, with photographs and descriptions of the intelligence and personalities of the people photographed. There is one particularly striking photo, of a young Xavante man

wearing a string necklace supporting a paper card on which the number "15" has been written. His hair is short, curly, and black. He has a dark line of stain, a decorative marking, straight across his cheeks and mouth. He stands before a stone surface broken by fractures. Later, after I had encountered it in the archives, I realized that this same photograph appeared in one of the 1967 papers, with the caption "Young Xavante male (0121015) short (154.3 cm), curly-haired, mentally dull with dental abnormalities as described in text. Digits appear stubby. Right parotid enlarged. No specific diagnosis was reached." In the text, the authors said, "One, a 19-year-old, was the most unusual appearing Xavante. He was short, stocky, had curly hair (the only such individual seen), a left Simian crease, and quaint, dull, smiling, sleepy facies" (Weinstein et al. 1967).

30. Yanomamö, 1968, Field Notes, Papers of JVN, APS. The book is a surrealist critique of Stalinist Russia, and the sort of novel that inspires entire courses. Bulgakov's work was banned in Russia, and he spent his later years as a stagehand in the Russian theater. But he kept writing.

31. Missionary Bob Shaylor to James V. Neel, 20 May 1968, in a letter describing the continuing impact of the measles epidemic, Papers of JVN, APS.

REFERENCES

Boyer, P. 1985. *By the Bomb's Early Light: American Thought and Culture at the Dawn the Atomic Age*. Pantheon, New York.

Bulgakov, M. 1967. *The Master and Margarita*. Translated from the Russian by Mirra Ginsburg. Grove Press, New York.

Easlea, B. 1983. *Fathering the Unthinkable: Masculinity, Scientists and the Nuclear Arms Race*. Pluto Press, London.

Lindee, M. S. 1994. *Suffering Made Real: American Science and the Survivors at Hiroshima*. University of Chicago Press, Chicago.

Merriweather, D. A. 1999. Freezer anthropology: New uses for old blood. *Philosophical Transactions of the Royal Society*, London, Series B 354: 121–129.

Neel, J. V. 1958. The study of natural selection in primitive and civilized human populations. *Human Biology* 30: 43–72.

———. 1994. *Physician to the Gene Pool*. Wiley, New York.

Neel, J. V., A. H. Andrade, G. E. Brown, W. E. Eveland, J. Goobar, W. A. Sodeman, G. H. Stollerman, E. D. Weinstein, and A. H. Wheeler. 1968b. Further studies on the Xavante Indians. IX. Immunologic status with respect to various diseases and organisms. *American Journal of Tropical Medicine and Hygiene* 17: 486–498.

Neel, J. V., E. O. Major, A. A. Awa, T. Glover, A. Burgess, R. Traub, B. Curfman, and C. Satoh. 1996. Hypothesis: "Rogue cell"–type chromosomal damage in lymphocytes is associated with infection with the JC human polyoma virus and has implications for oncogenesis. *Proceedings of the National Academy of Sciences (USA)* 93: 2690–2695.

Neel, J. V., W. M. Mikkelsen, D. L. Rucknagel, E. D. Weinstein, R. A. Goyer, and S. H. Abadie. 1968a. Further studies on the Xavante Indians. VIII. Some observations on blood, urine, and stool specimens. *American Journal of Tropical Medicine and Hygiene* 17: 474–485.

Neel, J. V., and F. M. Salzano. 1967. Further studies on the Xavante Indians. X. Some hypotheses-generalizations resulting from these studies. *American Journal of Human Genetics* 19: 554–574.

Neel, J. V., F. M. Salzano, P. C. Junqueira, F. Keiter, and D. Maybury-Lewis. 1964. Studies on the Xavante Indians of the Brazilian Mato Grosso. *American Journal of Human Genetics* 16: 52–140.

Oreskes, N. 1996. Objectivity or heroism? On the invisibility of women in science. *Osiris* 11: 87–113.

Rossiter, M. 1995. *Women Scientists in America: Before Affirmative Action, 1940–1972.* Johns Hopkins University Press, Baltimore.

Salzano, F. M. 1957. The blood groups of South American Indians. *American Journal of Physical Anthropology* 15: 555–579.

———. 2000. James V. Neel and Latin America—or how scientific collaboration should be conducted. *Genetics and Molecular Biology* 23: 557–561.

Santos, R. V. 2003. Indigenous peoples, the atomic bomb and human genome research: Reflections on late twentieth century human biology in/from Amazonia (1960/2000). In *Genetic Nature/Culture*, edited by A. Goodman, D. Heath, and M. S. Lindee. University of California Press, Los Angeles (in press).

Sherwin, M. J. 1977. *A World Destroyed: The Atomic Bomb and the Grand Alliance.* Vintage, New York.

Smith, A. K. 1965. *A Peril and a Hope: The Scientists' Movement in America, 1945–47.* MIT Press, Cambridge.

Weinstein, E. D., J. V. Neel, and F. M. Salzano. 1967. Further studies on the Xavante Indians. VI. The physical status of the Xavantes of Simões Lopes. *American Journal of Human Genetics* 19: 532–542.

3

JAMES V. NEEL AND JAPAN

Francisco M. Salzano

Any study that considers the charges made by Tierney (2000) against James V. Neel would not be complete without at least a brief presentation of Neel's studies in Japan. This is the reason for this chapter, although one of the contributors to this book (Lindee 1994) has already provided a detailed evaluation of these investigations some years ago.

Tierney's (2000) charges are particularly infamous because they relate Neel, on page 310 of his book, to no fewer than seven unethical experiments. Actually he confounds the agency with which Neel was connected for his Japanese studies, the Atomic Bomb Casualty Commission (ABCC), with the Atomic Energy Commission (AEC); and although the AEC provided support to the ABCC, it did not have any authority over the ABCC or its research programs. Nor did the ABCC ever participate, as the book suggests, in human experiments related or not related to radiation. This and other accusations were clearly rebutted by Bruce Alberts, president of the U.S. National Academy of Sciences (http://www4.nationalacademies. org/nas/nashome.nsf/b57ef1bf2404952b852566dd00671bfd/57065f16ff 258371852569920052d283?OpenDocument, accessed November 17, 2000); the academy was involved in the operation of ABCC since its beginning. In what follows I will present and document in part the studies performed by Neel and colleagues in Japan, also giving hints about the impact of their studies on genetic studies in that country. These investigations were always conducted in close collaboration with his Japanese colleagues, following strict ethical rules; they had a positive effect in Japan's scientific environment; and they contributed substantially to the knowledge and understanding of a major biomedical problem, namely, the genetic effects of ionizing radiation.

History

The atomic bombs dropped on Hiroshima on August 6, 1945, and on Nagasaki three days later, were a tremendous example of humans' capacity to kill and injure members of their own species. Within moments, thousands of buildings and vehicles were destroyed, bridges collapsed, and the water systems were badly damaged, making it impossible to fight the hundreds of fires that instantly erupted all over. Within two kilometers of the hypocenter only ferroconcrete structures remained. One hundred thousand persons perished instantly or within days, and tens of thousands were injured.

After the first impact of horror and perplexity, rescue operations started, with the treatment of the wounded, burial of those who had died, and other emergency measures. From the beginning, the Japanese recognized the importance of follow-up studies of the survivors. In Hiroshima they had planned to compare the present and future frequency of abnormal births in the city with the frequencies reported in their medical literature and vital statistics during the prewar years.

Independently of that, in November 1946 President Harry Truman directed the National Academy of Sciences and the National Research Council to undertake a long-range, continuing study of the biological and medical effects of the bombings. Two independent programs, one Japanese and one American, would involve needless duplication of effort. A joint undertaking was therefore implemented, the Atomic Bomb Casualty Commission (ABCC). The program was jointly operated by the U.S. National Academy of Sciences and the Japanese Institute of Health. In 1975, the ABCC was replaced by an independent binational foundation, the Radiation Effects Research Foundation (RERF), with joint supervision by the National Academy of Sciences and the Japanese Ministry of Health and Welfare. Throughout the entire period, funding for the U.S. contribution was derived from the Atomic Energy Commission and the agencies that replaced it, the Energy Research and Development Administration and the Department of Energy; the Japanese contribution was furnished by the Ministry of Health and Welfare.

James V. Neel was one of the first U.S. scientists involved in this project, and he was specifically worried about genetic effects. The main points established by him were presented to the Committee on Atomic Casualties of the U.S. National Research Council, which, with the help of distinguished geneticists of the time, approved them, recognizing, however, that significant genetic effects would be difficult to detect due to the limitations inherent in work with human subjects (Committee on Atomic Casualties, National Research Council 1947).

The primary focus of the first studies, which soon (1949) received the attention and scientific skills of William J. Schull, was the occurrence of congenital defects in newborn infants. This is, of course, a sensitive subject for parents everywhere, and the study had to take into consideration Japanese customs and beliefs. A dynamic tension was then established between the need to respect parents and their cultural conditioning and the need to determine pregnancy outcomes accurately. The success of the approach can be measured by the amount of information obtained, which was most gratifying. It was also gratifying to be able to accurately inform parents and children that the exaggerated rumors about possible after-effects were wrong.

The Investigation

Table 3.1 presents the main phases of the studies performed, and the Appendix a selected list of the publications that resulted from these efforts. This was the most extensive exercise in genetic epidemiology ever undertaken, and all the persons involved should be highly praised for persistence over more than half a century of investigation, always looking for new resources and strategies of study.

As indicated in table 3.1, the first two phases of the investigation were mainly of a medical-demographic nature. As new techniques were developed, however, they were extended to the cytological and molecular levels. The techniques involved obtaining blood samples from individuals thirteen years or older and of their parents still living in Hiroshima and Nagasaki many years after the bombing; a cooperation of 90 percent was achieved.

The complex set of data assembled can be viewed as an empirical exploration of the risks incurred by children of parents who had been irradiated. None of the analyses of these results yielded results suggestive of a significant difference between the children of exposed individuals and of controls. This, of course, does not imply that damage has not occurred,

TABLE 3.1   Main Phases of the Genetic Studies Related to the Children of Atomic Bomb Survivors

Phase 1 (1948–1954)
In conjunction with the operation of a national rationing system, almost all pregnant women living in Hiroshima and Nagasaki (more than 90%) were registered and data were collected, after the birth of the child, on sex, birth weight, viability, presence of congenital defect, and neonatal death. A cohort of 70,000 children was established and is being monitored up to the present.

Phase 2 (1955–1968)
Data collection was essentially limited to the sex ratio of newborn infants in the two cities and the survival of live-born children.

Phase 3 (1969–1990)
With the emergence of important new technologies, studies were conducted on (a) cytogenetics, looking for sex-chromosome aneuploidy and balanced chromosomal rearrangements; and (b) mutations resulting in electrophoretic variants of 30 proteins and in loss of activity of 11 erythrocyte enzymes. In addition: (c) the incidence of childhood malignancies; and (d) up-to-date data on rates of survival, were also obtained.

Phase 4 (1991–present)
Extension of the investigations to the DNA level involved (a) establishment of permanent cell lines of father/mother/one-or-more-child combinations; (b) two-dimensional DNA digests coupled with restriction fragment screening tests; and (c) Southern blot analysis of minisatellite systems and sequencing information.

Source: Neel and Schull (1991); Neel (1995b); unpublished data, Radiation Effects Research Foundation.

but its nature was certainly not sufficient to be detected with the techniques available at the time. The current molecular investigations, much more sensitive, may furnish new insights into this problem.

This question has to do with another charge raised by Tierney against Neel. He contended that Neel consistently underestimated the deleterious effects of radiation. This is a particularly difficult question that involves the comparison of both observational data on humans and experimental results in model organisms, especially in mice, the most studied species in this regard. Neel's evaluations were clearly exposed in a series of scientific papers (for instance, Neel et al. 1990; Neel and Lewis 1990; Neel 1995a,b, 1996). The main points involved relate to differences between acute and chronic irradiation, as well as to the most appropriate marker systems. The average combined gonadal doses of the exposed parents were of the same level of magnitude as values that on the basis of experiments with mice had been extrapolated as the gametic doubling dose of acute radiation for humans. A clear discrepancy therefore existed on the face of the negative A-bomb survivors' results. This was the reason that Neel and colleagues tried to revise the estimate of the genetic doubling dose of radiation. Be that as it may, criticisms have to be made on the basis of careful scientific evaluations, and not lightly with unsupported remarks as occurred in Tierney's (2000) book.

Relationships with Japanese Science

Another of Neel's achievements was his contribution to the progress of human genetics at a time when this field was not fully developed in Japan. This occurred through employment opportunities offered by the ABCC/RERF institutions, by close interaction with geneticists from other centers of Japan, and through training stays offered at his department in the United States. Many scientists were influenced by Neel and later embarked on the field of human genetics, including Toshiyuki Yanase, Norio Fujiki, and Koji Ohkura, who stayed in Ann Arbor for one year in the late 1950s.

Neel's work in Japan was not confined to radiation effects. He also developed an ambitious work on consanguinity effects, first in persons from Hiroshima and Nagasaki who had not been exposed to the bombs, published in book form (Schull and Neel, 1965), and then, later, in the island of Hirado (summary and interpretation in Schull and Neel, 1972). The Hirado studies, which covered the period 1964–1965, were from the start developed in close cooperation with personnel from four Japanese institutions of higher learning: Juntendo University, Kyushu University, Kyoto Prefectural University School of Medicine, and Tokyo Medical and Dental University.

Examples of work developed independently of the A-bomb effects and, at least at their earlier stages, influenced by Neel were the molecular investigations on two key proteins, albumin (Takahashi et al., 1987; Madison et al., 1991) and phosphoglucomutase (Takahashi et al., 2001). This work contributed not only to a better knowledge of the Japanese population but also to the understanding of how these molecules function.

The number of Japanese investigators who interacted with Neel was very large, as is apparent from the publications presented in the Appendix. A small list of main collaborators would include, in alphabetical order, Akio A. Awa, Jun-ichi Asakawa, Hiroo Kato, Masanori Otake, Chiyoko Satoh, Norio Takahashi, and Yasuhiko Yoshimoto.

Ethics and a Personal Touch

A difficult ethical problem that the ABCC researchers had to face was related to the treatment of the A-bomb survivors. The general policy of the U.S. government was that no wartime victims should receive treatment in any foreign country; therefore, no U.S. funds could be used for this purpose. Schull (1990) pointed out that by providing treatments to the victims of Hiroshima and Nagasaki, those who were unaffected by the A-bomb in those cities would be excluded from the benefits of health care programs. In addition, if treatment programs were provided for some period of time with U.S. funds, these funds would eventually run out. It was not clear whether the Japanese government would continue to fund such care.

On the other hand, it could be asked in what way Neel's studies in Japan would have contributed to the welfare of the Japanese and of humankind in general. First, the negative results obtained provided significant psychological support to the survivors, who were faced with all kinds of alarmist rumors. But the studies were also important to all humanity because they provided precious information about key issues related to our natural history, such as prenatal and postnatal development, morbidity and mortality, and the factors that are important for damage at the molecular and cytological levels. As a matter of fact, the insights gained through evaluations of our burden of mutations provide background material for the solution of one of the greatest challenges to biomedical research today: cancer.

Only insensitive persons, after reading the moving pages about Japan and the Japanese in both Schull's (1990) and Neel's (1994) autobiographies, would believe that these researchers regarded the A-bomb survivors merely as "guinea pigs" in a scientific experiment. I close by quoting a haiku Neel wrote for the ABCC's newsletter in 1972 to express his appreciation to those who had supported the commission's research: "Together, on a hill, we, you and I. Build our memory to peace."

REFERENCES

Committee on Atomic Casualties, National Research Council. 1947. Genetic effects of the atomic bombs in Hiroshima and Nagasaki. *Science* 106: 331–332.

Lindee, M. S. 1994. *Suffering Made Real: American Science and the Survivors at Hiroshima*. University of Chicago Press, Chicago.

Madison, J., K. Arai, Y. Sakamoto, R. D. Feld, R. A. Kyle, S. Watkins, E. Davis, Y. Matsuda, I. Amaki, and F. W. Putnam. 1991. Genetic variants of serum albumin in Amerindians and Japanese. *Proceedings of the National Academy of Sciences, USA* 88: 9853–9857.

Neel, J. V. 1994. *Physician to the Gene Pool: Genetic Lessons and Other Stories.* Wiley, New York.

———. 1995a. The genetic effects of human exposures to ionizing radiation. In *Radiation and Public Perceptions: Benefits and Risks,* edited by J. P. Young, and R. S. Yalow, pp. 115–131. American Chemical Society, Washington, D.C.

———. 1995b. New approaches to evaluating the genetic effects of the atomic bombs. *American Journal of Human Genetics* 57: 1263–1266.

———. 1996. *The Genetic Effects of Ionizing Radiation on Humans.* Department of Medical Genetics, University of South Alabama, Mobile.

Neel, J. V., and S. E. Lewis. 1990. The comparative radiation genetics of humans and mice. *Annual Review of Genetics* 24: 327–362.

Neel, J. V., and W. J. Schull. 1991. *The Children of Atomic Bomb Survivors: A Genetic Study.* National Academy Press, Washington, D.C.

Neel, J. V., W. J. Schull, A. A. Awa, C. Satoh, H. Kato, M. Otake, and Y. Yoshimoto. 1990. The children of parents exposed to atomic bombs: Estimates of the genetic doubling dose of radiation for humans. *American Journal of Human Genetics* 46: 1053–1072.

Schull, W. J. 1990. *Song among the Ruins.* Harvard University Press, Cambridge.

Schull, W. J., and J. V. Neel. 1972. The effects of parental consanguinity and inbreeding in Hirado, Japan. V. Summary and interpretation. *American Journal of Human Genetics* 24: 425–453.

Schull, W. J., and J. V. Neel, in collaboration with A. L. Drew, N. Fujiki, K. Iio, P. Ito, A. Kudô, R. W. Miller, M. Miyake, H. Nemoto, S. Neriishi, J. D. Niswander, K. Ohkura, A. Soni, J. N. Spuhler, C. Sujaku, H. Tanaka, N. Yanai, and T. Yanase. 1965. *The Effects of Inbreeding on Japanese Children.* Harper and Row, New York.

Takahashi, N., H. Omine, J. Kaneko, A. Miura, and C. Satoh. 2001. Identification of base substitutions in ten types of rare variants of phosphoglucomutase-1 (PGM1) encountered in Japanese. *Human Biology* 73: 755–762.

Takahashi, N., Y. Takahashi, T. Isobe, F. W. Putnam, M. Fujita, C. Satoh, and J. V. Neel. 1987. Amino acid substitutions in inherited variants from Amerindian and Japanese populations. *Proceedings of the National Academy of Sciences, USA* 84: 8001–8005.

Tierney, P. 2000. *Darkness in El Dorado: How Scientists and Journalists Devastated the Amazon.* Norton, New York.

APPENDIX

Some of the Main Papers Derived from the Hiroshima/Nagasaki Investigations (In Chronological Order)

1. Neel, J. V., and W. J. Schull, in collaboration with R. C. Anderson, W. H. Borges, R. C. Brewer, S. Kitamura, M. Kodani, D. J. McDonald, N. E. Morton, M. Suzuki, K. Takeshima, W. J. Wedemeyer, J. W. Wood, S. W. Wright, and J. N. Yamazaki. 1956. *The Effect of Exposure to the Atomic Bombs on Pregnancy Termination in Hiroshima and Nagasaki.* National Academy of Sciences–National Research Council, Washington, D.C.
2. Schull, W. J., and J. V. Neel. 1959. Atomic bomb exposure and the pregnancies of biologically related parents: A prospective study of the genetic effects of ionizing radiation in man. *American Journal of Public Health* 49: 1621–1629.
3. Schull, W. J., J. V. Neel, and A. Hashizume. 1966. Some further observations on the sex ratio among infants born to survivors of the atomic bombings of Hiroshima and Nagasaki. *American Journal of Human Genetics* 18: 328–338.
4. Kato, H., W. J. Schull, and J. V. Neel. 1966. A cohort-type study of survival in the children of parents exposed to atomic bombings. *American Journal of Human Genetics* 18: 339–373.
5. Neel, J. V., H. Kato, and W. J. Schull. 1974. Mortality in the children of atomic bomb survivors and controls. *Genetics* 76: 311–326.
6. Awa, A. A., T. Honda, S. Neriishi, T. Sufuni, H. Shimba, K. Ohtaki, M. Nakano, Y. Kodama, M. Itoh, and H. B. Hamilton. 1987. Cytogenetic study of the offspring of atomic bomb survivors, Hiroshima and Nagasaki. In *Cytogenetics*, edited by G. Obe and A. Basler, pp. 166–183. Springer-Verlag, Berlin.
7. Neel, J. V., C. Satoh, K. Goriki, J. Asakawa, M. Fujita, N. Takahashi, T. Kageoka, and R. Hazama. 1988. Search for mutations altering protein charge and/or function in children of atomic bomb survivors: Final report. *American Journal of Human Genetics* 42: 663–676.
8. Otake, M., W. J. Schull, and J. V. Neel. 1990. Congenital malformations, stillbirths, and early mortality among the children of atomic bomb survivors: A reanalysis. *Radiation Research* 122: 1–11.
9. Yoshimoto, Y., J. V. Neel, W. J. Schull, H. Kato, M. Soda, R. Eto, and K. Mabuchi. 1990. Malignant tumors during the first two decades of life in the offspring of atomic bomb survivors. *American Journal of Human Genetics* 46: 1041–1052.
10. Neel, J. V., W. J. Schull, A. A. Awa, C. Satoh, H. Kato, M. Otake, and Y. Yoshimoto. 1990. The children of parents exposed to atomic bombs:

Estimates of the genetic doubling dose of radiation for humans. *American Journal of Human Genetics* 46: 1053–1072.

11. Neel, J. V., and S. E. Lewis. 1990. The comparative radiation genetics of humans and mice. *Annual Review of Genetics* 24: 327–362.

12. Yoshimoto, Y., and K. Mabuchi. 1991. Mortality and cancer risk among the offspring (F1) of atomic bomb survivors. *Journal of Radiation Research* 32 (suppl.): 294–300.

13. Yoshimoto, Y., W. J. Schull, H. Kato, and J. V. Neel. 1991. *Mortality among the Offspring (F1) of Atomic Bomb Survivors, 1946–85*. Technical Report Series, Radiation Effects Research Foundation, Hiroshima and Nagasaki.

14. Neel, J. V., and W. J. Schull. 1991. *The Children of Atomic Bomb Survivors. A Genetic Study*. National Academy Press, Washington, D.C.

15. Neel, J. V., C. Satoh, and R. Myers. 1993. Report of a workshop on the application of molecular genetics to the study of mutation in the children of atomic bomb survivors. *Mutation Research* 291: 1–20.

16. Asakawa, J., R. Kuick, J. V. Neel, M. Kodaira, C. Satoh, and S. M. Hanash. 1994. Genetic variation detected by quantitative analysis of end-labeled genomic DNA fragments. *Proceedings of the National Academy of Sciences, USA* 91: 9052–9056.

17. Neel, J. V. 1995. The genetic effects of human exposures to ionizing radiation. In *Radiation and Public Perception: Benefits and Risks*, edited by J. P. Young and R. S. Yalow, pp. 115–131. American Chemical Society, Washington, D.C.

18. Neel, J. V. 1995. New approaches to evaluating the genetic effects of the atomic bombs. *American Journal of Human Genetics* 57: 1263–1266.

19. Kodaira, M., C. Satoh, K. Hiyama, and K. Toyama. 1995. Lack of effects of atomic bomb radiation on genetic instability of tandem-repetitive elements in human germ cells. *American Journal of Human Genetics* 57: 1275–1283.

20. Kuick, R., J. Asakawa, J. V. Neel, C. Satoh, and S. M Hanash. 1995. High yield of restriction fragment length polymorphisms in two-dimensional separations of human genomic DNA. *Genomics* 25: 345–353.

21. Satoh, C., N. Takahashi, J. Asakawa, M. Kodaira, R. Kuick, S. M. Hanash, and J. V. Neel. 1996. Genetic analysis of children of atomic bomb survivors. *Environmental Health Perspectives* 104 (suppl. 3): 511–519.

22. Neel, J. V. 1996. *The Genetic Effects of Ionizing Radiation on Humans*. Department of Medical Genetics, University of South Alabama, Mobile.

23. Kuick, R., J. Asakawa, J. V. Neel, M. Kodaira, C. Satoh, D. Thoraval, I. L. Gonzalez, and S. M. Hanash. 1996. Studies of the inheritance of human ribosomal DNA variants detected in two-dimensional separations of genomic restriction fragments. *Genetics* 144: 307–316.

24. Neel, J. V. 1998. Genetic studies at the Atomic Bomb Casualty Commission–Radiation Effects Research Foundation: 1946–1997. *Proceedings of the National Academy of Sciences, USA* 95: 5432–5436.

25. Neel, J. V. 1998. Reappraisal of studies concerning the genetic effects of the radiation of humans, mice, and *Drosophila*. *Environmental and Molecular Mutagenesis* 31: 4–10.

4

POLITICS AND SCIENCE

Paul R. Gross

On Exorcisms and Postmodernism

Innocents imagine that modern universities, the names of many of whose departments include "science" (as in social science), do not perform exorcisms. That is a mistake. Today, universities are among the busiest sites for the practice of intellectual exorcism. Ask any current student to define "investigate": you will get the definition for "indict." The latest outbreak of academic exorcism comes to us from anthropology. At issue are the Yanomamö, a Stone Age, indigenous people of the Amazon rain forest. The current repellent effort rests on poststructuralist-postmodern scripture: the doctrine that what we call science is just window dressing for Western hubris and colonialism.

About thirty years ago the distinction between technical disagreements and moral-political warfare began to dissolve. A whole generation of students and teachers became convinced that *everything*, including scientific inquiry, is inextricably political because knowledge itself was inextricably a social—therefore a political—phenomenon. Politics, meanwhile, becomes a matter far too important for niceties. The Berkeley anthropologist Nancy Scheper-Hughes exemplified these enthusiasms when she demanded from her colleagues, in 1995, a new, "militant anthropology," the education of a

new cadre of "barefoot anthropologists" that I envision must become alarmists and shock troopers—the producers of politically complicated and morally demanding texts and images capable of sinking through the layers of acceptance, complicity, and bad faith that allow the suffering and the deaths to continue.

The excuses for such self-righteousness are manifold: a concern for virtue, the environment, racism, sexism, imperialism—the list and the implied indignation are endless. The capo-exorcists are professors; the soldiers are students, junior faculty, and ambitious journalists. Self-criticism is a rarity. "Critical theory," Marxist or postmodern, is about *bad people*—that is, other people—never about oneself. The assassins believe themselves just, in public and in their hearts. This makes them political ruffians and intellectual terrorists, and academic terrorism is what we will see in the Yanomamö affair. But the thing is not new: there have been precedent demon-hunts in the last few decades. It is important first to recall their origins.

The Sociobiology Controversy

In the summer of 1975, E. O. Wilson, the distinguished Harvard zoologist, published *Sociobiology: The New Synthesis*. This was a work of exemplary scientific scholarship, a weaving together of threads from many biological subdisciplines. In some of those Wilson himself was already a leader: population biology, ecology, evolution, animal behavior. He was the authority on an enormous group of social animals: the ants. His purpose was to show that results and methods were already sufficient for a systematic account of animal social behavior and for expanded new research on the hard science of it.

Scores of qualified readers quickly gave praise and had no qualms about the closing chapter, in which Wilson extrapolated from his findings to speculate on *human* social behavior. He was laying out a program for future research, as well as recording achievements. No serious scientist denies that humans are at least animals. This part of *Sociobiology* was clearly more sowing than reaping, defining what should be meant henceforth by that word. Then, suddenly, came an earthquake of highly public denunciation, spreading from the Harvard epicenter, which only now has been properly chronicled. Ullica Segerstråle's impressive book *Defenders of the Truth* (2000) gives an excellent account of what has come to be called the "sociobiology controversy." Although Segerstråle is a sociologist, she has taken the trouble to comprehend fully the necessary detail of the science she writes about. It is worth noting, however, that the "battle" she writes about is really a case of attempted academic assassination, not, as is sometimes suggested, an argument over philosophy of science.

Segerstråle has attempted to provide "a view through the keyhole" to the inner workings of science and the means by which it changes. This scants the blatant politics of the attack she chronicles, emphasizing instead intellectual conflicts and alliances, opposed epistemologies, and different cognitive styles. But the real battle over sociobiology today is not an intellectual battle. It is a political battle, a moral—or rather a moralistic—crusade. Among the newest victims of this crusade are the late "father of human genetics," James V. Neel, and the renowned anthropologist Napoleon A. Chagnon. But to understand the attacks against them, we must return to E. O. Wilson and the charges made against him in 1975.

Wilson seems really to have been unaware of the full political implications of his final chapter. A respected member of the Cambridge (Massachusetts) community of able, ambitious, mostly leftish academics, he considered himself a good liberal on social issues. But he was and is, as Segerstråle notes, an energetic scientific planter as well as a weeder. He saw no more harm in deploying biology in the study of human behavior than in the study of ants or chimpanzees. Insistence on absolute animal-human discontinuity is, after all, reversion to eighteenth-century pop theology, or worse. In The Hub? In 1975? Never!

But Wilson had not been paying attention to the ideological storm clouds that had been gathering over Boston (Cambridge) and the other great academic centers of the West. Biology-phobia in the social sciences is a very old story, but from the end of World War II onward there was renewed fury on the academic left to expunge all vestiges of the idea that human behavior and sociality are, even in small part, products of our evolution (and hence of our genes). The reasons for this are easy to see. There was, first of all, a justified fear and hatred of Nazi eugenics. But there were also the increasingly vociferous demands for preferences and quotas for "minorities"—including women (an honorary minority who form a majority of the population)—because of prior racism or sexism. There was also the insistence among intellectuals on the West's moral inferiority to the Soviet "experiment" and to the Third World, a fixation on capitalist-colonial wrongdoing, and the cultural excellences of the wronged "Other."

The belief that "everything is political" implies that every problem can be fixed by political action. Biology introduces a few doubts to these beliefs and is therefore at best, in the view of believers, a diversion, and at worst an enemy. The attack on so-called biological determinism that is part and parcel of the regnant social-science mentality today really involves a blanket rejection of any significant biological contribution to human performance or behavior. (Note, too, that the term "biological determinism" is a calumny: no serious scientist believes that biology—heredity alone—"determines," that is *fixes*, human behavior). Instead of human nature, the champions of everything-is-political present us with the spectacle of an infinitely malleable potentiality. This idea is, of course, hardly new. It has been an important component of utopian thought for centuries. It figures prominently in the ideas of Karl Marx, for example, who insisted that it is not man's consciousness that makes social life, but society that makes consciousness. Thus, according to Marxists, their form of social thought is the "master science." Hence, there is not only Marxist economics but also Marxist everything, including *correct* (Marxist) science. To have been an academic in the 1970s and to have been unaware of this was most naïve; to have called upon biology, even if only as an aid to understanding culture, was more than likely to be judged a crime. It was this crime with which Wilson was charged. Segerstråle reports:

> In November 1975, a group called the Sociobiology Study Group, composed of professors, students, researchers, and others from the Boston area, launched an attack on Wilson's *Sociobiology*. . . . The first public statement by this group was a letter in *The New York Review of Books*. . . . The dramatic nature of this letter lay not only in its strong language, but also in the fact that among the co-signers could be found the names of some of Wilson's colleagues, working in the same department at Harvard, particularly Richard C. Lewontin and Stephen J. Gould.

And of what was E. O. Wilson accused? Well, of doing bad (incorrect) science, of course, but also of being a voice of racism, sexism, and even genocide. Segerstråle notes that "Wilson was presented as an ideologue supporting the status quo as an inevitable consequence of human nature, because of his interest in establishing the central traits of a genetically controlled human nature."

The Sociobiology Study Group merged with the Boston area New Left's Science for the People and attracted and recruited support from other radical-left fraternities such as the Committee Against Racism (CAR). In due course CAR members attacked Wilson—once physically—hounding and shouting him down in public. Although the shouting has abated, the slurs have never really ended. Meanwhile, Wilson has gone on to win every honor and international prize available to a scientist of his interests and has steadily published important new work far outside the field of sociobiology.

But the artillery still growls by night. There are now a few real scientific issues. The descendant of sociobiology flourishes—an interdisciplinary field for anthropologists, psychologists, cognitive scientists, geneticists, even economists—but it no longer calls itself "sociobiology." In an attempt to purchase immunity from political stink bombs, it calls itself "evolutionary psychology." Segerstråle's attempt to make an epistemology of the continuing debate fails:

> In any case, the lack of [a genuine] scientific critique was only temporary: soon Gould and Lewontin changed their strategy and went full steam ahead with various scientific attacks on sociobiology. Arguably, though, Gould and Lewontin's new focus on the field's scientific shortcomings was not a real substitute for the continuing lack of genuinely scientific critique. In their writings, these two Harvard critics never quite abandoned their original moral/political condemnation of sociobiology.

Nor have they and their followers abandoned it yet. There are new assassins and targets. The "scientific" objections now take this form: sociobiology *cannot* be good science because data gathering or theorizing insensitive to the harm it might do victim groups is ipso facto bad science. This impresses the young, the aged New Left, and other contemporary philosophical naïfs. But it is tautologic nonsense. There is no connection between quality of inquiry and social decorousness of result. More: a possible role for biology in human behavior implies that political action alone might not, perhaps, change *everything* for the better. For the political *engagé*, that alone is absolute heresy.

A New Storm

Terence S. Turner is a professor of anthropology at Cornell University who has studied Amazonian indigenes. So has Chagnon, though he has been immensely more successful (by the standard measures of recognition). A self-identified political anthropologist and defender of human rights, Turner abhors "sociobiology" and has for years denounced both it and Chagnon. For him it is vicious, rightist, and reductionist (the latter now being a favorite derogative term shared by leftist demagogues and rightist mystics). He is a vocal enemy of Chagnon, who thinks (and writes) that human evolution can help explain some of our doings, including—horror of horrors—our tendencies toward aggression. Leslie E. Sponsel, a professor of anthropology at the University of Hawaii, also specializing in "peace studies," shares Turner's hostility to sociobiology, indeed toward science in anthropology generally. These two represent the "cultural" ("social" in the United Kingdom) branch of the subject, which has in many places divorced itself from physical anthropology. Stanford University, for example, has separate departments.

In September 2000, Turner and Sponsel wrote a five-page e-mail message to the president and president-elect of the American Anthropological Association (AAA). Somehow, this epistle was immediately sent on to many others in the field; overnight it was made public on the Internet. No word describes it better than "hysterical." "We write to inform you," it begins,

> of an impending scandal that will affect the American anthropological profession. . . . In its scale, ramifications, and sheer criminality and corruption it is unparalleled in the history of anthropology. . . . This nightmarish story—a real anthropological heart of darkness beyond the imagining even of a Joseph Conrad (although not, perhaps, a Josef Mengele)—will be seen (rightly in our view) . . . as putting the whole discipline on trial.

Turner and Sponsel had just seen proofs, they averred, of a book by Patrick Tierney, an investigative journalist, called *Darkness in El Dorado: How Scientists and Journalists Devastated the Amazon* (2000). This book contains horrifying revelations about which Turner and Sponsel, ostensibly fearing for their colleagues, were sounding the alarm.

There is something wrong with these claims. Turner and Sponsel seem to have known Tierney and to have been aware of this book for a long time before they ever saw such proofs. In the book, Tierney thanks Turner for his help. Turner and Sponsel are also on record citing prior versions of Tierney's claims. But never mind that. Their tocsin sounded for colleagues in anthropology: publication is imminent! *Darkness* was about to be excerpted in the *New Yorker*. (It was also, in fact, a candidate for the National Book Award.)

The Charges

What does Tierney charge? Well, I proceed from the ridiculous to the merely defamatory: Chagnon was a draft dodger; he exploits ethnographic studies among the Yanomamö for his, but not their, profit; he is careless of human rights; he is a right-wing ideologue, out to make sociobiological points; he faked the Yanomamö fierceness made famous in his ethnography; thirty years ago, he joined the American medical geneticist (and physician and coinvestigator, with Japanese colleagues, of the genetic consequences of the atomic bomb) James V. Neel in inoculating the Yanomamö with a "virulent" vaccine in order to induce a measles epidemic, thereby testing sociobiological and "eugenic" theories; and, finally, that Neel was a right-wing eugenicist who performed illegal radiation experiments on the Yanomamö for the Atomic Energy Commission (now the U.S. Department of Energy). Most of this was supposed to have taken place in 1968. And it is only a partial list of the charges.

The media jumped. Before anybody had seen even the *New Yorker* extract, let alone the book, a full-blown character assassination was under way, with no epistemological quibbling to confuse the audience. In England, the *Guardian*'s headline read "Scientist 'Killed Amazon Indians to Test Race Theory.'" The book's publisher had obviously never allowed the manuscript to be read by reviewers competent to evaluate the evidence— not even those from the institutions where all the facts lay open for examination: the Universities of Michigan and of California at Santa Barbara; the National Academy of Sciences (Dr. Neel was an honored member); the Department of Energy; and the several federal vaccine safety and distribution agencies. Turner and Sponsel also arranged a suitable denouement: the national meeting of their association was scheduled for mid-November 2000, in San Francisco.

The writers, both emeritus members of the Committee for Human Rights, had arranged

> that the Open Forum put on by the Committee this year be
> devoted to the Yanomami case. This seemed the best way to
> provide a public venue for a public airing of the scandal, given
> that the program is of course already closed. . . . [W]e *have invited*
> *Patrick Tierney to come to the Meetings and to be present at the*
> *Forum.* (emphasis added)

Reaction and Reality

Things did not turn out as expected. Serious scholars, of whom some remain even in cultural anthropology (with more in adjacent fields), read the *New Yorker* piece. They got hold, with difficulty, of original proof copies of the book. And then all hell broke loose.

Tierney's "investigative reporting"—he claims to have given it ten years, some of them in the Amazon—is a tissue of misrepresentation, scientific ignorance, and groundless insinuation. The book is densely "documented," but, among the 5,000 notes, many refer to informants who cannot be checked, most others to known enemies of Chagnon or to locals in Brazil and Venezuela who are in fact exploiters of the indigenes. Citations of documents or conversations say the opposite of what is found in the documents, or of what the interviewees report independently. The entire "induced" epidemic horror story, central to Tierney's bill of indictment, is part innuendo and part gross incomprehension of the science. Turner was forced to withdraw publicly his endorsement of *that* part of *Darkness in El Dorado*. There were also *no* "illegal radiation experiments."

What of Dr. Neel's racist "eugenics"? It is clear from their comments that none of the three—Messrs. Tierney, Turner, Sponsel—knows what "eugenics" means. It looks as though Tierney was unaware that Dr. Neel, a physician as well as a scientist, had advice and assistance, in his effort to abort an *existing* measles epidemic among the Yanomamö, from the world's best-qualified sources. Neel's lifelong commitment—and great success—was in fact to *defeating* "eugenics"! All this is recorded—even, thanks to the aroused institutions, on the Internet. The "draft dodger" charge against Chagnon is simple slander.

By the time the *New Yorker* extract appeared, Tierney had muffled some of its most outrageous claims—in language but not intent. Old proof copies of the book were out, and it was clear from what extreme assertions the backing down was being done. The book, as published, uses still weaker language, reduced in many places to mere innuendo. But the tendentiousness is unremitting. No longer, for example, does Tierney invoke crazy sociobiological experiments and an induced epidemic. Instead, he is content with statements like this:

> The Venezuelan Yanomami experienced the greatest disease
> pressure in their history during a 1968 measles epidemic. The
> epidemic started from the same village where the geneticist James
> Neel had scientists inoculate the Yanomami with a live virus that
> had proven safe for healthy American children but was known to
> be dangerous for immune-compromised people. The epidemic
> seemed to track the movements of the investigators.

The virus was not "live" in the trivial sense. The vaccine used by Neel was the standard *attenuated* virus preparation (a process first systematized by Louis Pasteur), multiple millions of doses of which had and have been given around the world, not just to "healthy American children." Among the millions of vaccinations, known serious consequences number three, all in children with prior severe immunodeficiency disease. The vaccine Neel and Chagnon obtained was the best available at the time; and no vaccine was available for measles before 1963. The creation of effective antiviral vaccines was one of the great biomedical achievements of the twentieth century. The measles vaccine was developed by Dr. Samuel L. Katz (a distinguished Duke pediatrician) and Nobelist John Enders, inter alios. Dr. Katz has quietly shown since the scandal broke that the Tierney charges are unrelieved nonsense. There is no case on record of such a vaccine *ever* having *transmitted* measles. Better vaccines are available today, but this was thirty years ago.

That so delicious a story could be a complete fiction may seem unlikely, but then, many otherwise normal people think that Hollywood's version of the Kennedy assassination was a courageous exposé rather than imaginative political nonsense. Believers in vast right-wing conspiracies can get, however, a proper account of the measles epidemic from a long letter by William J. Oliver, M.D. (retired chairman of the Department of Pediatrics at the University of Michigan), which dissects the Tierney-Turner-Sponsel account point by point. It was (and may still be) available on-line, in company with much related material, from the University of Michigan (www.umich. edu/~urel/Darkness/oliver.html).

This letter, along with the dozens of other contributions from competent physicians and scientists, pushed Turner to recant his passionate endorsement of both Tierney's early and then-weakened stories of the Yanomamö measles epidemic. In an e-mail response to Dr. Katz on September 28, 2000, Turner excuses himself and Sponsel, and at the same time abandons Tierney, as follows:

> We did set about doing our best to check on its more shocking allegations. . . . One of the authorities we consulted was Dr. Peter Aaby, a well-known medical anthropologist and member of the Scandinavian medical team that has been working on measles in West Africa for some twenty years. He has gone over the claims about the vaccine made by Tierney and refuted them point by point, in very much the same terms that you [Katz] have used. We are in the process of preparing a memo that will state our

understanding of this matter, to help correct the confusion that the unauthorized circulation of our earlier memo [sic].

No matter: the activist Tierney still gets his word in: "I sensed that the injustice done to the Yanomamö was matched by the distortion done to science and the history of evolution. Yet the incredible faith the sociobiologists had in their theories was admirable."

Impact and Consequences

It looks as though this particular exorcism of "sociobiology" has, for the moment, failed again. But decent scholars have been hounded and besmirched. Perhaps they, too, will recover in strength, as E. O. Wilson has done. But Dr. Neel is dead, and the energetic Chagnon has retired from the field in which he is both an eminence and the target of bitter obloquy. (Some of his detractors justify this by saying that he is not a nice man.) At the AAA meetings in November 2000, most of the speakers exposed the conceits and deceits of *Darkness in El Dorado*. And thus far there have been no serious rebuttals from the book's promoters. Patrick Tierney's feeble and largely irrelevant written responses to the critical revelations could be found, along with links to many other important documents, on-line at http://www.anth.uconn.edu/gradstudents/dhume/darkness_in_el_dorado/index.htm.

The discussion has not ended. For a good example of the general response of highly respected scholars to the book, the reader is referred to the multiple-author review of Tierney's (2000) work in the April 2001 issue of *Current Anthropology* (Coronil et al. 2001); Sponsel's (2002) reaction to it; and the replies given to him by F. Coronil, A. G. Fix, M. S. Lindee, and P. Pels. The American Anthropological Association task force established to examine the whole affair has a site (http://www.aaanet.org/edtf/) in which many documents related to different aspects of the charges can be examined. Heated debates related to the work of this task force occurred at the AAA meetings in 2001.

Yet the dirty work is done. However far the exorcists retreat, they have damaged indigenous peoples, who are already afraid of outsiders (and should be, of some outsiders) and of what we know as medicine, and who see only conspiracy—of both men and gods—against them. Science and preventive medicine suffer already; stung by the worldwide attention to this false horror story, the Venezuelan government is moving to stop all future scientific contacts with such peoples as the Yanomamö. At the AAA meetings in 2000, however, Tierney received enthusiastic applause, presumably for *caring*. Those who applauded, the barefoot anthropologists and activists, are and will be teaching your children.

NOTES

This chapter constitutes a very slightly modified and updated version of an article originally published in *New Criterion* 19, no. 6 (February 2001). We thank the journal's managing editor for allowing us to reproduce it here.

REFERENCES

Coronil, F., A. G. Fix, P. Pels, C. L. Briggs, C. E. Mantini-Briggs, R. Hames, S. Lindee, and A. R. Ramos. 2001. Perspectives on Tierney's *Darkness in El Dorado*. *Current Anthropology* 42: 265–276.

Segerstråle, U. 2000. *Defenders of the Truth: The Battle for Science in the Sociobiology Debate and Beyond*. Oxford University Press, Oxford.

Sponsel, L. E. 2002. On reflections on *Darkness in El Dorado*. *Current Anthropology* 43: 149–152.

Tierney, P. 2000. *Darkness in El Dorado: How Scientists and Journalists Devastated the Amazon*. Norton, New York.

Wilson, E. O. 1975. *Sociobiology: The New Synthesis*. Harvard University Press, Cambridge.

5

WHY GENETIC STUDIES IN TRIBAL POPULATIONS?

Francisco M. Salzano

Worthless Information?

Incorrect and pernicious notions permeate Tierney's book (2000), which claims that human population genetic studies have little value, and they harm tribes like the Yanomamö. To the contrary, information on the genetic composition of a population can be useful to the group under investigation, and to humanity, in at least two ways: (1) by describing the genetics of a population, we are able to better understand its origins, its distinct evolutionary history, and the inherited peculiarities that result from them; and (2) by identifying possible genetic susceptibility to illnesses and adverse reactions to foods or drugs, we may be able to intervene early and prevent adverse health outcomes in the future.

The objective of this chapter is twofold. First, I will argue that tracing population origins and evolutionary histories of populations is an invaluable tool for understanding biological variation in general and the distribution of infectious, chronic, or drug-induced illness. Second, I propose that full appreciation for the implications of population history and health in any one population is best realized in the context of genetic knowledge drawn from a large, diverse sample of genetic data from all continents. Therefore, I will consider efforts developed internationally to obtain standardized, fully comparable population genetic information on a worldwide scale, as well as the antiscience movements that are hampering such endeavors.

Genetic and Evolutionary Research in South American Natives

Over the past several decades, scientists have conducted analyses of the genetics of South American natives in hopes of understanding their population history and its implications for cultural and biological diversity. Researchers do so by characterizing differences and similarities between the gene pools of native communities or populations, which they do in a variety of ways. Geneticists have relied on a large number of markers, including traditional markers of the blood (i.e., blood group systems such as ABO, rhesus, Diego, and others); electrophoretic markers (i.e., serum proteins, red cell proteins); immunoglobulins (i.e., gamma globulins, KM system); histocompatibility systems or human leukocyte antigens (HLAs); and more recently DNA polymorphisms. With novel techniques such as restriction fragment length polymorphisms and others, the precision of measurements of genetic variation has greatly increased (Crawford 1998). It is now possible to describe the variation of the DNA molecule itself rather than to have to infer genetic variation from the measurement of gene products such as markers of the blood and immunoglobulins. Salzano and Callegari-Jacques (1988) and Crawford (1998) summarized most of the data on South American native populations available from the pre-DNA era, while Salzano (2002) reviewed the most recent DNA polymorphism data.

Amerindian communities in general meet conditions favorable for the investigation of population history and susceptibility to disease and adverse reactions to food and drugs. This is the case for several reasons: (1) the date of their entry into the continent and their putative ancestors can be traced though genetic research with a reasonable degree of certainty; (2) they tend to have lower genetic diversity than other populations; (3) it is easier to quantitatively assess genetic variation across South American native groups due to small population size; and (4) they have been subjected to a wide array of physical, biotic, and cultural environments, providing ample material for comparative investigations.

The pattern of genetic relationships observed among South American Indians indicates the absence of a few large genetic clusters; instead, we find greater homogeneity across populations, with more gradual, stepwise differences between them. These genetic characteristics track geographic and linguistic factors in ways that suggest that females may be more mobile than males (Fagundes et al. 2002).

In order to adequately characterize genetic relationships between South American native populations, researchers have worked long and hard for seventy-five years, an undertaking that has not been attempted in most other ethnic groups. In spite of such effort, the amount of genetic information available for Amerindians is still quite uneven. For instance, while for mitochondrial DNA there are data on ninety samples involving 3,829 individuals, data on nuclear DNA variants are much more sparse, sometimes consisting of a few dozen subjects studied in a population only (Salzano 2002). This is unfortunate because the use of mitochondrial DNA is limited in that it cannot be used to investigate selection of genes in the nucleus, and only female migration can be studied, since mitochondrial DNA is transmitted through mothers. Moreover, nuclear DNA holds much greater genetic variation than does mitochondrial DNA (Crawford 1998).

Population History

Human population variability is of decisive importance for understanding the biological history of a group (be it local or of continental size), as well as for humankind in general. Why are humans so diverse? What factors influence this variability? Why are some genetic variants ubiquitous, whereas others are restricted to one or a few population groups? In which ways do these differences reflect the morphology and physiology of their carriers? These questions can only be answered through careful, well-delineated investigations.

Three types of factors influence population variability: (1) genetic origins and demographic history, namely, the size, degree of isolation, and movement of the population under study; (2) natural selection (deterministic factors) or random genetic drift (stochastic factors), which contribute to the frequencies of genetic variants; and (3) external sources of variation, or the factors that may alter the genetic material; these involve both natural (intrinsic levels of errors in DNA duplication, soils with high background radiation) and artificial (exposition to drugs manufactured by ourselves, for example) agents.

Although there is general agreement that the ancestral Amerindian populations migrated from Asia into America through Beringia during the Pleistocene, many questions remain, including the age and number of these migrations, as well as the size of the colonizing groups. It is not possible to discuss these problems in detail here (see general evaluations in Salzano and Callegari-Jacques 1988; Crawford 1998), but both mitochondrial DNA and Y chromosome data suggest that a single early wave of migration occurred during the peopling of the Americas, and that this event took place about 20,000 years ago (Bonatto and Salzano 1997a,b; Santos et al. 1999; Silva et al. 2002).

Similarly, geneticists study single populations to determine how natural selection, random drift, and natural or artificial agents may have played a role in the distribution of the cultural and biological traits that characterize them today. The Aché, Tupi-Guarani speakers of eastern Paraguay, had sporadic contacts with non-Indians since the seventeenth century and began having more extensive contact with the surrounding population in the late 1960s. They show marked morphological differences when compared with other Amerindians that may have become fixed in the population through random genetic drift. Unlike most other Amerindians, the Aché tend to have very oriental features, fair skin and eye color, and distinctive beards. Some anthropologists who first made their acquaintance believed that they were descendants of an early Viking colonization or of a lost tribe of Japanese. Other more likely possibilities are that they are the descendants of a Guarani group, or of a Ge group that preceded the Guarani colonization of Paraguay (Battilana et al. 2002).

Table 5.1 lists some of the genetic peculiarities of the Aché that are certainly related to their past history of isolation in the woods. They are being used to test the hypothesis that the Aché are a Guarani group that reverted to life in the woods, as opposed to the early Ge origin (a question not yet settled). Additionaly, this information can be used to explain eventual peculiarities of medical significance to be detailed in the next section.

It is clear, then, that *genetic history matters*. Both deterministic and stochastic elements contribute to a given unique gene pool in ways that may determine different degrees of adaptation of their carriers to distinct environmental and biological challenges. It should also be mentioned that most members of any given ethnic group are curious about their past.

Differential Susceptibility to Diseases, Drug Reactions

Amerindians present a series of distinctive genetic features. One of the most exciting differences between them and other groups is related to the HLA system. Molecular studies have indicated (1) a limited amount of genetic variability; (2) novel B locus variants, especially in South America; (3) the phenomenon of "allele turnover," that is, new alleles tend to sup-

TABLE 5.1   Genetic Peculiarities of the Aché of Paraguay, Certainly Related to Their History

Genetic System	Description	References
Blood groups plus proteins	Markedly distinct from other South American Indians. In a study that involved 58 populations of this ethnic group and seven genetic systems, the Aché presented the highest average genetic distance (0.84; others: 0.33–0.77). These results were confirmed with a more limited number of populations, but with a higher number of markers	Salzano and Callegari-Jacques (1988); Battilana et al. (2002)
Alu insertions	Considering 12 insertions ($n = 31$–75), the average genetic distance between the Aché and three other Brazilian Indian groups was 2.4 times higher than the others	Battilana et al. (2002)
CGG repeats, FMR1 gene	They show only two types (28, 29) of the 26 that occur in cosmopolitan populations ($n = 15$)	Mingroni-Netto et al. (2002)
FRAXAC1 alleles	They present only two (154 bp, 152 bp) of the six that occur in other populations ($n = 36$)	Mingroni-Netto et al. (2002)
DXS548 alleles	Only one (194 bp) of the nine that are found in other populations occur among them ($n = 38$)	Mingroni-Netto et al. (2002)
GST, CYP, TP53	Average heterozygosity: 35 ($n = 67$); interval, in relation to six other South American Indian populations: 19–38	Gaspar et al. (2002)
HLA	Allele frequencies clearly different from those of the other groups analyzed ($n = 89$)	Tsuneto et al. (2002)
Seven biallelic polymorphisms, Y chromosome	They show just one haplotype (no. 2) of the seven found in 19 other Amerindian populations ($n = 53$)	Bortolini et al. (2002)
Mitochondrial DNA	Only two (A, B) of the four haplotypes usually found in Amerindians were observed; low nucleotide diversity ($n = 42$)	Schmitt et al. (2001)

plant older alleles rather than supplementing them; and (4) an antigen-driven evolution of HLA-B molecules of Central and South American natives that generated novel peptide specificities not provided by the limited repertoire of founder allotypes postulated to have been present in the first migrants to the continent (review in Salzano 2002). Since this system is involved with the immune response, these results help to explain a series of characteristics about it discussed in other chapters of this book.

HLA is different from many other systems in humans due to its function, which is to collect peptide fragments inside the cell and transport them to the cell surface, where the peptide-HLA complex is surveyed by immune system T cells. This key function demands a versatile adaptation regime, in which new variants are actively tested, to cope with the vast amount of variability among pathogenic agents. In this case, therefore, we have a beautiful example as how limitation imposed by history may be overcome by positive natural selection.

The search for factors responsible for susceptibility or resistance to diseases is much influenced by the amount of recombination that occurs in a given genetic region, since it is necessary to observe linkage between the traits under consideration. It has been established that this amount of recombination is also related to the history of the population under study (Frisse et al. 2001; Reich et al. 2001). For instance, a group that originated from a small number of founders carries much less diversity, or opportunity for segregation of genetically diverse regions, than another that has a more diversified origin. Therefore, results obtained in a given ethnic group cannot be easily extrapolated to another.

Human serum albumin, the most abundant protein in blood plasma, is physiologically important because of its unique ability to reversibly bind an extensive series of endogenous and exogenous compounds, thereby helping in the metabolization or excretion of these substances. Studies at the molecular level associated with population surveys disclosed distinct distribution patterns for two variants of this protein. Albumin Yanomamö 2 is restricted to members of this tribe, where it reaches a relatively high (7 percent) frequency. Homozygotes for this variant show a lower ability for bilirubin binding, while heterozygotes cannot be distinguished from individuals who have normal (A) albumin only. Therefore, these carriers can increase in numbers, but when homozygotes for the variant start to appear, their decreased adaptation may provide a check to the spread of this allele. Albumin Maku, on the other hand, shows a widespread distribution both in South American Indians and in populations with mixed Indian and non-Indian ancestry. This variant is clearly more efficient than albumin A in relation to binding to several nonesterified fatty acids, independently of their composition. This may explain its wide occurrence (Franco et al. 1999).

Our group is actively involved in the investigation of the genetic and environmental aspects of lipid metabolism (how our body deals with the fat substances ingested in the diet), and a series of studies in systems that may influence it had been performed in South American natives (Kaufman et al. 1999; Hutz et al. 2000, 2002; De Andrade et al. 2000, 2002; Mattevi et al. 2000). A special and important aspect of this subject is obesity. This condition presently constitutes a generalized problem, which is particularly acute among acculturated aboriginal populations throughout the world, and many factors are involved in it. The first candidate gene for obesity identified in native Brazilians was the low-density lipoprotein receptor (*LDLR*). Mattevi et al. (2000) verified in members of four tribes (Xavante, Gavião, Suruí, Zoró) a haplotype derived from four restriction site polymorphisms that was highly associated with the body-mass index (weight in kilograms/(stature in meters)^2), skinfold thickness, and the arm fat index (which relates triceps skinfold thickness and upper arm circumference measurements). Members of these four tribes, plus Kaingang subjects, were also tested by Hutz et al. (2002) in relation to another genetic region, the dopamine D2 receptor gene. The results were even more interesting because they indicated that variants in this system might influence obesity through the dopaminergic reward pathway. Food consumption, of course, is essential for survival, and the feeling of pleasure and satisfaction after the provision of nutrients strongly reinforces this action. Stimulation of this pathway may reduce the effectiveness of satiety factors, promoting overeating and leading to obesity.

Contemporary Brazilian native societies are experiencing drastic changes in their diet and ways of living. Santos and Coimbra (1996) and Gugelmin and Santos (2001) verified among the Suruí and Xavante, respectively, that there was a clear positive association between these factors (lifestyle changes) and indicators of obesity. It is important to correlate these environmental changes to a background of genetic predisposition, since individuals from these populations may develop an increased prevalence of metabolic diseases (like diabetes) as their lifestyles become more westernized.

The Fragile X syndrome is one of the most frequent inherited forms of mental retardation. It results from expansions in the CGG (cytosine, guanine, guanine) repeat of the 5' untranslated region of the *FMR1* gene. This CGG region is polymorphic in the normal population and varies in size from six to fifty repeats. Mingroni-Netto et al. (2002) verified that the Aché and Wai Wai Indians of South America, unlike populations of African or European derivation, present extremely reduced variability in this region, and that the number of repeats conditions a low probability that they may be affected by the syndrome.

In addition to disease susceptibility and resistance, populations differ in the ways that they metabolize and are sensitive to drugs and foods. The biochemical compositions of individuals and populations differ; therefore, observations of unusual reactions to drugs or food could most easily be explained by this fact. In the 1950s, several abnormal and adverse drug reactions were shown to be determined by specific genetic enzymatic variation. This now well-recognized area of study, known as pharmacogenomics, examines the genetic factors that that determine the elimination and kinetics of drugs in the organism.

Two systems that are important in this regard are those denominated by cytochrome P-450 (CYP), a superfamily of enzymes that act on phase I of xenobiotic metabolic transformation), and glutatione S-transferases (GST), a group of phase II enzymes that detoxify endogenous and exogenous electrophiles). Studies of variants in these systems among seven South American tribes by Gaspar et al. (2002) disclosed high frequencies of CYP1A1*2A and CYP1A1*2C alleles and mostly low values of the null deletions GSTM1*0/*0 and GSTT1*0/*0. The enzymes codified by CYP1A1*2A and CYP1A1*2C have higher catalytic activities than the products of the most common alleles, producing a larger amount of toxic metabolites, which are mainly detoxified by the GSTM1 and GSTT1 proteins. Since carriers of the GSTM1*0/*0 and GSTT1*0/*0 genotypes produce no enzyme activity, toxic products induced by the action of CYP enzymes can accumulate in these individuals.

It is possible, therefore, that CYP1A1*2A and CYP1A1*2C frequencies had increased during America's colonization either by genetic drift or by selection in response to new environmental challenges. These high CYP prevalences could have acted as selective factors reducing GSTM1*0/*0 and GSTT1*0/*0 frequencies, since the ratio between CYP and GST activities is critical to avoid the accumulation of toxic reactive intermediates. Since both the CYP1 and GST systems are involved in cancer susceptibility and development, Amerindians may need differentiated surveillance and treatment in relation to these conditions.

It is clear, therefore, that there is a continuum of variation in humans, with sometimes difficult distinctions between healthy and disease states. Results obtained in populations of a given ethnic group do not necessarily apply to those of distinct affiliation. Therefore, efforts have been developed to obtain the amount of genetic variability data needed for all these analyses on an orderly, worldwide basis. Two such programs are described in the following.

Attempts at Coordinated Efforts

The International Biological Programme (IBP)

This project, coordinated by the International Council of Scientific Unions, was developed between 1964 and 1975. A full history of its Human Adaptability (HA) section was provided by Collins and Weiner (1977). The studies involved work in forty-six countries, which were examined in thirty meetings or symposia. Twenty books coordinated at the international level have described the results. In addition, twenty-five others, edited in eight countries, provided further information. Special mention should be given to the book that described the papers presented at an international symposium held in Burg Wartenstein, Austria, during the organizational phase (Baker and Weiner 1966); the *A Guide to Human Adaptability Proposals* (Weiner 1969) and the *Human Biology* (Weiner and Lourie 1969), published in the operational phase; and the book by Harrison (1977), in which multidisciplinary studies developed using the IBP philosophy were carried out from the tundras of Siberia to the Pacific Islands, from the Amazon to the savannas of Africa, in the deserts and hills of Israel, and from small, isolated settlements to modern cities.

Bioethics is not a recent invention. In the ethical norms issued in two World Health Organization documents of that time, which served as guidelines in the IBP (WHO 1964, 1968), clear statements were given in relation to the need to protect and respect the dignity of the subjects under study, about the services and rewards that could be provided, and concerning appropriate rules of conduct in the field (see chapter 1, this volume).

The Human Genome Diversity Project (HGDP)

The starting point for this project was a paper by Cavalli-Sforza et al. (1991), who made a plea for a worldwide survey of human genetic diversity. The Human Genome Organization (HUGO) responded to this proposal with the formation of an ad hoc committee that would consider how such an international project could be developed. At the outset, the complexity of the project became clear, since it would be of interest to biomolecular scientists, human geneticists, anthropologists, archaeologists, evolutionists, linguists, and historians.

A series of three main workshops was planned to discuss these problems in depth. At the first, which organized by L. Luca Cavalli-Sforza and Marc Feldman and took place at Stanford University in July 1992, forty participants discussed statistical issues related to sampling problems. The second was organized by Kenneth M. Weiss and took place at Pennsylvania State University in November 1992. At that workshop forty-four participants discussed the issues most pertinent to the selection of representative populations from each area of the world, indicating those that could meet the defined criteria. Finally, at the third workshop, organized by HUGO Europe and held in Porto Conte, Sardinia, Italy in September 1993, eighty researchers attended and considered the scientific aspects of the project (sample collection, long-term storage of samples, analysis of these samples, development of a database); ethical issues; and organization and management.

The aims of the project were twofold: to investigate the variation in the human genome by studying samples collected from populations that are representative of all peoples of the world, and to create a resource for the benefit of all humanity and for the scientific community worldwide. The project's enormous potential for illuminating our understanding of human history and identity was emphasized, as well as the valuable information it could provide for the elucidation of differential susceptibilities to disease. Its international and interdisciplinary scope and its potential for the proper dissemination of genetic knowledge and elimination of racism were also stressed.

Unlike the almost universal acceptance of IBP three decades earlier, the HGDP met with considerable resistance at the outset. The two main criticisms were that the project, by emphasizing on genetic diversity, would encourage racism (just the opposite of one of its aims), and that it would do nothing to improve the welfare of indigenous people (ignoring its potential medical value; see, e.g., Lewin 1993).

These ideas were widely circulated through nongovernmental organizations, by political activists, and by other means, reaching the local populations and their leaders. Although this opposition had no effect in Europe (the European Human Genome Diversity Project is thriving; its third biennial conference was held in 1999, and the resulting papers have been edited by Renfrew and Boyle 2000; see Harpending 2001), this was not true elsewhere. The South American Committee of the Program, organized by the initiative of Sergio D. J. Pena in 1994–1995, decided to cease the program's existence in September 1996, due to the generalized rejection of HGDP by indigenous and indigenist leaders, as well as to a lack of funds.

The variety of reactions to the HGDP can be well appreciated from a discussion promoted by the *Journal of Politics and the Life Sciences*. David B. Resnik was first asked to provide a paper that was later submitted to twenty researchers (eleven from the United States; two each from South Africa and the United Kingdom; one each from Brazil, Canada, Denmark, Israel, and Japan), with a request for a written opinion. Although eleven of the twenty replies emphasized the positive sides of the project, nine were generally opposed to it (Resnick 1999; several 1999). Santos (2002) analyzed in depth the similarities and differences between the HA/IBP and HGDP initiatives. He concluded that HGDP, which had the same basic philosophy as the HA/IBP project, did not make the realignments in its fundamental dimensions to match the social and economic transformations, as well as the aggressive political activism, of the 1990s.

Science and Antiscience

The reaction to the HGDP is not an isolated phenomenon but is related to a vast world movement that is questioning science and its values. Other striking aspects of this movement are the antievolutionist position of several religious groups, especially in the United States, as well as the world campaign against the use of genetically modified organisms. In the first case, religious people remain impervious to the huge amount of data compiled by Charles Darwin (1859) and the scientists who followed him in the years since the publication of his seminal work. In relation especially to transgenic food, political activists have naively related it to capitalism and do not take into account the considerable amount of data that point to its safety and importance, as emphasized by a report released by seven academies of sciences (Royal Society of London, National Academy of Sciences [United States], Third World Academy of Sciences, and the Brazilian, Chinese, Indian, and Mexican academies of sciences; several 2000).

In the specific case of the studies in human variation, the several ethical principles that are being demanded and followed by research groups (since now institutional ethics committees occur everywhere) have already been emphasized (see chapter 1, this volume). But a second point that needs to be considered is the duty of any community (or its leaders) to appropriately disclose its history, to provide a better understanding of our biological and cultural nature. Presently, this history can be obtained not only through documents but also by investigating the genetic material of the community's members. Actively preventing the acquisition of such data (sometimes based on mythical, erroneous beliefs) should be considered as unethical as procuring this information by inappropriate means (Salzano 1998, 1999).

Perspectives

It is clear that future fieldwork in the area of human population genetics is becoming increasingly problematic. The bureaucratic demands of the several normative committees will certainly increase, and the action of political activists at the local level will make the development of future biological surveys difficult or impossible. Without these surveys, our understanding of human nature will be limited. Most of the biological knowledge we have about our species is based on limited samples obtained primarily from First World countries. Although there are many biological universals, changes are occurring everywhere in our genome, and the view that they are, from the practical point of view, negligible is untenable. If there is one single lesson that modern molecular biology has taught us, it is that our gene pool is incredibly more dynamic than was previously supposed. By ignoring this diversity, generalizations based on First World population biology only will certainly lead to increased problems (such as adverse responses to drugs, to name just one) among minority populations, exactly those who in principle should need more protection.

It could be argued that the fantastic development of laboratory and computing methods could compensate for the lack of appropriate new biological samples. Presently it is possible to establish, based on genetic variation only, inferences about demographic events that occurred in the distant past, and these methods, are being extended, making feasible the study of ancient, prehistoric DNA. These techniques certainly will be improved in the future. New electronic devices will also lead to ever more sophisticated hypotheses and simulation studies. A whole new set of possibilities is being opened for science, but it would be a pity if they could not be tested using actual biological samples.

Therefore, students of human variation are facing a dilemma. In parallel with fantastic scientific progress, significant segments of our society stubbornly remain attached to old, unscientific views. Not only that, but they are actively developing a strong antiscience campaign that may hamper future development. It is important for the area of studies of human variation to take deliberate action against such a campaign. In addition, the development of a relationship between students and those individuals studied of the type indicated by Engelhardt (1996) as of "moral friends," not "moral strangers," is needed.

REFERENCES

Baker, P. T., and J. S. Weiner. 1966. *The Biology of Human Adaptability*. Clarendon Press, Oxford.

Battilana, J., S. L. Bonatto, L. B. Freitas, M. H. Hutz, T. A. Weimer, S. M. Callegari-Jacques, M. A. Batzer, K. Hill, A. M. Hurtado, L. T. Tsuneto, M. L. Petzl-Erler, and F. M. Salzano. 2002. *Alu* insertions versus blood group plus protein genetic variability in four Amerindian populations. *Annals of Human Biology* 29: 334–347.

Bonatto, S. L., and F. M. Salzano. 1997a. Diversity and age of the four major mtDNA haplogroups, and their implications for the peopling of the New World. *American Journal of Human Genetics* 61: 1413–1423.

———. 1997b. A single and early origin for the peopling of the Americas supported by mitochondrial DNA sequence data. *Proceedings of the National Academy of Sciences, USA* 94: 1866–1871.

Bortolini, M.-C., F. M. Salzano, C. H. D. Bau, Z. Layrisse, M. L. Petzl-Erler, L. T. Tsuneto, K. Hill, A. M. Hurtado, D. Castro-de-Guerra, G. Bedoya, and A. Ruiz-Linares. 2002. Y-chromosome biallelic polymorphisms and Native American population structure. *Annals of Human Genetics* 66: 255–259.

Cavalli-Sforza, L. L., A. C. Wilson, C. R. Cantor, R. M. Cook-Degan, and M.-C. King. 1991. Call for a worldwide survey of human genetic diversity: A vanishing opportunity for the Human Genome Project. *Genomics* 11: 490–491.

Collins, K. J., and J. S. Weiner. 1977. *Human Adaptability: A History and Compendium of Research in the International Biological Program*. Taylor and Francis, London.

Crawford, M. H. 1998. *The Origins of Native Americans: Evidence from Anthropological Genetics*. Cambridge University Press, Cambridge.

Darwin, C. 1859. *On the Origin of Species by Means of Natural Selection, or the Preservation of Favoured Races in the Struggle for Life*. John Murray, London.

De Andrade, F. M., C. E. A. Coimbra Jr., R. V. Santos, A. Goicoechea, F. R. Carnese, F. M. Salzano, and M. H. Hutz. 2000. High heterogeneity of apolipoprotein E gene frequencies in South American Indians. *Annals of Human Biology* 27: 29–34.

De Andrade, F. M., G. M. Ewald, F. M. Salzano, and M. H. Hutz. 2002. Lipoprotein lipase and *APOE/APOC-I/APOC-II* gene cluster diversity in native Brazilian populations. *American Journal of Human Biology* 14: 511–518.

Engelhardt, H. T., Jr. 1996. *The Foundations of Bioethics*. Oxford University Press, New York.

Fagundes, N. J. R., S. L. Bonatto, S. M. Callegari-Jacques, and F. M. Salzano. 2002. Genetic, geographic, and linguistic variation among South American Indians: Possible sex influence. *American Journal of Physical Anthropology* 117: 68–78.

Franco, M. H. L. P., S. O. Brennan, E. K. M. Chua, U. Kragh-Hansen, S. M. Callegari-Jacques, M. Z. P. J. Bezerra, and F. M. Salzano. 1999. Albumin genetic variability in South America: Population distribution and molecular studies. *American Journal of Human Biology* 11: 359–366.

Frisse, L., R. R. Hudson, A. Bartoszewicz, J. D. Hall, J. Donfack, and A. Di Rienzo. 2001. Gene conversion and different population histories may explain the contrast between polymorphism and linkage disequilibrium levels. *American Journal of Human Genetics* 69: 831–843.

Gaspar, P. A., M. H. Hutz, F. M. Salzano, K. Hill, A. M. Hurtado, M. L. Petzl-Erler, L. T. Tsuneto, and T. A. Weimer. 2003. Polymorphisms of *CYP1A1*, *CYP2E1*, *GSTM1*, *GSTT1*, and *TP53* genes in Amerindians. *American Journal of Physical Anthropology* (in press).

Gugelmin, S. A., and R. V. Santos. 2001. Human ecology and nutritional anthropology of adult Xavante Indians in Mato Grosso, Brazil. *Cadernos de Saúde Pública* 17: 313–322.

Harpending, H. C. 2001. Book review. *American Journal of Physical Anthropology* 116: 177–178.

Harrison, G. A. 1977. *Population Structure and Human Variation*. Cambridge University Press, Cambridge.

Hutz, M. H., S. Almeida, C. E. A. Coimbra Jr., R. V. Santos, and F. M. Salzano. 2000. Haplotype and allele frequencies for three genes of the dopaminergic system in South American Indians. *American Journal of Human Biology* 12: 638–645.

Hutz, M. H., V. S. Mattevi, S. Almeida, V. M. Zembrzusky, and F. M. Salzano. 2003. Association of the dopamine D2 receptor gene with obesity in Native Brazilians. *Progress in Obesity Research* (in press).

Kaufman, L., A. F. Vargas, C. E. A. Coimbra Jr., R. V. Santos, F. M. Salzano, and M. H. Hutz. 1999. Apolipoprotein B genetic variability in Brazilian Indians. *Human Biology* 71: 87–98.

Lewin, R. 1993. Genes from a disappearing world. *New Scientist* 29 May: 25–29.

Mattevi, V. S., C. E. A. Coimbra Jr., R. V. Santos, F. M. Salzano, and M. H. Hutz. 2000. Association of the low-density lipoprotein receptor gene with obesity in Native American populations. *Human Genetics* 106: 546–552.

Mingroni-Netto, R. C., C. B. Angeli, M. T. B. M. Auricchio, E .R. Leal-Mesquita, A. K. C. Ribeiro dos Santos, I. Ferrari, M. H. Hutz, F. M. Salzano, K. Hill, A. M. Hurtado, and A. M. Vianna-Morgante. 2002. Distribution of CGG repeats and FRAXAC1/DXS548 alleles in South American populations. *American Journal of Medical Genetics* 111: 243–252.

Reich, D. E., M. Cargill, S. Bolk, J. Ireland, P. C. Sabeti, D. J. Richter, T. Lavery, R. Kouyoumjian, S. F. Farhadian, R. Ward, and E. S. Lander. 2001. Linkage disequilibrium in the human genome. *Nature* 411: 199–204.

Renfrew, C., and K. Boyle. 2000. *Archaeogenetics: DNA and the Population Prehistory of Europe.* Oxbow Books, Oxford.

Resnick, D. B. 1999. The Human Genome Diversity Project: Ethical problems and solutions. *Politics and the Life Sciences* 18: 15–23.

Salzano, F. M. 1998. The nature of human genetic diversity. *Dialogo* (UNESCO) 23: 26–27.

———. 1999. Global human diversity and ethics. *Politics and the Life Sciences* 18: 330–332.

———. 2002. Molecular variability in Amerindians: Widespread but uneven information. *Anais da Academia Brasileira de Ciências* 74: 223–263.

Salzano, F. M., and S. M. Callegari-Jacques. 1988. *South American Indians: A Case Study in Evolution.* Clarendon Press, Oxford.

Santos, F. R., A. Pandya, C. Tyler-Smith, S. D. J. Pena, M. Schanfield, W. R. Leonard, L. Osipova, M. H. Crawford, and R. J. Mitchell. 1999. The Central Siberian origin for Native American Y chromosomes. *American Journal of Human Genetics* 64: 619–628.

Santos, R. V. 2002. Indigenous peoples, postcolonial contexts and genomic research in the twentieth century: A view from Amazonia (1960–2000). *Critique of Anthropology* 22: 81–104.

Santos, R. V., and C. E. A. Coimbra Jr. 1996. Socioeconomic differentiation and body morphology in the Suruí of southwestern Amazonia. *Current Anthropology* 37: 851–856.

Schmitt, R., N. J. R. Fagundes, V. C. Muschner, L. B. Freitas, S. L. Bonatto, and F. M. Salzano. 2001. Baixa variabilidade genética no mtDNA da tribo Aché do Paraguai. *Abstracts, 47°. Congresso Nacional de Genética* (available in CD-ROM).

Several. 1999. Comments on the Human Genome Diversity Project. *Politics and the Life Sciences* 18: 285–340.

————. 2000. *Plantas Transgênicas na Agricultura*. Academia Brasileira de Ciências, Rio de Janeiro.

Silva, W. A. Jr., S. L. Bonatto, A. J. Holanda, A. K. C. Ribeiro-dos-Santos, B. M. Paixão, G. H. Goldman, K. Abe-Sandes, L. Rodriguez-Delfin, M. Barbosa, M. L. Paçó-Larson, M. L. Petzl-Erler, V. Valente, S. E. B. Santos, and M. A. Zago. 2002. Mitochondrial genome diversity of Native Americans supports a single early entry of founder populations into America. *American Journal of Human Genetics* 71: 187–192.

Tierney, P. 2000. *Darkness in El Dorado: How Scientists and Journalists Devastated the Amazon*. Norton, New York.

Tsuneto, L. T., C. M. Probst, F. M. Salzano, M. H. Hutz, and M. L. Petzl-Erler. 2002. HLA class I and class II alleles in five Amerindian populations: Guarani-Ñandeva, Guarani-Kaiowá, Guarani-M'Bya, Kaigang and Aché. *Tissue Antigens* 59 (suppl. 2): 97–98.

Weiner, J. S. 1969. *A Guide to the Human Adaptability Proposals*. Blackwell, Oxford.

Weiner, J. S., and J. A. Lourie. 1969. *Human Biology: A Guide to Field Methods*. Blackwell, Oxford.

WHO. 1964. *Research in Population Genetics of Primitive Groups*. World Health Organization, Geneva.

————. 1968. *Research on Human Population Genetics*. World Health Organization, Geneva.

Part III

Epidemiological Contexts

6

EMERGING HEALTH NEEDS AND EPIDEMIOLOGICAL RESEARCH IN INDIGENOUS PEOPLES IN BRAZIL

Carlos E. A. Coimbra Jr. & Ricardo Ventura Santos

The health of indigenous peoples throughout Latin America is the complex outcome of violent sociocultural and environmental changes forged by expansionist population movements. The advance of these frontiers has had an overwhelming effect on indigenous health by introducing novel pathogens that caused serious epidemics, by usurping territory, making subsistence difficult or impossible, and by persecuting and killing individuals, and even entire communities.

It is important to point out that this picture does not apply only to past interethnic relations in Brazil. We have only to look at the recent events that have so severely affected the Yanomamö, whose lands have been invaded by gold miners, and lives shattered by epidemics and massacres, to realize that, as indigenous peoples in Brazil today struggle for physical and cultural survival, they face challenges no less demanding than those of the past. Nor do these problems occur only in the Amazon; they can be found, sometimes in even more intractable form, affecting the daily lives of indigenous groups that live in the more industrialized southern and southeastern regions of the country.

All too little is known about the epidemiological conditions of indigenous peoples in Latin America; relatively little research has been conducted, surveys and censuses are largely nonexistent, and the information systems that report on morbidity and mortality are unreliable. Moreover, any discussion about health or disease processes among indigenous peoples must take into consideration their enormous social diversity, as well as the dynamics of their epidemiology and demography. For example, in Brazil, there are approximately 200 ethnic groups, which speak about 170 distinct languages and have had diverse interactions with the national society. A few groups are still relatively isolated in the Amazon, while a significant proportion of others live in urban areas. Although we do not have the quantitative information on which to base a broad, detailed epidemiological analysis, there can be little doubt that the health conditions of indigenous peoples in Brazil are precarious, placing them at a disadvantage relative to other segments of the national society.

Our intent in this chapter is to present a general overview of the health status of the indigenous peoples of Brazil, with a focus on linkages to the processes of social, economic, and environmental change in which they are involved. We will emphasize the need for understanding how these developments interact with health, since this knowledge is essential, among other reasons, for planning and evaluating health programs and services intended to serve the needs of these populations.

Demography

The demographic situation of indigenous peoples in Brazil at the present time is a clear result of the multiple impacts caused by interaction with Western society over a period that extends back to the arrival of European colonists in the sixteenth century. Although they number around 300,000 today, in 1500 a population of 6 million or more may have inhabited a region that now includes the territory of Brazil (Denevan 1976; Cunha 1992). As in other parts of the Americas, epidemics of infectious disease, massacres, and slave labor were the main causes of depopulation.

Until recently, especially between 1950 and 1970, pessimistic forecasts about the future of indigenous peoples in Brazil were common. The possibility was even raised that indigenous peoples in Brazil might become extinct (Davis 1977; Ribeiro 1977, among others). In recent decades more optimistic voices have been heard. According to Gomes,

> Independent of any other cultural or political variable—in the last thirty or forty years, the Indians have been experiencing a new, unexpected, and extraordinary development that we may unabashedly call "the Indian demographic turnaround." This notion is meant to express the fact that most extant Indian

peoples have interrupted their former propensity to lose population and have actually been growing in numbers. (2000: 2)

The reversal of pessimistic predictions about the future of indigenous peoples was based on the realization that the population of a number of ethnic groups had been growing for some time (Ricardo 1996; Coimbra et al. 2002)

Although the need to produce and disseminate more information is widely recognized, almost nothing is known about the basic demographic parameters of most indigenous groups in the country. Such vital statistics as infant mortality rate, life expectancy at birth, and crude birth and death rates, which are essential for monitoring health and disease and for planning health and education programs, are seldom available. Even when they exist, as Ricardo points out, the data

are very heterogeneous in terms of origin, date, and collection procedure. . . . Even when the data are derived from a direct count, the census takers usually do not know the language, do not understand the social organization nor the spatial and seasonal dynamics of the indigenous society, and therefore produce inconsistent and erroneous totals, either over or under counted. (1996: v)

Coimbra and Santos (2000) have called attention to the implications of this lack of demographic information, which makes it impossible to carry out in-depth analyses of the mortality, fertility, migration, or population growth of indigenous peoples.

It is important to understand how this absence of demographic data for indigenous peoples in Brazil has been "produced." Although for a long time it was the institutional responsibility of the National Indian Foundation (FUNAI) to collect and organize demographic data, in practice these data either were completely missing or were unreliable because they were not systematically collected and updated. Up to the present this lack of data has not been remedied, even though a specific classification for Indians was placed in the "color" item of the 1991 national census. Beyond the confusion in classification, since "Indian" obviously is not a color, a number of other problems with the census have been identified (Azevedo 1997; Coimbra and Santos 2000; Silva 1994). For example, the only people counted in the 1991 census were those living at Indian posts or religious missions, so an unknown, but undoubtedly significant, number of individuals living in villages without government agents or missionaries was excluded from the count. Moreover, since the census based its count on "generic Indians," information about specific groups (Xavante, Kayapó, Yanomamö, etc.) is not available. Some indigenous associations were so dissatisfied with the results of the 1991 census that they organized their own independent census counts, partly with the aim of revealing the defects of the official census.

According to data from the Instituto Socioambiental (ISA), there are 216 indigenous groups in Brazil, totaling some 350,000 individuals. This constitutes less than 0.5 percent of the total Brazilian population (Ricardo 2000: 10–15). If we look at ethnic groups, we find that 68.4 percent belong to "microsocieties," those with fewer than 1,000 members. Following Ricardo (2000: 15), the few groups with more than 10,000 members (Guaraní, Kaingáng, Makuxí, Guajajára, Teréna, Tikúna, and Yanomamö) together add up to 148,000 individuals, or approximately half of the total indigenous population in the country. Therefore, a large proportion of the total indigenous population is concentrated in a few ethnic groups.

Detailed demographic studies have been done on only a few groups. Even those studies suffer from important limitations, such as the short time interval analyzed. Moreover, some of the more detailed studies report data from the 1960s and 1970s and focus almost exclusively on Amazonian groups (see Salzano and Callegari-Jacques 1988 for a detailed review of these studies). More recent publications that can be cited are Early and Peters (1990), Baruzzi et al. (1994), Flowers (1994), and Souza and Santos (2001) (see also the collection of case studies edited by Adams and Price 1994). To compare the results presented in these works, as well as others on indigenous peoples, is a difficult task due to different methodologies of collecting data, reporting vital statistics, grouping age cohorts, and so on. Nevertheless, these studies tend to be consistent in pointing to a demographic pattern characterized by a combination of high fertility and high mortality. In such indigenous populations young people predominate, sometimes with more than 50 percent of the population under the age of fifteen.

A recent demographic study of the Xavante of Sangradouro, in Mato Grosso state, exemplifies these points (Souza and Santos 2001). In a community of 825 people the authors found a high crude death rate (9.1/1,000 in the 1993–1997 period), higher than the national rate (6.7/1,000 in 1996), and even above the highest regional rate, that of the Northeast (7.8/1,000 in 1996). It is necessary, however, to use caution in comparing crude rates because these are markedly influenced by the age composition of the population, which in the case of the Xavante is quite different from that of the national population. A little more than half (56 percent) of the Xavante population was under the age of fifteen (average thirteen years). For Brazil as a whole, the percentage was approximately 30 percent in 1991.

The infant mortality rate for the Xavante (87.1/1,000) in the period between 1993 and 1997 was much higher than the figure for Brazil (37.5/1,000 in 1996). The greater number of deaths (55 percent) in Sangradouro occurred in children under one year of age, an age-group that made up 5 percent of the total population. Because of very high mortality in the first years, only 86 percent of Xavante children survive to the age of ten.

Souza and Santos (2001) argue that the high mortality rate of the Xavante, like those reported in case studies of other indigenous groups in Brazil, reflects the socioeconomic marginality to which indigenous peoples are relegated, which is demonstrated, among other disadvantages, by lack of sanitation in their villages and inadequate health services, which especially compromise the health and survival of children.

The total fertility rate (TFR) calculated for the Xavante of Sangradouro was 8.6 children. This pattern of high fertility, with TFRs in the order of 7 to 8 children, has been observed among other indigenous populations in the country (Werner 1983; Meireles 1988; Early and Peters 1990; Picchi and College 1994). It is associated with short birth intervals and child-bearing that begins early, at the age of thirteen to fourteen, and often continues to forty or forty-five. The TFRs reported for different indigenous groups, including the Xavante, are invariably much higher than that of the Brazilian population in general. In 1996 the TFR for Brazil was 2.3.

Subsistence and Nutrition

In the past, indigenous peoples in Brazil depended for their subsistence on horticulture, hunting, fishing, and gathering, usually emphasizing one or another of these resources. Interaction with expanding frontiers, which brought new economic systems and diminished the land available to the Indians, drastically altered their subsistence patterns; the usual result was impoverishment and hunger. For indigenous peoples the guaranteed right to land subsumes subsistence itself and is an important condition for cultural continuity. While landholding and the nutritional status of indigenous populations are certainly interconnected, little is known in Brazil about this relationship. One remarkable statistic is that 40 percent of Brazil's indigenous population lives in the Northeast, Southeast, and South regions of the country, where only 2 percent of the land demarcated as indigenous reservations is located. Ninety-eight percent of demarcated reservation territory and 60 percent of the indigenous population are in the Center West and North regions (Ricardo 1996: xii). Not surprisingly, a survey carried out in the mid-1990s revealed serious problems of food supply in at least one-third of the country's indigenous reservations, especially affecting those in the Northeast, Southeast, and South (Verdum 1995).

Very little is known about the nutritional status of indigenous peoples in Brazil. The three principal nationwide surveys that included the collection of data on the nutritional status of the country in recent decades, the National Study of Family Expenditure, carried out in 1974–1975, the National Investigation of Health and Nutrition in 1989, and the National Investigation of Demography and Health in 1996, did not include indigenous populations as a specific category for analysis. Yet these surveys are the main sources for analyzing the transformations that have taken place in the nutritional configuration of the country in the late twentieth century. This lack of information about the nutritional status of indigenous peoples is cause for concern, since the social and economic upheavals these are undergoing may bring about conditions that favor the appearance of malnutrition.

What we know about the occurrence of protein-energy malnutrition (PEM) in indigenous children is derived from anthropometric studies in a few communities, most of them in the Amazon. The results in general show a high frequency of deficits in height-for-age (below –2 z-scores from NCHS curves), a measure of chronic malnutrition. Several studies show that indigenous children are more likely to have low height-for-age than nonindigenous children throughout Brazil (15.7 and 10.5 percent in children 0–5 years of age in 1989 and 1996, respectively; Monteiro 2000: 379). These studies were conducted in the late 1980s and 1990s among Suruí, Gavião, and Zoró children (Coimbra and Santos 1991; Santos and Coimbra 1991, 1998), and among Xavante (Gugelmin et al. 2001), Parakanã (Martins and Menezes 1994), Teréna (Ribas et al. 2001) and Xingú children (Mattos et al. 1999). There is, however, current discussion in the literature about the validity of using the recommendations of international agencies, such as the endorsement by the WHO of the NCHS growth curves, in nutritional evaluations of indigenous children (see Santos 1993; Stinson 1996).

Anemia is another serious nutritional problem among indigenous populations, mainly affecting children, as well as women of reproductive age. In the 1960s and 1970s, investigators found high frequencies of anemia among the Xavante (Neel et al. 1964), the Krenakaróre (or Panará; Baruzzi et al. 1977), and in populations of the Upper Xingu River (Fagundes-Neto 1977). In other parts of the Amazon, recent studies have found that this nutritional deficiency is widespread. Among the Suruí, for example, approximately 71 percent of children zero to nine years of age suffered from anemia (Coimbra and Santos 1991). Among the Xavante, Leite (1998) reported that 74 percent of children one to ten years of age, as well as 53 percent of the total population, were anemic.

This brief review reveals wide gaps in information about nutrition among indigenous peoples in Brazil. The little that we do know comes mainly from studies done in the Amazon. It is likely that nutritional problems are even more serious among groups living in the Northeast, Southeast, and South regions of the country, where obtaining food tends to be more difficult than in the North and Center West because people have so little land and many live on the outskirts of urban centers.

Infectious and Parasitic Diseases and Environmental Health

During most of their postcontact history the main threats to the health of indigenous peoples in Brazil have been infectious and parasitic diseases. Until recently, epidemics of viral disease, like measles and influenza, could decimate populations within a short time, endangering the biological and social continuity of the affected groups. Although epidemics of this magnitude do not occur as frequently as in the past, infectious and parasitic diseases continue to put great stress on the health and well-being of indigenous populations.

Tuberculosis stands out as one of the principal infectious diseases affecting indigenous peoples in Brazil. It is important not only because of its historical role as a factor in depopulation but also because it is still widespread. As an example, during the first half of the 1990s, 329 new cases of tuberculosis were registered among Indians in the state of Rondônia, in the southwestern Amazon. This represents about 10 percent of the total cases reported in the state during the same period, even though the indigenous population accounts for only about 1 percent of the state's total population (Escobar et al. 2001). A high incidence of tuberculosis has also been registered in other indigenous groups (Sousa et al. 1997; Buchillet and Gazin 1998; Baruzzi et al. 2001).

The place of malaria as a major scourge of indigenous peoples is indisputable. It affects, above all, groups in the Amazon, especially those in the paths of migration, gold mining, or development projects. Considering the differences in local environments and socioeconomic factors, as well as sociocultural diversity and variation in access to health services, it is not hard to understand why malaria is so unevenly distributed in the Amazon. Such differences contribute to large discrepancies between areas that are near one another or even contiguous (see Ianelli 2000).

The Yanomamö case illustrates the effects of an epidemic of malaria that began when thousands of gold miners invaded indigenous territory at the end of the 1980s and beginning of the 1990s. According to Pithan et al. (1991), during the worst phase of the epidemic, around 40 percent of all Yanomamö deaths were due to malaria. There are no reliable statistics on the impact of malaria in the more isolated Yanomamö communities, but it is known that many persons died without having received any medical assistance. Other investigations on malaria in indigenous areas have revealed that the epidemiological profile of the disease may vary widely among different groups (Arruda et al. 1989; Burattini et al. 1993; Sampaio et al. 1996; Ianelli et al. 1998).

A striking characteristic of the majority of indigenous villages is the absence of safe sanitary conditions, with no infrastructure for disposing of waste or supplying pure drinking water. Under these conditions, it is hardly surprising to find that infection by intestinal parasites is extremely widespread (see Salzano and Callegari-Jacques 1988 for a review of work published up to the 1980s). Recent investigations have confirmed previous findings according to which the most frequent helminth species are *Ascaris lumbricoides* (roundworms), *Trichuris trichiura* (whipworms), and hookworms. These studies also found varying prevalences of infection by pathogenic protozoans such as *Giardia lamblia* and *Entamoeba hystolitica* (Coimbra and Santos 1991; Ferrari et al. 1992; Santos et al. 1995; Miranda et al. 1998, Carvalho et al. 2001).

The same environmental conditions that favor the transmission of helminths and protozoans also lead to the contamination of water and food by enterobacteria and rotavirus, which are important causes of diarrhea. The presence of various species of enterobacteria and the occurrence of high rates of seropositivity for rotavirus have been widely reported for the indigenous population in general, especially in the Amazon (Linhares et al. 1986; Linhares 1992). At times gastrointestinal infections account for almost half the hospitalizations and up to 60 percent of deaths of indigenous children under one year of age, as in the Xavante (Coimbra et al. 2002).

There are few studies on the epidemiology of cutaneous leishmaniasis among indigenous groups, even though the great majority of these groups inhabit endemic areas under living conditions likely to place them in contact with the enzootic cycles of the parasite. Intradermal tests for *Leishmania* infection (Montenegro skin tests) point to a pattern characterized by strong reactions to the test (around 60 to 80 percent) but with only rare cases of clinical disease (Lainson 1988; Coimbra et al. 1996b). Relatively serious outbreaks of visceral leishmaniasis have been described among the Makuxí and Yanomamö in the far north of the Brazilian Amazon (Castellón et al. 1998).

Different kinds of hepatitis are important causes of sickness and death among indigenous peoples in Brazil. For instance, various studies have found a high prevalence of serological markers for hepatitis B (A. K. Santos et al. 1995; Azevedo et al. 1996; Coimbra et al. 1996a). Certain cultural practices, cosmetic or therapeutic, such as scarification, tattooing, and bloodletting, which can transmit the virus, make these populations particularly vulnerable to its transmission. This is also true of other viruses transmitted through bodily fluids, such as hepatitis D virus, HIV, and HTLV (Soares and Bensabath 1991; Ishak et al. 1995; Black et al. 1996).

We have concluded that the contexts of sociocultural and economic change in which indigenous peoples in Brazil are enmeshed at present have great potential to reshape their epidemiological configuration. In this brief overview, we have only touched on the surface of a broad, complex, and multifaceted picture. The lack of reliable statistics does not permit us to go beyond reviewing a relatively limited (from a geographic, ethnic, and epidemiological standpoint) collection of case studies. For example, we have not mentioned infectious diseases about which there is little information, nor those restricted to specific areas or a small number of ethnic groups or villages. Some that deserve attention are schistosomiasis and tracoma among Indians in the Northeast, leprosy and AIDS in the indigenous population in general, and river blindness in the far north of the country. In addition, very little is known about the health of indigenous women, but the few findings that we have suggest that sexually transmitted diseases and cervical and uterine cancer occur at disturbingly high rates (Brito et al. 1996; Taborda et al. 2000; Ishak and Ishak 2001).

Another concern that is relevant to the health situation of indigenous peoples is the impact of the environmental changes that accompany the construction of hydroelectric dams on or near their territory, mining activities, and even the introduction of new agricultural technology that involves replacing traditional horticulture with monoculture. Koifman (2001) has mapped the location of the principal hydroelectric plants in the country in relation to indigenous lands and has called attention to their possible impacts on health. In another study, the same author discusses the possible association between constant exposure to electromagnetic fields generated by high-tension electric power lines and cancer in indigenous populations (Koifman et al. 1998).

Another environmental offense with grave consequences for health is contamination of rivers and streams with the mercury used in placer mining for gold, principally in the Amazon. This is related to the consumption of fish, an important part of indigenous diets. For example, among the Munduruku, Brabo et al. (1999) found high levels of methylmercury in the fish species they most frequently consume. Other recent studies have revealed widespread environmental contamination by mercury in the rivers that flow through indigenous lands in the Amazon (Sing et al. 1996; Barbosa et al. 1998).

Disease and Death in Transition

A particularly little-known dimension of the epidemiology of indigenous peoples in Brazil, but one that has broad implications for their present and future health, is the emergence of chronic noncontagious diseases such as obesity, hypertension, and diabetes mellitus. The rise of these diseases as important threats to indigenous health is recent and closely associated with ongoing changes in subsistence, diet, and physical activity. In addition, there has been an increasing number of reports of mental disturbances, including depression, suicide, and drug addiction, in different ethnic groups (Morgado 1991; Meihy 1994; Langdon 1999; Poz 2000; Viertler 2000; Erthal 2001). Deaths by external causes also appear to be on the increase, whether from accidents involving automobiles or agricultural machinery or from violence—in many cases murders and even massacres perpetrated by loggers, gold miners, and other invaders of indigenous territory (CIMI 1997).

Very little is known about the epidemiology of hypertension among indigenous populations in Brazil. Most of the studies on blood pressure have been done on groups that were still relatively "isolated" (Oliver et al. 1975; Fleming-Moran and Coimbra 1990; Crews and Mancilha-Carvalho 1993). Little investigation has taken into account the effects of sociocultural and environmental changes on blood pressure (Fleming-Moran et al. 1991; Cardoso et al. 2001; Coimbra et al. 2001).

The case of the Xavante of the village of Etéñitépa (or Pimentel Barbosa), in Mato Grosso, provides a useful illustration of this process. In the early 1960s, a team that included physicians and anthropologists studied these Xavante (Neel et al. 1964). About thirty years later a restudy was done of the same group, and the results clearly showed a tendency toward increase in systolic and diastolic blood pressure levels (Coimbra et al. 2001). In 1962, systolic and diastolic blood pressures fell in the range of 94 to 126 and 48 to 80 mm Hg, respectively, and there were no cases of hypertension. In 1990, average systolic and diastolic blood pressures were higher in both sexes, and cases of hypertension were found. In 1990, a correlation was also found between age and blood pressure that did not exist previously. Coimbra et al. (2001) argue that during the nearly fifty years that the Xavante have been in permanent contact with the national society, lifestyle changes have taken place that predispose them to hypertension and other cardiovascular diseases. Physical activity has declined, and the average body mass index (BMI) of adults has increased significantly (Santos et al. 1997; Gugelmin and Santos 2001). At present, rice is the staple food, and salt is consumed daily. Moreover, a good number of the men smoke, which was not the case in the past (Coimbra et al. 2001).

References to obesity among Brazilian Indians were rare until recently. Before the early 1990s, reviews of nutritional problems primarily stressed protein-energy malnutrition and its effects on children (Dufour 1992; Santos 1993). At present, it is not possible to describe the prevalence and distribution of obesity among indigenous populations in Brazil. However, a number of studies show that this health problem is rapidly emerging in some groups (Santos and Coimbra 1996; Capelli and Koifman 2001; Gugelmin and Santos 2001).

Toward the end of the 1980s, one study among Suruí adults showed that individuals who were no longer directly involved in traditional subsistence activities consumed a diet basically made up of industrialized foods low in fiber and high in sugars and fats; they also had lower levels of physical activity (Santos and Coimbra 1996). The average weight of these individuals was considerably higher than that of the Suruí population in general, with the differences reaching 7.6 kilograms in women and 5.7 kilograms in men. The researchers concluded that the members of the Suruí population who gained the most weight were those most directly involved in certain recently introduced economic activities that could be rapidly capitalized (coffee growing and timber trading, for example), leading to drastic changes in diet and physical activity.

Accounts of non-insulin-dependent diabetes mellitus (NIDDM) in indigenous peoples in Brazil are anecdotal and limited to a few case studies. The first report of NIDDM in an indigenous group dates to the 1970s, when physician João Paulo Vieira-Filho (1977) described the disease among the Palikúr and Karipúna, in the northeastern Amazon. The emergence of diabetes in these populations was linked to changes in their diet, in which manioc flour and refined sugar (two food items unknown to them before contact) had become basic foods. These dietary changes were connected to commercialization of the indigenous economies, as they had become much involved with the local market, primarily through the production and sale of manioc flour.

The image of obese Indians suffering from diabetes was foreign to most Brazilian anthropologists and physicians until recently (Coimbra et al. 2002). Research conducted in the Upper Xingu region depicted a complex of culturally rich societies with physically fit members practicing a subsistence economy based on horticulture, hunting and fishing, and gathering wild foods. The team led by Roberto G. Baruzzi, which for three decades has been carrying out research and providing medical assistance to indigenous peoples in that region, has found no diabetes (Baruzzi and Franco 1981; Franco 1992). A number of other studies on glucose metabolism have been carried out in indigenous groups that adhered to traditional diets and maintained relatively high levels of physical activity. None of these found any indications of diabetes (Vieira-Filho 1975; Spielman et al. 1982; Bloch et al. 1993).

Vieira-Filho has called attention to the health implications of dietary changes for indigenous peoples and the emergence of obesity and NIDDM in various populations of eastern Amazonia and Central Brazil (Vieira-Filho 1981, 1996; Vieira-Filho et al. 1984). Vieira-Filho's observations of the occurrence of diabetes mellitus at Sangradouro and São Marcos are particularly important because he has made regular visits and given medical assistance to the Xavante on those reservations since the 1970s. They give us a qualitative view of how the situation of the Xavante has changed over recent decades:

> Twenty years ago I observed that [the Xavante] were slim and very active physically, and there was not one case of diabetes mellitus among them. . . . In recent years we have seen cases with declared symptoms, and the Xavante have become obese. . . . [Rice] became the basis of their diet. . . . Soft drinks were consumed in families that had access to cash. The adults increased in weight, with many individuals developing a heavy layer of fat on the abdomen. (Vieira-Filho 1996: 61)

To fully understand epidemiological transitions among indigenous populations of Brazil, regional and ethnic diversity must be considered. We have stressed elsewhere that epidemiological changes in these populations differ from those experienced by nonindigenous peoples in Brazil (Coimbra et al. 2002). To effectively influence the development, implementation, and evaluation of services, health care professionals must take these observations into account.

Final Comments

Until recently, the services that provide health care to indigenous populations in Brazil were under the management of the National Indian Foundation (FUNAI), which provided mainly curative medical care. There was little continuity in providing basic preventive health care to indigenous communities. Even in the 1960s and 1970s, when vaccines, antibiotics, and other resources were available to deal with a number of diseases, the government services failed to prevent epidemics of malaria, tuberculosis, or even measles from killing hundreds of Indians recently contacted in central Brazil and the Amazon. This happened especially in areas where highways such as the Transamazon were under construction, as well as in regions like Rondônia and Roraima where the cattle-raising frontier was advancing. Even in the absence of serious epidemics, with few exceptions, services managed by FUNAI tended to be disorganized and, in many areas, sporadic. Since 1999 the National Health Foundation (FUNASA), a branch of the federal Ministry of Health, has been responsibile for providing health care to indigenous peoples. It has set up health services designed especially for indigenous peoples, and districts were divided according to ethnic and geographic criteria (the so-called Special Indigenous Health Districts) linked to the national public health system, known as Unified Health System (SUS). Thirty-four districts are now in place throughout the country (Langdon 2000; Athias and Machado 2001).

Among the strategies for restructuring the health services for indigenous peoples, one of the most important is the establishment of the Indigenous Health Information System (SIASI), whose role is to monitor health activities in the various districts. Following FUNASA,

> This system will collect information according to the requirements of each level of management, providing the information needed to construct indices for evaluating health conditions and, indirectly, to evaluate the quality of health care, such as the organization of services in the Health Districts, with special attention to access, coverage, and effectiveness. (http://www.funasa.gov.br/ind/ind01.htm#6 accessed January 25, 2002)

The implementation of information services for indigenous health is vital for many reasons. Throughout this chapter, we have mentioned the lack of reliable information on health and disease among indigenous peoples in Brazil. It is unnecessary to emphasize the value of accessible and systematic epidemiological records for planning, implementing, and evaluating health services and programs. Trustworthy information is also essential to make it possible to analyze the many and complex interrelationships among social inequalities, health and disease processes, and ethnicity. As we have previously pointed out, "Higher coefficients of disease and death . . . hunger and malnutrition, occupational risk and social violence, are but a few of the many repercussions on health that come from the persistence of inequality" (Coimbra and Santos 2000: 131, see also Coimbra 1998). Knowledge generated by partnerships of indigenous leaders, researchers, public health services, and nongovernment organizations must become the basis for political action, including that of indigenous communities, to promote measures leading to greater equity in health. We hope that, with growing indigenous participation in the operations of the health system, the Indians themselves will make increasing use of this information to define priorities and devise more appropriate strategies to guide the activities of health services in their communities.

REFERENCES

Adams, K., and D. Price, eds. 1994. *The Demography of Small-Scale Societies: Case Studies from Lowland South America*. Special Issue of *South American Indian Studies* 4. Bennington College, Bennington, Vt.

Arruda, M., E. Nardin, R. S. Nussenzweig, and A. H. Cochrane. 1989. Sero-epidemiological studies of malaria in Indian tribes and monkeys of the Amazon basin of Brazil. *American Journal of Tropical Medicine and Hygiene* 41: 379–385.

Athias, R., and M. Machado. 2001. A saúde indígena no processo de implantação dos Distritos Sanitários: Temas críticos e propostas para um diálogo interdisciplinar. *Cadernos de Saúde Pública* 17: 425–431.

Azevedo, M. M. 1997. Fontes de dados sobre as populações indígenas brasileiras da Amazônia. *Cadernos de Estudos Sociais* 13: 163–177.

Azevedo, R. A., A. E. Silva, M. L. G. Ferraz, L. F. Marcopito, and R. G. Baruzzi. 1996. Prevalência dos marcadores sorológicos dos vírus da hepatite B e D em crianças das tribos Caiabi e Txucarramãe do Parque Indígena do Xingu, Brasil Central. *Revista da Sociedade Brasileira de Medicina Tropical* 29: 431–439.

Barbosa, A. C., S. R. Silva, and J. G. Dorea. 1998. Concentration of mercury in hair of indigenous mothers and infants from the Amazon Basin. *Archives of Environmental Contamination and Toxicology* 34: 100–105.

Baruzzi, R. G., V. L. Barros, D. Rodrigues, A. L. M. Souza, and H. Plagiaro. 2001. Saúde e doença em índios Panará (Kreen-Akarôre) após vinte e cinco anos de contato com o nosso mundo, com ênfase na ocorrência de tuberculose (Brasil Central). *Cadernos de Saúde Pública* 17: 407–412.

Baruzzi, R. G., and L. J. Franco. 1981. Amerindians of Brazil. In *Western Diseases: Their Emergence and Prevention*, edited by H. C. Trowell and D. P. Burkitt, pp. 138–153. Edward Arnold, London.

Baruzzi, R. G., L. F. Marcopito, M. L.C. Serra, F. A. A. Souza, and C. Stabile. 1977. The Kren-Akorore: A recently contacted indigenous tribe. In *Health and Disease in Tribal Societies*, edited by K. Elliot and J. Whelan, pp. 179–211. Elsevier, Amsterdam.

Baruzzi, R. G., H. Pagliaro, S. S. Silva, V. Schivartche, and H. Meziara. 1994. Os índios Panará: A busca pela sobrevivência. In *IX Encontro Nacional de Estudos Populacionais, Annals*, vol. 2, pp. 225–242. Associação Brasileira de Estudos Populacionais, Brasília.

Black, F. L., R. Biggar, R. B. Lal, A. A. Gabbai, and J. P. B. Vieira-Filho. 1996. Twenty-five years of HTLV type II follow-up with a possible case of tropical spastic paraparesis in the Kayapó, a Brazilian Indian tribe. *AIDS Research and Human Retrovirus* 12: 1623–1627.

Bloch, K. V., E. S. F. Coutinho, M. E. C. Lôbo, J. E. P. Oliveira, and A. Milech. 1993. Pressão arterial, glicemia capilar e medidas antropométricas em uma população Yanomámi. *Cadernos de Saúde Pública* 9: 428–438.

Brabo, E. S., E. Santos, I. M. Jesus, A. F. Mascarenhas, and K. F. Faial. 1999. Níveis de mercúrio em peixes consumidos pela comunidade indígena de Sai Cinza, na reserva Mundurukú, Estado do Pará, Brasil. *Cadernos de Saúde Pública* 15: 325–331.

Brito, E. B., R. C. Menezes, S. J. Martins, M. G. M. Bastos, and A. Sousa. 1996. Estudo preliminar para detecção de cérvico-vaginites e lesões precursoras do câncer de colo uterino em índias da tribo Parakanã. *Revista da Associação Médica Brasileira* 42: 11–15.

Buchillet, D., and P. Gazin. 1998. A situação da tuberculose na população indígena do Alto Rio Negro (Estado do Amazonas, Brasil). *Cadernos de Saúde Pública* 14: 181–185.

Burattini, M. N., E. Massad, F. A. B. Coutinho, and R. G. Baruzzi. 1993. Malaria prevalence amongst Brazilian Indians assessed by a new mathematical model. *Epidemiology and Infection* 111: 525–537.

Capelli, J. C. S., and S. Koifman. 2001. Avaliação do estado nutricional da comunidade indígena Parkatêjê, Bom Jesus do Tocantins, Pará, Brasil. *Cadernos de Saúde Pública* 17: 433–437.

Cardoso, A. M., I. E. Mattos, and R. J. Koifman. 2001. Prevalência de fatores de risco para doenças cardiovasculares na população Guaraní-Mbyá do Estado do Rio de Janeiro. *Cadernos de Saúde Pública* 17: 345–354.

Carvalho, E. F., A. K. Fontbonne, G. A. Sá, and E. P. Cesse. 2001. Fatores de risco para poliparasitismo intestinal em uma comunidade indígena de Pernambuco, Brasil. *Cadernos de Saúde Pública* 17: 367–373.

Castellón, E. G., J. O. Guerra, and Y. C. Costa. 1998. A leishmaniose visceral (calazar) no Estado de Roraima. In *Homem, Ambiente e Ecologia no Estado de Roraima*, edited by R. I. Barbosa, E. J. Ferreira, and E. G. Castellón, pp. 157–179. Instituto Nacional de Pesquisas da Amazônia, Manaus.

CIMI (Conselho Indigenista Missionário). 1997. *A Violência Contra os Povos Indígenas no Brasil—1996*. CIMI, Brasília.

Coimbra, C. E. A., Jr. 1998. Minorías étnico-raciales, desigualdad y salud: Consideraciones teóricas preliminares. In *Salud, Cambio Social y Política: Perspectivas desde América Latina*, edited by M. N. Bronfman and R. Castro, pp. 151–161. Edamex, México.

Coimbra, C. E. A., Jr., D. Chor, R. V. Santos, and F. M. Salzano. 2001. Blood pressure levels in Xavánte adults from the Pimentel Barbosa Indian Reserve, Mato Grosso, Brazil. *Ethnicity and Disease* 11: 232–240.

Coimbra, C. E .A., Jr., N. M. Flowers, F. M. Salzano, and R. V. Santos. 2002. *The Xavante in Transition: Health, Ecology and Bioanthropology in Central Brazil*. Michigan University Press, Ann Arbor.

Coimbra, C. E. A., Jr., and R. V. Santos. 1991. Avaliação do estado nutricional num contexto de mudança sócio-econômica: O grupo indígena Suruí do estado de Rondônia, Brasil. *Cadernos de Saúde Pública* 7: 538–562.

———. 2000. Saúde, minorias e desigualdade: Algumas teias de inter-relações, com ênfase nos povos indígenas. *Ciência & Saúde Coletiva* 5: 125–132.

Coimbra, C. E. A., Jr., R. V. Santos, N. M. Flowers, C. Yoshida, M. Baptista, and A. C. F. Valle. 1996a. Hepatitis B epidemiology and cultural practices in Amerindian populations of Amazonia: The Tupí-Mondé and the Xavánte of Rondônia and Mato Grosso. *Social Science and Medicine* 42: 1738–1743.

Coimbra, C. E. A., Jr., R. V. Santos, and A. C. F. Valle. 1996b. Cutaneous leishmaniasis in Tupí-Mondé Amerindians from the Brazilian Amazonia. *Acta Tropica* 61: 201–211.

Crews, D. E., and J. J. Mancilha-Carvalho. 1993. Correlates of blood pressure in Yanomami Indians of Northwestern Brazil. *Ethnicity and Disease* 3: 362–371.

Cunha, M. C. 1992. Introdução a uma história indígena. In *História dos Índios no Brasil,* edited by M. C. Cunha, pp. 9–24. Companhia das Letras, São Paulo.

Davis, S. H. 1977. *Victims of the Miracle*. Cambridge University Press, Cambridge.

Denevan, W. M. 1976. *The Native Populations of the Americas in 1492*. University of Wisconsin Press, Madison.

Dufour, D. 1992. Nutritional ecology in the tropical rain forests of Amazonia. *American Journal of Human Biology* 4: 197–207.

Early, J. D., and J. F. Peters. 1990. *The Population Dynamics of the Mucajai Yanomama*. Academic Press, San Diego.

Erthal, R. 2001. O suicídio Tikúna no Alto Solimões: Uma expressão de conflitos. *Cadernos de Saúde Pública* 17: 299–311.

Escobar, A. L., C. E. A. Coimbra Jr., L. A. Camacho, and M. C. Portela. 2001. Tuberculose em populações indígenas de Rondônia, Amazônia, Brasil. *Cadernos de Saúde Pública* 17: 285–298.

Fagundes-Neto, U. 1977. Avaliação do estado nutricional das Crianças Índias do Alto Xingu. Ph.D. diss., Escola Paulista de Medicina, São Paulo.

Ferrari, J., M. U. Ferreira, L. M. Camargo, and C. S. Ferreira. 1992. Intestinal parasites among Karitiana Indians from Rondonia state, Brazil. *Revista do Instituto de Medicina Tropical de São Paulo* 34: 223–225.

Fleming-Moran, M., and C. E. A. Coimbra Jr. 1990. Blood pressure studies among Amazonian native populations: A review from an epidemiological perspective. *Social Science and Medicine* 31: 593–601.

Fleming-Moran, M., R. V. Santos, and C. E. A. Coimbra Jr. 1991. Blood pressure levels of the Suruí and Zoró Indians of the Brazilian Amazon: Group- and sex-specific effects resulting from body composition, health status, and age. *Human Biology* 63: 835–861.

Flowers, N. M. 1994. Crise e recuperação demográfica: Os Xavánte de Pimentel Barbosa, Mato Grosso. In *Saúde e Povos Indígenas*, edited by R. V. Santos and C. E. A. Coimbra Jr., pp. 213–242. Editora Fiocruz, Rio de Janeiro.

Franco, L. 1992. Diabetes in Brazil: A review of recent survey data. *Ethnicity and Disease* 2: 158–165.

Gomes, M. P. 2000. *The Indians and Brazil*. University Press of Florida, Gainesville.

Gugelmin, S. A., and R. V. Santos. 2001. Ecologia humana e antropometria nutricional de adultos Xavánte, Mato Grosso, Brasil. *Cadernos de Saúde Pública* 17: 313–322.

Gugelmin, S. A., R. V. Santos, and M. S. Leite. 2001. Crescimento físico de crianças indígenas xavantes de 5 a 10 anos de idade, Mato Grosso. *Jornal de Pediatria* 77: 17–22.

Ianelli, R. V. 2000. Epidemiologia da malária em populações indígenas da Amazônia. In *Doenças Endêmicas: Abordagens Sociais, Culturais e*

Comportamentais, edited by R. B. Barata and R. Briceño-León, pp. 355–374. Editora Fiocruz, Rio de Janeiro.

Ianelli, R. V., H. A. Honório, D. C. Lima, R. Lourenço-de-Oliveira, R. V. Santos, and C. E. A. Coimbra Jr. 1998. Faunal composition and behavior of Anopheline mosquitoes on the Xavánte Indian Reservation of Pimentel Barbosa, Central Brazil. *Parasite* 5: 37–46.

Ishak, M. G., and R. Ishak. 2001. O impacto da infecção por *Chlamydia* em populações indígenas da Amazônia brasileira. *Cadernos de Saúde Pública* 17: 385–396.

Ishak, R., W. J. Harrington, V. N. Azevedo, N. Eiraku, M. O. Ishak, and W. W. Hall. 1995. Identification of human T cell lymphotropic virus type IIa infection in the Kayapó, an indigenous population of Brazil. *AIDS Research and Human Retrovirus* 11: 813–819.

Koifman, S. 2001. Geração e transmissão de energia elétrica: Impacto nas nações indígenas do Brasil. *Cadernos de Saúde Pública* 17: 413–423.

Koifman, S., I. Ferraz, T. S. Vianna, C. L. Silveira, M. T. Carneiro, R. J. Koifman, C. Fernández, and A. C. Bulcão. 1998. Cancer clusters among young Indian adults living near power transmission lines in Bom Jesus do Tocantins, Pará, Brasil. *Cadernos de Saúde Pública* 14 (suppl. 3): 161–172.

Lainson, R. 1988. Ecological interactions in the transmission of leishmaniasis. *Philosophical Transactions of the Royal Society of London* 321(B): 389–404.

Langdon, E. J. 1999. O que beber, como beber e quando beber: O contexto sociocultural no alcoolismo entre as populações indígenas. In *Saúde, Saberes e Ética: Três Conferências sobre Antropologia da Saúde,* edited by E. J. Langdon, pp. 1–17. Programa de Pós-Graduação em Antropologia Social, Universidade Federal de Santa Catarina, Florianópolis.

———. 2000. Salud y pueblos indígenas: Los desafíos en el cambio de siglo. In *Salud y Equidad: Una Mirada desde las Ciencias Sociales,* edited by R. Briceño-León, M. C. S. Minayo, and C. E. A. Coimbra Jr., pp. 107–117. Editora Fiocruz, Rio de Janeiro.

Leite, M. S. 1998. *Avaliação do Estado Nutricional da População Xavánte de São José, Terra Indígena Sangradouro-Volta Grande, Mato Grosso.* M.P.H. thesis, Escola Nacional de Saúde Pública, Rio de Janeiro.

Linhares, A. C. 1992. Epidemiologia das infecções diarréicas entre populações indígenas da Amazônia. *Cadernos de Saúde Pública* 8: 121–128.

Linhares, A. C., E. V. Salbe, Y. B. Gabbay, and C. M. Nakauth. 1986. Prevalence of rotavirus antibody among isolated South American Indian communities. *American Journal of Epidemiology* 123: 699–709.

Martins, S. J., and R. C. Menezes. 1994. Evolução do estado nutricional de menores de 5 anos em aldeias indígenas da tribo Parakanã, na Amazônia oriental brasileira. *Revista de Saúde Pública* 28: 1–8.

Mattos, A., M. B. Morais, D. A. Rodrigues, and R. G. Baruzzi. 1999. Nutritional status and dietary habits of Indian children from Alto Xingu (Central Brazil) according to age. *Journal of the American College of Nutrition* 18: 88–94.

Meihy, J. C. S. B. 1994. A morte como apelo para a vida: O suicídio Kaiowá. In *Saúde e Povos Indígenas*, edited by R. V. Santos and C. E. A. Coimbra Jr., pp. 243–251. Editora Fiocruz, Rio de Janeiro.

Meireles, D. M. 1988. Sugestões para uma análise comparativa da fecundidade em populações indígenas. *Revista Brasileira de Estudos Populacionais* 5: 1–20.

Miranda, R. A., F. B. Xavier, and R. C. Menezes. 1998. Parasitismo intestinal em uma aldeia indígena Parakanã, sudeste do Estado do Pará, Brasil. *Cadernos de Saúde Pública* 14: 507–511.

Monteiro, C. A. 2000. Evolução da nutrição infantil nos anos 90. In *Velhos e Novos Males da Saúde no Brasil*, edited by C. A. Monteiro, pp. 375–392. Hucitec, São Paulo.

Morgado, A. F. 1991. Epidemia de suicídio entre os Guaraní-Kaiwá. *Cadernos de Saúde Pública* 7: 585–598.

Neel, J. V., F. M. Salzano, P. C. Junqueira, F. Keiter, and D. Maybury-Lewis. 1964. Studies on the Xavante Indians of the Brazilian Mato Grosso. *American Journal of Human Genetics* 16: 52–140.

Oliver, W. J., E. L. Cohen, and J. V. Neel. 1975. Blood pressure, sodium intake and sodium related hormones in the Yanomamo Indians, a "no-salt" culture. *Circulation* 52: 146–151.

Picchi, D., and F. P. College. 1994. Observations about a central Brazilian indigenous population: The Bakairi. *South American Indian Studies* 4: 37–46.

Pithan, O. A., U. E. Confalonieri, and A. Morgado. 1991. A situação de saúde dos índios Yanomami. *Cadernos de Saúde Pública* 7: 563–580.

Poz, J. D. 2000. Crônica de uma morte anunciada: Do suicídio entre os Sorowahá. *Revista de Antropologia* (São Paulo) 43: 89–144.

Ribas, D. L., A. Sganzerla, J. R. Zorzatto, and S. T. Philippi. 2001. Nutrição e saúde infantil de uma comunidade Teréna da região Centro-Oeste do Brasil. *Cadernos de Saúde Pública* 17: 323–331.

Ribeiro, D. 1977. *Os Índios e a Civilização*. Editora Vozes, Petrópolis.

Ricardo, C. A. 1996. A sociodiversidade nativa contemporânea no Brasil. In *Povos Indígenas no Brasil 1991/1995*, edited by C. A. Ricardo, pp. i–xii. Instituto Socioambiental, São Paulo.

———. 2000. Apresentação. In *Povos Indígenas no Brasil 1996/2000*, edited by C. A. Ricardo, pp. 7–15. Instituto Socioambiental, São Paulo.

Salzano, F. M., and S. M. Callegari-Jacques. 1988. *South American Indians: A Case Study in Evolution*. Clarendon Press, Oxford.

Sampaio, M. R., S. Turcotte, V. F. Martins, E. M. Cardoso, and M. N. Burattini. 1996. Malaria in the Indian reservation of "Vale do Javarí," Brasil. *Revista do Instituto de Medicina Tropical de São Paulo* 38: 59–60.

Santos, A. K., M. O. Ishak, S. E. Santos, J. F. Guerreiro, and R. Ishak. 1995. A possible correlation between the host genetic background in the epidemiology of hepatitis B virus in the Amazon region of Brazil. *Memórias do Instituto Oswaldo Cruz* 90: 435–441.

Santos, R. V. 1993. Crescimento físico e estado nutricional de populações indígenas brasileiras. *Cadernos de Saúde Pública* 9 (suppl. 1): 46–57.

Santos, R. V., and C. E. A. Coimbra Jr. 1991. Socioeconomic transition and physical growth of Tupí-Mondê Amerindian children of the Aripuanã Park, Brazilian Amazon. *Human Biology* 63: 795–820.

———. 1996. Socioeconomic differentiation and body morphology in the Suruí of southwestern Amazonia. *Current Anthropology* 37: 851–856.

———. 1998. On the (un)natural history of the Tupí-Mondé Indians: Bioanthropology and change in the Brazilian Amazon. In *Building a New Biocultural Synthesis: Political-Economic Perspectives on Human Biology*, edited by A. H. Goodman and T. Leatherman, pp. 269–294. University of Michigan Press, Ann Arbor.

Santos, R. V., C. E. A. Coimbra Jr., N. M. Flowers, and J. P. Silva. 1995. Intestinal parasitism in the Xavante Indians, Central Brazil. *Revista do Instituto de Medicina Tropical de São Paulo* 37: 145–148.

Santos, R. V., N. M. Flowers, C. E. A. Coimbra Jr., and S. A. Gugelmin. 1997. Tapirs, tractors, and tapes: The changing economy and ecology of the Xavánte Indians of Central Brazil. *Human Ecology* 25: 545–566.

Silva, M. F. 1994. A demografia e os povos indígenas no Brasil. *Revista Brasileira de Estudos Populacionais* 11: 261–264.

Sing, K. A., D. Hryhorczuk, D. C. Paschal, and E. H. Chen. 1996. Environmental exposure to organic mercury among the Makuxí in the Amazon Basin. *International Journal of Occupational and Environmental Health* 2: 165–171.

Soares, M. C., and G. Bensabath. 1991. Tribos indígenas da Amazônia Oriental como população de risco para a hepatite D (delta). *Revista do Instituto de Medicina Tropical de São Paulo* 33: 241–242.

Sousa, A. O., J. I. Salem, F. K. Lee, M. C. Verçosa, P. Cruaud, B. R. Bloom, P. H. Lagrange, and H. L. David. 1997. An epidemic of tuberculosis with a high rate of anergy among a population previously unexposed to tuberculosis, the Yanomami Indians of the Brazilian Amazon. *Proceedings of the National Academy of Sciences, USA* 94: 13227–13232.

Souza, L. G., and R. V. Santos. 2001. Perfil demográfico da população indígena Xavánte de Sangradouro–Volta Grande, Mato Grosso, Brasil (1993–1997). *Cadernos de Saúde Pública* 17: 355–365.

Spielman, R. S., S. S. Fajans, J. V. Neel, S. Pek, J. C. Floyd, and W. J. Oliver. 1982. Glucose tolerance in two unacculturated Indian tribes of Brazil. *Diabetologia* 23: 90–93.

Stinson, S. 1996. Early childhood growth of Chachi Amerindians and Afro-Ecuadorians in northwest Ecuador. *American Journal of Human Biology* 8: 43–53.

Taborda, W. C., S. C. Ferreira, D. Rodrigues, J. N. Stávale, and R. G. Baruzzi. 2000. Rastreamento do câncer de colo uterino em índias do Parque Indígena do Xingu, Brasil Central. *Revista Panamericana de Salud Pública* 7: 92–96.

Verdum, R. 1995. Mapa da fome entre os povos indígenas no Brasil. In *Mapa da Fome entre os Povos Indígenas no Brasil: Contribuição à Formulação de Políticas de Segurança Alimentar Sustentáveis*, edited by Instituto de Estudos Sócio-Econômicos (INESC), pp. 7–15. INESC, Brasília.

Vieira-Filho, J. P. B. 1975. Análise das glicemias dos índios das aldeias Suruí, Gaviões e Xikrín. *Revista da Associação Médica Brasileira* 21: 253–255.

———. 1977. O diabetes mellitus e as glicemias de jejum dos índios Caripuna e Palikur. *Revista da Associação Médica Brasileira* 23: 175–178.

———. 1981. Problemas de aculturação alimentar dos Xavante e Bororo. *Revista de Antropologia* (São Paulo) 24: 37–40.

———. 1996. Emergência do diabetes melito tipo II entre os Xavantes. *Revista da Associação Médica Brasileira* 42: 61.

Vieira-Filho, J. P. B., E. M. K. Russo, and Y. Juliano. 1984. A hemoglobina glicosilada (HbA1) dos índios Bororo. *Arquivos Brasileiros de Endocrinologia e Metabologia* 28: 87–90.

Viertler, R. B. 2000. Alcoolismo entre os Bororos. In *Ciências Sociais e Saúde para o Ensino Médico*, edited by A. M. Canesqui, pp. 243–261. Editora Hucitec, São Paulo.

Werner, D. 1983. Fertility and pacification among the Mekranoti of Central Brazil. *Human Ecology* 11: 227–245.

7

THE NEXUS OF YANOMAMÖ GROWTH, HEALTH, AND DEMOGRAPHY

Raymond Hames & Jennifer Kuzara

Our goal in this chapter is to provide a synthetic overview of studies on Yanomamö health from an ecological perspective, with a special emphasis on emerging medical problems that are primarily a consequence of recent contact with non-Yanomamö. As we shall document, throughout most of their recent history the Yanomamö can be characterized as a high-mortality and high-fertility population that has been subjected to a variety of infectious and parasitic diseases common to other Amazonian populations. Ecologically, these illnesses appear to be the primary factors limiting Yanomamö population growth. Our goal is to begin an assessment of the degree to which diet and disease affect Yanomamö growth and development and morbidity and mortality rates. Just as important, we hope to document the consequences of the introduction of novel diseases on an already highly parasitized people and the steps the governments of Brazil and Venezuela are taking to regulate contact with outsiders and how they are responding to introduced diseases.

We begin with a description of Yanomamö anthropometrics and diet. The Yanomamö are one of the smallest people in all of Amazonia. The cause of their short stature as well as some interesting variation among Yanomamö populations is unknown. In the 1970s a number of anthropologists (e.g., Gross 1974; Harris 1977) suggested that the Yanomamö were suffering from an inadequate protein intake, which may account for their short stature. Research by Lizot (1977) and Chagnon and Hames (1979) demonstrated that protein intake was more than adequate, and Lizot (1977) documented overall caloric and micronutrient sufficiency. Nevertheless, the causes of short stature are unclear, and dietary insufficiency in the form of inadequate calories may play a role in some areas.

We next turn to an examination of the traditional infectious and parasitic diseases that afflict the Yanomamö. Throughout human history such diseases have had an enormous impact on human population structure, and the Yanomamö are no exception. As we shall demonstrate, the Yanomamö are afflicted by a wide variety of diseases, but their degree of affliction is probably no greater than that of other native peoples who live in an equatorial environment, the most disease-ridden of all human habitats (see Low 1990 and references therein; Mackintosh 2001). We distinguish between traditional and introduced diseases. By traditional diseases we mean those diseases that appear to predate regular contact with non-Indian populations. Most important, they include a variety of intestinal parasites and malaria. Introduced diseases are those that seem not to have afflicted the Yanomamö until they came in contact with whites. Some of these diseases, such as measles and influenza, seem to sweep rapidly through the population and disappear, only to reappear through continued contact with outsiders. Other introduced diseases such as tuberculosis and hepatitis are chronic illnesses that spread slowly from village to village causing widespread illness, debilitation, and death. Unlike measles and influenza, these chronic infectious diseases persist in villages indefinitely unless public health officials mount well-designed campaigns for their eradication.

Finally, two richly detailed demographic investigations of the Yanomamö (Melancon 1982; Early and Peters 2000) have the ability to inform us about mortality and survivorship, two fundamental dimensions of life that are correlated with health. These studies indicate that infectious disease is the main health problem, and it appears to have a major effect in the early years of life.

Throughout, we consider the responses of anthropologists, missionaries, nongovernmental organizations, and state bureaucracies in treating diseases over the short and long term and in controlling Yanomamö contact with outsiders who habitually introduce diseases. Regulation of outside contact and effective monitoring and treatment are critical dimensions for enhancing Yanomamö health.

Yanomamö Growth

By Amazonian and world standards the Yanomamö are of small stature. The general literature on growth has consistently demonstrated a negative correlation between socioeconomic status and adult stature and weight (Huss-Ashmore and Johnston 1985; Bogin 1999). The implication is that poverty leads to reduced dietary quality, an increase in disease, or both (Garn 1980). It is particularly difficult to untangle the role of nutritional intake and disease and their synergistic relationship. One attempt to document this relationship (Martorell et al., 1980, cited in Huss-Ashmore and Johnston [1985: 486]) reports that common illnesses were associated with a reduction of 20 percent in food intake. Jenkins's study of children in Belize (1981) demonstrates the negative growth effects of chronic diarrhea, as do Hodge and Dufour (1991) for Shipibo Indians.

A consistent finding of the several studies of Yanomamö growth is that the Yanomamö are small even by tropical forest standards. Comparative research on this topic was undertaken by Holmes (1995). Table 7.1 contains the ethnic groups Holmes compared to her two Yanomamö groups (Parima and Coyoweteri). To this we have added other Yanomamö studies (Spielman et al. 1972; Coco 1973; Hames, field data 1987; Crews and Mancilha-Carvalho 1991) and data reported by Santos and Coimbra (1996) on the Surui. Table 7.1 clearly indicates that of the sixteen tropical and subtropical native South Americans surveyed, Parima Yanomamö men and women are the second smallest and lightest in the sample. Notably, the two villages surveyed by Holmes contain the lightest and shortest Yanomamö ever documented. We will return to this finding later.

Dietary insufficiency is an obvious hypothesis for small stature. Basing her assessment on weight-for-height curves and arm and fatfold measures, Holmes (1985) notes that children from ages one through twelve are moderately to severely malnourished, whereas older children "are relatively heavy, indicating stocky body proportions." She also notes that young children and older adults do not manifest good nutritional status. In an earlier report based on the same survey, published in 1984, she makes the following assessment: "Few clinical signs of malnutrition were present in the population. It was not uncommon to find very small children (that is, short or light for their age) who would be classified anthropometrically as malnourished, traveling through the forest for several hours carrying heavy loads without signs of physical exhaustion" (Holmes 1985: 387).

Recent research by Hagen et al. (2001) on fatfold thickness in the lowland village of Cejal undergoing short-term food scarcity may provide a

TABLE 7.1   Anthropometric Statistics for the Yanomamö and
Other Populations

Group[1]	Male Stature (cm)	Female Stature (cm)	Male Weight (kg)	Female Weight (kg)	Male BMI	Female BMI
Motilon[1]	146.2	138.1	nd	nd	nd	nd
Parima Yanomamö[1]	146.9	136.9	43.7	37.9	20.22	20.22
Yanomamö Surucucu[2]	151.1	142.0	46.9	43.0	20.40	21.30
Yanomamö: Coyoweteri[1]	152.3	139.6	44.4	38.2	19.22	19.60
Yanomamö (18 highland and lowland villages)[3]	153.2	142.4	nd	nd	nd	nd
Auca[1]	154.0	144.0	nd	nd	nd	nd
Apalai-Waiana[1]	154.2	142.8	nd	nd	nd	nd
Bari[1]	154.5	nd	nd	nd	nd	nd
Guahibo[1]	155.4	nd	54.1	nd	22.52	nd
Mundurucu[1]	155.6	145.4	nd	nd	nd	nd
Ye'kwana[1]	156.0	146.0	62.0	53.0	25.48	24.86
Tucano[1]	156.0	146.0	nd	nd	nd	nd
Yanomamö: Ocamo[4]	156.0	148.0	nd	nd	nd	nd
Yanomamö Kedi-Washawa[5]	156.5	145.1	51.8	44.4	21.01	21.09
Surui[6]	156.5	147.0	53.3	49.9	nd	nd
Karina[1]	156.6	146.7	56.6	nd	23.26	nd
Warao[1]	157.3	nd	50.8	nd	19.60	nd
Curripaco[1]	157.3	144.4	59.2	50.2	24.02	24.08
Pemon[1]	159.0	146.7	nd	nd	nd	nd
Guajiro[1]	159.2	nd	60.5	nd	23.93	nd
Yaruro[1]	165.6	nd	58.8	nd	21.34	nd
Mekranoti[1]	166.4	153.1	66.6	56.4	24.17	24.06
Xirkin[1]	168.7	155.9	63.6	56.0	22.53	23.04
Venezuela Peasant[1]	166	157	65	57	23	23.1
United States[1]	172	159	75	65	25.4	25.5
Caracas Elite[1]	172.9	161.1	61.4	52.8	20.75	20.34

Communities in boldface are Yanomamö communities.

Sources: [1]Holmes (1995); [2]Crews and Mancilha-Carvalho (1991); [3]Spielman et al. (1972); [4]Coco (1973); [5]Hames, field data (1987); [6]Santos and Coimbra (1996).

context for interpreting Holmes's results. The village of Cejal, located near the mouth of the Casiquiare Canal on the Orinoco, suffered a shortage of horticultural crops as a consequence of garden flooding brought on by the El Niño weather phenomenon in 1998. Children (ages four to sixteen years) had triceps skinfolds in the range of three to eight millimeters (boys) and three to sixteen millimeters (girls). A figure from Holmes (1985: 252, her figure 6) on triceps measurements from highland groups shows a similar range (this assessment is interpolated from the figure, since no tabular or summary measures are presented). Data collected earlier in two non-food-stressed lowland villages by one of us (Hames) indicates that boys in these villages had significantly greater skinfolds ($p < .001$) than those of the food-stressed village of Cejal (Hagen et al. 2001: 14). The difference between the girls in the two villages was not statistically significant ($p = .59$), although they were greater in the nonstressed village and appear to be greater than measurements in Holmes's highland villages. These comparative findings show that the skinfolds of children in the food-stressed village of Cejal are similar to those found by Holmes in her highland groups, and the skinfolds of children in non-food-stressed lowland villages are greater than either. This suggests that food may be scarcer in highland villages and is reflected in the skinfold measures of children.

Interestingly, Holmes (1984: 388, her figure 3) documents an apparent lack of relationship between an individual's parasite load and nutritional status. To explain this unlikely finding, Holmes speculates that low nutritional status may protect against parasitic infection, although, if this is correct, Holmes should have found a positive association between parasite load and nutritional status. This mirrors an argument made by Kent and Weinberg (1989) concerning low iron levels in Third World women as a mechanism to protect against bacterial infections. We will return to this hypothesis later.

In a comparative examination of growth and nutrition in more than a dozen Amazonian groups, Dufour observes for the Yanomamö: "Indeed, they are the shortest people in Amazonia" (Dufour 1994: 156). In reference to the small stature of Yanomamö adults, Tierney (2000: 60) quotes Dufour as generalizing that this is evidence of "long term nutritional inadequacy or generally poor environmental conditions, especially ones in which chronic or repeated infections are prevalent." The quotation is accurate but misleading, since Dufour is speaking of height for age, which is a measure of stunting in children and not indicative of "poor environmental conditions" for adults. Indeed, height for age, measurements are never made for adults as indicators of relative health. The proper measure for adults is weight-for-height (i.e., BMI). The body-mass indices shown in table 7.1 indicate that the Yanomamö are in the healthy range (18.5–24.9) according to the Centers for Disease Control (Centers for Disease Control 2002).

How do we account for this result in light of the fact that most biomedical researchers (e.g., Neel et al. 1977; Neel 1979) report that the Yanomamö are well nourished and healthy, and the main dietary study we have (Lizot 1977) suggests that the Yanomamö diet meets or exceeds international dietary standards? Research on two exceptionally small populations, the Pygmies and the Mountain Ok of New Guinea (sum-marized in Bogin 1999), has implicated genetic variation in the pro-duction of a growth hormone (IGF-1) or sensitivity to its effects. At this point there is nothing to suggest that hormonal variation plays a role among the Yanomamö, for no such studies have been done. The three Yanomamö villages with smallest statures come from highland areas (Parima and Coyoweteri in Venezuela and Surucucu in Brazil, both at about 1,000 meters), whereas those with the tallest statures (Kedi-Washawa and Ocamo) are in the Mavaca lowlands (see table 7.1). The men in lowland villages are seven to ten centimeters taller than Holmes's Parima population.[1] This implies a negative altitude gradient that may be correlated with dietary and disease patterns. There is suggestive evi-dence that lowland villages (Chagnon 1997) may have better access to food resources. Other than onchocerciasis, which seems more prevalent at high altitudes, our review of epidemiological investigations suggests that there is no discernible relationship between altitude and disease pressure.

Rebecca Holmes is the only anthropologist who has attempted to deal with the issue of small stature among the Yanomamö. In her most re-cent assessment of their stature, weight, and growth, she argues that the Yanomamö may be "small and adaptive" (Holmes 1995: 140). In part, her argument parallels the "small but healthy" position taken by Stini (1971) and Seckler (1982): small body size is an adaptation to chronic undernutrition and disease. This hypothesis states that populations under food and disease stress facultatively adjust their growth to adapt to these problems. As Holmes herself notes, this perspective has gener-ated considerable criticism (e.g., Martorell 1989). Holmes also believes that there also may be a genetic component to Yanomamö stature (Holmes 1995: 132, 138).

In an attempt to explain small stature among native South Americans, Salzano and Callegari-Jacques (1988: 116, their table 6.1) demonstrate that of the forty-three native ethnic groups they surveyed, only three are shorter than the Yanomamö. They note a statistically significant north-south geographic patterning such that northern groups such as the Yanomamö are significantly smaller than southern groups (Salzano and Callegari-Jacques 1988, their figure 6.1). The meaning of this pattern is unclear. The authors do not correlate this geographic pattern with genetic markers, linguistic grouping, or ecological factors. The only interpreta-tion at this point is that the small stature of the Yanomamö is consistent with their geographic position in South America. Consequently, it is uncertain what roles disease, nutrition, and genetics play separately or jointly in determining Yanomamö stature in comparison to that of other Amazonian peoples or within the Yanomamö. Nevertheless, it is an important finding that may help us identify the ecological or genetic factors that underlie this relationship.

Disease Patterns

The most important threat to Yanomamö health and quality of life is the presence of infectious diseases, the most threatening of which are those of European and African origin. Some of these diseases have spread to the Yanomamö through recent direct contact, while others may have been introduced prior to actual contact through trade with neighboring Amerindian groups. The most important of these are the mycobacterial infection tuberculosis, the hepatitis viruses (both B and delta), other viral infections such as measles, and parasitic infections such as onchocerciasis and a variety of intestinal helminths. Finally, although malaria has been present in the Amazon for hundreds of years, contact with non-Indians appears to lead to the introduction of new strains that have a devastating effect on the Yanomamö.

The presence of infectious agents among the Yanomamö is a perpetual drain on the body's nutritional and defensive resources. Whether this drain is marginal or detrimental depends on the severity of the symptoms of each species, possible interaction between infectious agents, the number of species infecting each individual, and the severity of each infection. Many infections that would not be fatal if those infected had access to proper medical care can cause severe problems and even be life threatening in the absence of such care.

Knowing which diseases affect the Yanomamö and the overall prevalence of these diseases in each village is only the first stage in developing adequate health care programs. One must be able to predict the changes that are likely to occur in the patterns of disease and pathogen dispersion as the Yanomamö become more sedentary and have greater exposure to Western diet and lifestyle. For this purpose, acculturated native Amerindian peoples of the same region may provide a model for the effects on health of the acculturation process; indeed, some Yanomamö groups that have begun this transition, such as those near mission stations, may also serve for comparison to those groups that still have limited exposure to Westerners. We will attempt to synthesize some of the data currently available on each of these groups in order to make a preliminary comparison of this nature.

Hepatitis

Of grave concern among the Yanomamö are the hepatitis viruses. Both hepatitis B (HBV) and hepatitis delta (HDV) have been identified among the Yanomamö. According to infectious disease experts in the United States, most cases of HBV worldwide (94 percent of adult infections, 70 percent of infections among children; see http://www.cdc.gov/ncidod/diseases/hepatitis/b/fact.htm) are overcome after about six months, after which the carrier becomes immune (antibodies to the virus are present in their blood, but the viral antigens are not) and may no longer become ill with the infection or transmit the infection to others. For infants infected at birth, about 90 percent become chronically infected, and up to 6 percent of adult infections may become chronic. In 15 to 25 percent of all cases that remain chronic, liver damage can be a life-threatening concern. This danger is even greater for those infected with HDV, which is more severe. HDV requires the presence of HBV to replicate and seems to reduce the likelihood that concomitant HBV infection will become chronic. However, it also causes a more acute infection. Of cases of individuals who are chronic for both HBV and HDV, 70 to 80 percent develop liver damage, rather than the 15 to 25 percent of carriers of HBV alone. Given the fact that the Yanomamö generally do not have immediate access to the type of emergency care necessary for those suffering from severe liver damage, they are undoubtedly more susceptible to mortality associated with the disease than are people who live elsewhere.

In Ocamo and Mavaca villages, HBV was first introduced in 1968 by an American missionary who had reused needles in administering multivitamin complexes to himself and to the Yanomamö in the village (Torres and Mondolfi 1991). It is unlikely that the viruses were present prior to this time. By the time of a 1986 study in these villages (Torres and Mondolfi 1991), 84 percent of eighty Yanomamö who were randomly tested had been infected. A full 30 percent of the samples showed active infection (hepatitis B surface antigen or [HbsAg] was present in their blood), meaning that they either were chronically or newly infected. Over half (54 percent) of the samples from the two villages were from persons who had been infected and already developed immunity at the time of the study. One can see from figure 7.1 that the number of active infections (either chronic or new) does not decrease appreciably with

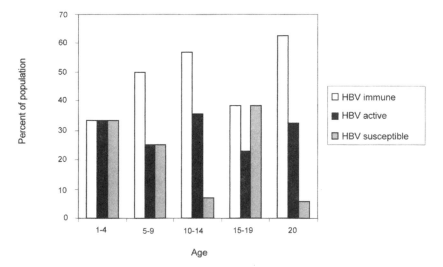

FIGURE 7.1   Hepatitis B virus prevalences in the Yanomamö village of Mavaca (Torres and Mondolfi 1991).

age, which one would expect in a population where the virus is endemic. Furthermore, in the same study, 40 percent of those infected with HBV also tested positive for HDV. As noted previously, those with HBV infection who otherwise showed no symptoms can develop liver damage associated with HDV.

Torres and Mondolfi (1991) also studied thirty-six serum samples that had been collected in 1975 and preserved. In this case, samples had been collected only from individuals with acute liver damage; thus the prevalence of HBV or HDV infections in this group is likely to be higher than among the general population. Of these individuals, 97 percent had been exposed to HBV, and 53 percent had active infection at the time the samples were collected. After the test for HBV, enough serum remained to test for HDV in only six of the samples. These were tested for the presence of anti-delta antigens, which were present in all six (this prior even to its description in the medical literature in 1977).

The risks posed by the presence of HBV and HDV among the Yanomamö are serious. The damage associated with chronic HBV is severe, and that with HDV even more so. Because the viruses are spread through contact with saliva, blood and sexual fluids, the intimate nature of interactions among the Yanomamö makes it likely that the disease will spread more quickly than in groups where this contact is not as common.

Intimate contact among the Yanomamö includes the universality of breast feeding, premastication of food for infants, body paint mixed with saliva, early onset of sexual activity, and the sharing of chewing tobacco and instruments used to pierce the body.

Tuberculosis

Tuberculosis, like the hepatitis viruses, was very unlikely to have existed among the Yanomamö prior to contact and is currently a major threat to their health. Although tuberculosis affects primarily the lungs, it can also spread to the gastrointestinal, genitourinary, nervous, and lymphatic systems, as well as to the bones and skin. This range makes it a particular threat. Tubercles, which form when macrophages attempt to engulf the *Mycobacterium tuberculosis* bacilli, may heal through fibrosis and calcification, and in this state, the infection can remain arrested until reinfection or other exacerbation of the disease, when a chronic and progressive form may develop.

Drug therapies for tuberculosis are very often successful, and, though less effective than treatment, inoculation with bacille Calmette-Guérin (BCG) vaccine can prevent infection. However, some drug-resistant strains of the bacterium have developed. These are often associated with improper use of drug therapies, but the formation of resistant strains is preventable if proper care is taken with the administration of treatment.

For some groups of Yanomamö, particularly those in Brazil, the disease is likely being contracted through contacts with Brazilians, although some suspect that tuberculosis was first introduced among some Yanomamö through contacts with other Yanomamö from the Apiau and Ajarani region (Peters 1980), who had likely first contracted the disease from contacts with whites or with other native groups. However the disease was first introduced, directly or indirectly through non-Yanomamö, its prevalence is high. Sousa et al. (1997) found a prevalence of 6.4 percent (40 cases out of 625 people) in a study of five Yanomamö villages in Brazil, which is 100 times higher than the average for Amazonas State, Brazil. Peters (1980) found that among 280 Yanomamö, 3.6 percent had active disease (1980: 276). In addition, he noted there were "40–50 [of 280 Yanomamö examined] suspect cases, either of the pulmonary or intestinal variety" (Peters 1980: 276), or about 16 percent of the population. Apparently these diagnoses were made by "a doctor from the National Division of Tuberculosis" (Peters, 1980: 246).

Measles

Measles and other introduced viral infections can present severe health risk to the Yanomamö. The historical record clearly shows that New World peoples experienced massive population reductions when infected by many Old World diseases. This is certainly due to the fact that, unlike the Europeans, they did not have prior experience with the infections. Whether this is the result of a genetic immunity that is present in Europeans and lacking in Amerindians (see Black et al. 1982) or a consequence of lack of acquired immunity in the community (Neel et al. 1977) is still debated. According to Neel (1979), the high rate of mortality among Amerindians is mostly likely a consequence of their inexperience with the illness that causes nearly all residents of a village to become ill. This leads to a breakdown in the economic and health systems: there is scarcely anyone available to provide food and water to enable the afflicted to fight the illness. Tropical forest horticulturalists have a fundamentally different economic system than temperate land agriculturalists. In temperate environments food is stored in the home for most of the year. Consequently, if an epidemic strikes, the ill can easily procure food from stores within their dwellings. In contrast, tropical forest horticulturalists rely on root crops and plantains which cannot be processed to store for any length of time. In a sense, food is stored in the garden. To acquire food, adults must travel to gardens, harvest the food, transport it home, and prepare it. In addition, on a daily basis they tend to spend even more time hunting, gathering, and fishing than they do gardening (Hames, 1989). The successful acquisition of these foraged resources is beyond the abilities of someone who is ill. In this sort of economic system, villagewide illness is much more likely to prevent the ill from "curing" themselves through adequate caloric consumption and hydration. In experienced populations, however, large numbers of adults have gained some measure of immunity through previous contact with the illness, and they are able to care for those who lack such immunity. Also in modern populations, easy availability of water, food, and medications mitigates the symptoms of disease and associated complications.

In a specific instance described by Neel et al. (1970), it was suggested that the Yanomamö were unlikely to have been exposed to measles in the past. Lack of previous infection was confirmed in 1966 and 1967 with serological evidence: in only two out of eighteen villages did a significant number of individuals test positive for measles antibodies. One of these villages was located near a mission and had been known to have experienced a measles epidemic; in the other, none of the positive responders was younger than twenty-eight years, suggesting that this village had sustained an epidemic of measles prior to direct contact with non-Indians.

Alarmed by this evidence, Neel obtained measles vaccine so he could vaccinate the Yanomamö in 1968. However, measles was introduced to some of these villages by a Brazilian missionary prior to Neel's expedition. Thus they began a vaccination campaign in the midst of a measles epidemic.

Throughout this epidemic, most villages were visited by a government team or by missionaries, and antibiotics were supplied to help prevent secondary infections. For some, especially distant, villages, these were provided late in the infection, however. Neel et al. (1970) estimated that of about 170 cases, 29, or 17.7 percent, proved fatal. Most of these were due to secondary pulmonary infection. This toll would certainly have been far worse had the team not been able to vaccinate so many people and provide antibiotics to those infected. It also shows what a devastating effect such an outbreak could potentially have in the future if health care workers do not maintain constant vigilance.

Onchocerciasis

Onchocerciasis was probably introduced to the Yanomamö in the early 1970s (Salzano and Callegari-Jacques 1988: 97) and is now very common in highland communities, where infection in some villages is widespread (Grillet et al. 2001). It has been present in the Americas since the introduction of immigrants and slaves from Africa, where it is endemic in certain regions. Caused by the filarial parasite *Onchocerca volvulus*, it is rarely fatal. However, it can be disfiguring and debilitating; at its worst, it can lead to blindness and to disorders of the lymphatic system.

Some of the most adverse consequences of this infection are related to the host's immune response to the microfilariae. The symptoms of this disease are often similar to a mild to severe allergic reaction, such as itching, cracking, and thickening of the skin, related bacterial infection, and eventual fibrosis. Hanging groin can also result from inflammation of lymph nodes associated with the infection.

Blindness results when nodules form in the cornea or retina of the host. Because symptoms develop over time, however, uninvasive diagnosis of infection can be difficult. Palpable nodules may not be found in all infected individuals; Rassi et al. (1976), for example, found only seventeen Yanomamö with palpable nodules out of seventy-five Yanomamö subjects who had tested positive for microfilariae in skin biopsies.

Species of black fly of the genus *Simulium* serve as the vector for the parasite, including *S. guianense*, *S. oyapockense*, and *S. incrustatum*, although the role of the latter as a vector is undetermined. The prevalence of onchocerciasis seems to be greater at higher altitudes. In a study of biting rates of these three species of black fly, the biting rates of both *S. guianense* and *S. incrustatum* increased with altitude (Grillet et al. 2001). This may be related to the fact that the larval stage of the fly requires fast-flowing, highly oxygenated water, which is more likely to be found at higher altitudes.

Prevalence of this disease can vary greatly from one village to another. Rassi et al. (1976) found that onchocerciasis had not yet appeared in several villages inhabited by the Yanomamö. In Toototobi, however, prevalence of the disease, as determined by palpation, vision tests, skin biopsy, and reactivity to Hetrazan,[2] was 61 percent. In Auaris, prevalence was 25 percent, and in Surucucu, it was 24 percent.

Onchocerciasis may be on the rise, however. Grillet et al. (2001) measured the prevalence of the disease in several villages as well. Although these were not the same villages as those examined by Rassi et al. (1976), prevalence was much higher. They found high rates of infection in highland villages (24 to 80 percent), although in at least one lowland village (Ocamo), the rate was considerably lower (2.4 percent).

Treatment of onchocerciasis is relatively straightforward; ivermectin can rid an individual of infection. However, the real likelihood of reinfection makes vigilance and repeated treatment necessary to prevent long-term physical damage. For this to occur, health care workers must be available to administer medications and to ensure that they are used effectively.

Malaria

Malaria is one of the most serious threats to Yanomamö health. In several studies conducted among the Yanomamö, *Plasmodium falciparum* has proven to be the most common malaria pathogen (Perez Mato 1998; Torres et al. 1988, 2000). This species accounted for 68.6 percent of all infections in one study (Torres et al. 2000) and 57.1 percent in another (Perez Mato 1998). Torres et al. (1988) found that the titers of antibody to *P. falciparum* were higher than those to *P. vivax* in all but two cases out of fifty-nine studied.

This contrasts with the species distribution common elsewhere, even in Venezuela itself: the average Venezuelan distribution of infections in 1992 was 76 percent *P. vivax* and only 24 percent *P. falciparum*. This is significant to the Yanomamö because, although *P. vivax*, unlike *P. falciparum*, can remain dormant in the liver and thus relapse, the infection caused by *P. falciparum* is often much more acute, sometimes fatally so.

Among some Yanomamö groups, virtually everyone has been infected with malaria at some point. Torres et al. (1988; see also Torres et al. 1997 for additional details) found that of 59 serum samples taken from individuals in Ocamo and Mavaca, all had antibodies to both *P. falciparum* and *P. vivax*. The presence of active infection (determined by the detection of *Plasmodium* species in thick blood smears) with any of the *Plasmodium* species, however, was found in only 3 out of 110 samples, suggesting either a high level of immunity among adults in this area or a pattern of (perhaps frequent) periodic epidemics.

Indeed, Perez Mato (1998) found higher levels of *P. falciparum* and *P. vivax* in younger age-groups than in adults in Ocamo and Mavaca in 1992 (figure 7.2). Out of 35 individuals between age six months and ten years of age, 17.1 percent had active *P. falciparum* infection, and 14.3 percent had active *P. vivax* infection. Of twelve individuals between the ages of ten and fifteen years, none were infected with either species. Of those over fifteen years of age, 3.6 percent had *P. falciparum* infection, and only 1.8 percent had *P. vivax* infection. This suggests, though not with certainty,

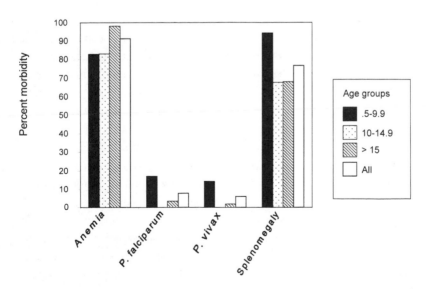

FIGURE 7.2   Malaria and malaria-related morbidity in the Yanomamö village of Mavaca (Source of data: Perez Mato 1998).

that some of those in the older age-groups have acquired immunity to active malaria infection.

This immunity may have some benefits for the village as a whole. If adults do not become ill, they can give better care to ill children. Basic economic functions continue to be fulfilled, such as procurement of food and water. On the other hand, the prolonged or repeated infection required to acquire immunity takes a heavy toll on those living in hyperendemic areas such as Ocamo and Mavaca.

In contrast, areas that are not hyperendemic, while spared from high prevalence of infection much of the time, may experience severe periodic outbreaks of the disease. In a study comparing malaria outbreaks in Coyoweteri and Matoweteri, Laserson et al. (1999) found that the prevalence of active malaria was very low in August and September 1993, and again in May and July 1994. During these two sampling periods, a total of 14 cases of active *P. falciparum* infections were found in 320 (4.4 percent) samples from both villages. After severe outbreaks in October and November 1994, however, Coyoweteri had a prevalence of active *falciparum* malaria of 45.2 percent (out of 62 individuals) and Matoweteri of 45.7 percent (out of 70 individuals). With this proportion of the population of a village ill, severe economic hardship is a likely result. Ill parents, particularly nursing mothers, cannot provide as well for ill children. Procurement of food and water becomes problematic. Those who are well may flee the village rather than staying on to care for the sick and risking infection themselves.

The most immediately life-threatening complication of malaria is the often extreme febrile state reached by those suffering current infection and associated dehydration. Many other complications are common, however. These include splenomegaly, or enlargement of the spleen; acute hemolytic anemia, a form of anemia caused by the destruction of a large quantity of red blood cells; hepatomegaly, or enlargement of the liver, which can lead in turn to hypertension of the portal vein, which conducts blood from digestive organs to the liver, and potentially cirrhosis, a disease in which the tissue of the liver becomes fibrous, resulting in a loss of normal function. Torres et al. (1988) found that 44 percent of individuals in the villages of Ocamo and Mavaca suffered some degree of splenomegaly. An estimated 23 percent of all malaria cases resulted in hyperreactive malarial splenomegaly. This syndrome was associated with hemolysis in the same villages (Torres et al. 2000). Prior to the study, in just one year, 38 of the 550 inhabitants (7 percent) of Ocamo and Mavaca had required evacuation for emergency transfusion, due to severe hemolytic anemia.

Perez Mato (1998) found that anemia was ubiquitous in Mavaca in 1992. Of the total population of 103 individuals, 91 percent suffered from anemia. Adults, particularly women, were more likely to suffer from anemia than were children. On the other hand, children aged six months to ten years were more likely, at 94 percent of 33 individuals in the age range, to suffer from splenomegaly than were adults, at 68 percent of 38 individuals. The presence of splenomegaly in this population was strikingly high, at 77 percent, and 45 percent suffered from moderate to severe splenomegaly (see figure 7.2). This is most likely due to repeated infection with *Plasmodium* parasites.

Other Parasites

One of the most ubiquitous and persistent health problems facing the Yanomamö is the presence of a vast range of parasitic infections. Some of these, such as *Entamoeba coli*, are nonpathogenic and common to the intestinal flora. Others reach an equilibrium within their hosts; while they do sap nutrients and can cause some serious health problems, they are generally not life-threatening. These include many species of intestinal helminth, such as *Ancylostoma duodenale* and *Ascaris lumbricoides*, as well as a variety of roundworms, flatworms, tapeworms, and filarial worms and protozoans.

Many of these parasites are contracted primarily through oral-fecal contact; often this involves soil in which eggs or larvae (in the case of worms) or cysts (in the case of protozoan infections) have been deposited. Many of these are equipped to enter the new host through the skin, particularly that of bare feet, but they can also infect hands and subsequently be ingested. The other primary mode of transmission is through infected water. Thus, sanitation practices are of great import in determining the severity and prevalence of infection. The Yanomamö, being swidden agriculturalists, have been prone to move periodically, thus evading areas in which infective agents have built up in the soil for several years. As the Yanomamö become more sedentary, unless concomitant measures are taken to ensure proper sanitation such as pit latrines, these infections are likely to increase.

Macroparasites

Ancylostoma duodenale   The genus *Ancylostoma* includes the hookworms, of which *A. duodenale* is one of the most common. Hookworm is contracted through the skin, from fecal material deposited in the soil. Once resident in the intestine, it attaches itself to the mucous membrane and consumes the blood of its host. The most severe effect of hookworm infection is loss of blood, which can result in iron deficiency anemia and, in very severe cases, malnutrition. In the case of a mild infection, the side effects may be minimal.

Holmes (1984) found that in two Yanomamö Venezuelan villages the rates of infection were, respectively, 39 percent and 67 percent, somewhat lower than the rates of 76 percent and 80 percent found by Lawrence et al. (1980) in Mavaca and Patanowateri.

Ascaris lumbricoides   *Ascaris lumbricoides* is the most common roundworm worldwide, currently infecting nearly 1.5 billion people. It is also the most common to the Yanomamö. Passed through feces, it requires a two-week incubation period in the soil, after which, if ingested, the eggs are infective. They hatch in the intestinal tract, and the larvae enter the venous circulation and pass to the lungs, from which they migrate up the subject's upper respiratory passages and are swallowed. The parasite can cause pneumonia during this stage in its life cycle. Another complication is intestinal obstruction, although most cases are asymptomatic. (http://www.nematode.net/Species.Summaries/Ascaris.lumbricoides/).

This infection is quite common among the Yanomamö; prevalence rates ranged from 73 to 99 percent in four villages (Lawrence et al. 1980; Holmes 1984). Only Confalonieri et al. (1989; cited in Confalonieri et al. 1991) found a range of 6.6 to 14.3 percent, for which the specific villages were not named.

Strongyloides stercoralis   This parasite, like the hookworm, is contracted through the skin. The filariform larvae travel to the lungs, from whence they may be swallowed, to take up residence in the intestine and there mature. It may be symptomatic during the pulmonary stage of infection but is frequently asymptomatic. Unlike some other helminth species, *Strongyloides stercoralis* does not require an incubation period in the soil; autoinfection is possible, and in some individuals, particularly those who are immunosuppressed, fever and abdominal pain may occur.

Holmes (1984) found from 0 to 1 percent in two villages, while Lawrence et al. (1980) observed from 3 to 11 percent in two others. Confalonieri et al. (1989; cited in Confalonieri et al. 1991) observed a rate of 0 to 3.3 percent in several unidentified villages.

Capillaria   Three species of roundworm of the genus *Capillaria* can infect humans, one of which, *C. phillipinensis*, is most common, and two of which, *C. hepatica* and *C. aerophila*, are rare. *C. hepatica* causes hepatic capillariasis, which may result in hepatitis and eosinophilia; *C. aerophila* causes pulmonary capillariasis, which may result in asthma and pneumonia. Both of these illnesses may be fatal.

According to the Centers for Disease Control (http://www.dpd.cdc.gov/dpdx/HTML/Capillariasis.htm), the geographic distribution of *Capillaria* species is limited primarily to the Philippines and Thailand, with rare cases reported in the Middle East and Colombia. Confalonieri et al. (1989; cited in Confalonieri et al. 1991) report a prevalence of unspecified *Capillaria* species of 2.8 to 6.6 percent among the Yanomamö, a finding that illustrates the extent to which even very remote peoples may be exposed to diseases and parasites thought to be locally specific to distant areas.

Hymenolepis nana   *Hymenolepis nana*, a tapeworm that completes its life cycle within its host, is common worldwide. It is most often asymptomatic, although in the case of heavy infection, it can cause abdominal pain and diarrhea, and possibly sap nutrients from its host. Of three villages studied (Hurtado et al. 1997), it was found only in the Venezuelan village of Coyoweteri, with an overall prevalence of 5.3 percent.

Mansonella ozzardi   *Mansonella ozzardi*, a filarial nematode similar to *Onchocerca volvulus*, is transmitted by black flies and midges. Symptoms of this infection can include hepatomegaly and adenopathy. Torres et al. (1988) found a low prevalence, 1.8 percent in 110 individuals, of this parasite in the Venezuelan villages of Ocamo and Mavaca.

Trichuris trichiura   *Trichuris trichiura* is a frequently asymptomatic nemathelminth, although in some cases and especially in small children it may cause pain, diarrhea, or rectal prolapse. There seems to be considerable variation in the prevalence of this parasite. Holmes (1984) found only 9.5 percent in Parima B, but Orinoquito had a prevalence of 53.3 percent. Lawrence et al. (1980) found a prevalence ranging from 68 to 92 percent.

Microparasites

Entamoeba histolytica   This parasite, the only member of the genus *Entamoeba* that is pathogenic, is responsible for amebic dysentery and tropical liver abscess. It seems to be common among the Yanomamö, but not in all locations. Lawrence et al. (1980), for example, found rates as low as 28 percent in one village and as high as 77 percent in another. Confalonieri et al. (1991) found rates ranging from 28.5 to 40 percent.

Giardia lamblia   *Giardia lamblia* infection can cause severe symptoms, such as diarrhea, vomiting, and weight loss that generally lasts for one to three weeks but may last longer. In two Yanomamö villages it was present, respectively, in 4 percent and 5 percent of individuals, (Lawrence et al. 1980), but Holmes (1984) found a prevalence of 20 percent in both Parima B and Orinoquito.

Toxoplasma gondii   *Toxoplasma gondii* is a fairly common infection worldwide that most often is asymptomatic in adults, although it may produce blindness in severe cases. If contracted by a pregnant woman, it can cause congenital damage to the heart, brain, or lungs of the fetus. The only study (Sousa et al. 1997) that has tested for the presence of *Toxoplasma gondii* among the Yanomamö found it in 39 percent of 202 individuals examined.

Nonpathogenic Parasites

Several studies have also tested for the presence of parasites that are nonpathogenic, normal denizens of the human intestine. The effects of these infections on the general health of the host are minimal, except in those with the most severely compromised immune systems. However, while specific symptoms may not appear, chronic or severe infection may result in the draining of energy resources from the host. Of these, *Entamoeba hartmanni* had a prevalence of 0 percent in one Yanomamö village and of 19 percent in the other. *Chilomastix mesnili* was prevalent in about 10 percent of individuals in one village but was found in more than half of another (Lawrence et al. 1980). *Endolimax nana* infected a quarter to a third of the Yanomamö tested for it (Lawrence et al. 1980). *Balantidium coli* was not found among the Yanomamö (Lawrence et al. 1980); these authors found *Entamoeba coli* to be nearly ubiquitous in two Yanomamö villages, with 91 percent and 100 percent prevalence. Holmes (1984), however, found somewhat lower rates (70 to 84 percent) in several villages.

The Effects of Acculturation

It is clear that virtually all Yanomamö studied bear a heavy parasite burden. Figures 7.3 and 7.4 display the variety of diseases carried by indi-

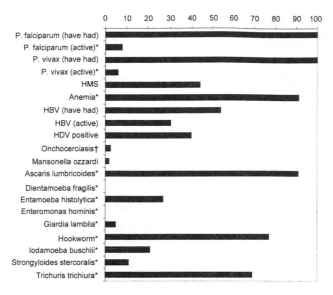

FIGURE 7.3   Disease profile in the Yanomamö villages of Mavaca and Ocamo (Sources of data: Grillet et al. 2001; Lawrence et al. 1980; Perez Mato 1988; Torres and Mandolfi 1991; Torres et al. 2000). Note: diseases without* or † indicate combined mean incidence for Mavaca and Ocamo.

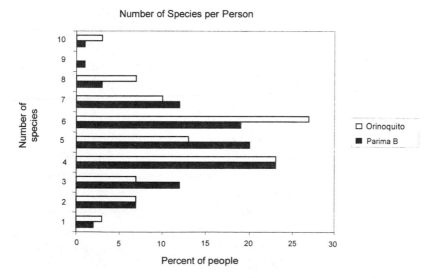

FIGURE 7.4   Number of species of parasites per person in the Yanomamö villages of Orinoquito and Parima B (Source of data: Holmes 1984).

viduals of this tribe. Figure 7.3, compiled from Grillet et al. 2001, Lawrence et al. 1980, Perez-Mato 1988, and Torres and Mondolfi 1991, Torres et al. 2000, shows the incidence of debilitating and life-threatening parasitic and viral diseases at the mission villages of Mavaca and Ocamo in Venezuela. As indicated, everyone sampled had contracted both types of malaria, even though only 5 to 10 percent had active cases. The consequences of malaria, such as anemia (90 percent) and hyperreactive malarial splenomegaly (42 percent, indicated as HMS in Figure 7.3), were common. In addition to malaria and associated conditions, about half of those sampled had hepatitis, and about 40 percent had HDV active cases. The load of intestinal parasites can also be quite high. Figure 7.4, derived from Holmes (1984), shows that members of the highland mission villages of Parima B and Orinoquito carry from one to ten intestinal parasites, with a median range of four to six.

Comparative health data on the Yanomamö at missions and in villages some distance from missions, as well as health data on acculturated native people who are neighbors to the Yanomamö in Venezuela, may allow us to detect changes in health profiles as the Yanomamö become more acculturated. Many of the parasites that afflict the Yanomamö require an incubation period in the soil and are spread through oral-fecal contact or through contact between bare skin and fecal material. As villages undergo acculturation and their inhabitants become more sedentary, it is possible that parasites build up in the soil and water sources, and rates of infection may increase. In addition, population density around missions tends to be much higher than in nonmission areas. For example, one of us (Hames) noted that the Yanomamö population around Mavaca in the mid-1970s was no more than 150 people. By 1986 there were more than 525 scattered in small settlements around the mission (see also Chagnon 1997: 228–229). At the same time, acculturation may lead to the development of sanitation facilities (e.g., latrines) and the availability of vermicides and other medications from missions or governmental health outposts that may moderate any increase in infection that occurs as a consequence of a more sedentary life. Yet it is undoubtedly the case that greater sedentariness and higher population density increase the potential for the spread of infectious and parasitic diseases. How missions or governmental health workers mitigate these effects is key to Yanomamö well-being.

Lawrence et al. (1980) were able to compare parasite infection in two Yanomamö villages with that in three non-Yanomamö (but native) acculturated villages in the same region of the Upper Orinoco Basin of Venezuela. The results are somewhat mixed (Lawrence et al. 1980: 534, their figure 2). For example, they found that hookworm infection (not identified by species) was very common in both Yanomamö villages, with infection rates of about 76 percent in one and about 80 percent in the other. At 93 percent, it was even more common in the acculturating villages, however, suggesting that Yanomamö groups may incur an increase in the already high rates of hookworm infection. These researchers also found *Trichuris trichiura* to be more common in acculturating villages than in Yanomamö villages, although, again, even in the Yanomamö villages, rates were fairly high, at 68 to 70 percent in one village and 90 to 92 percent in another. *Dientamoeba fragilis*, believed to cause vomiting and diarrhea, was found in acculturating villages but not at all among the Yanomamö. *Giardia lamblia* was also less common in Yanomamö villages, at 4 percent and 5 percent in two villages than in acculturating villages, in which about a quarter of the people were infected. However, another study found rates of around 20 percent in the Yanomamö villages of Parima B and Orinoquito (see Holmes 1984).

On the other hand, *Entamoeba histolytica*, responsible for amebic dysentery and tropical liver abscess, had a much higher prevalence among the Yanomamö, from 28 percent in one village to 78 percent in another, than it did in the acculturating villages, where prevalence ranged from 0 to 30 percent. Whereas *Ascaris lumbricoides* was common in both Yanomamö and acculturating villages, in the Yanomamö villages, with prevalence of 90 percent and 100 percent, infection rates did not diminish in adulthood. In the acculturating villages, infection rates of 100 percent were found in children but declined to less than 10 percent in adults. Little difference was found between rates of infection with *Strongyloides stercoralis* in the acculturating villages and the Yanomamö villages.

These results are difficult to interpret. No straightforward generalization can be made about whether the acculturation process leads to a heavier or lighter parasite burden. There was no apparent pattern dependent on the mechanism by which parasites are spread, such as those that build up in the soil versus those that are autoinfective.

It is also difficult to interpret differences in overall parasite load and age-related changes in parasite load. In the Yanomamö villages, a higher average number of species were found per adult person, ranging from 4.2 to 6.8, compared with 3.0 to 4.5 in the acculturated non-Yanomamö communities. This range is nearly identical to what Holmes (1984) found in highland Yanomamö populations (see figure 7.4). In one Yanomamö village, the average number of parasites decreased with age among adults, whereas in the other the average was fairly constant across age-groups.

In acculturating communities, the average number of species per person was lower, from 1.3 to 6.0, with no real trend across age-groups. Finally, in acculturating villages, fourteen different species of intestinal parasites were found, while only twelve species were found in Yanomamö villages.

Another study allows us to compare the Yanomamö to Venezuelan nationals who live in the same area. In this case, the Yanomamö are compared with poor Venezuelan nationals who are more or less fully integrated into the state economy and social system but who live in the same area. Holmes (1984: 389, her table II) was able to compare helminth (*Ascaris lumbricoides, Trichuris trichiura, Ancylostoma duodenale, Strongyloides stercoralis*) and protozoan (*Entamoeba coli* and *Giardia lamblia*) infection rates in two highland Parima Yanomamö groups with those among the Spanish-speaking residents of San Carlos de Rio Negro. San Carlos has been settled for decades; its residents have access to medical care and schools, and they purchase most of the food they consume. The comparison is useful because both groups occupy the same general area of the Upper Orinoco, although the Yanomamö are at a significantly higher altitude. Except for the fact that the Yanomamö have a larger fraction of the population infected by *Ancylostoma duodenale* and both kinds of *Entamoeba*, there are no striking differences. However, the number of parasites per person is much greater among the Yanomamö than it is for the residents of San Carlos. For example, in San Carlos only 5 percent of the population is infected by four or more parasites; in the Parima villages, more than 50 percent of the population is infected by four or more parasites (Holmes 1984: 389, her table I).

It may also be useful to compare Yanomamö villages at different stages in the acculturation process. One of us (Hames), based on research visits to nearly all the villages surveyed, has rated the villages studied by Lawrence et al. (1980), Holmes (1984), and others summarized in Hurtado et al. (1997) from most to least acculturated. This rating informs our discussion below.

The results of such a comparison are inconclusive (see figure 7.5, which compares the lightly contacted village with one of the most acculturated mission villages). The lightly contacted village, Patanowäteri (Lawrence et al. 1980), was an exercise in extremes. For almost every species tested, Patanowäteri had either the highest prevalence (*Ancylostoma* sp., *A. lumbricoides, T. trichiura, E. coli,* and *E. hystolitica*) or the lowest (*G. lamblia,* and nearly the lowest rate of *Strongyloides* sp.). In the case of *Ancylostoma* sp. and *E. coli,* the margin by which they exceeded their neighbors is insignificant: 1.5 percent and 4.5 percent, respectively.

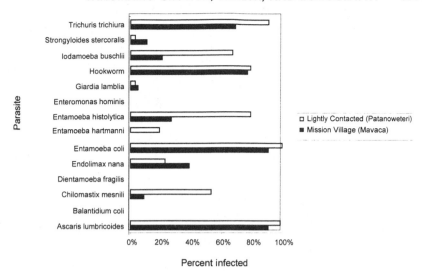

FIGURE 7.5   Parasite loads in two Yanomamö villages with different degrees of acculturation (Source of data: Lawrence et al. 1980).

The prevalence of *A. lumbricoides* was higher by 8 percent in the lighly contacted village. The prevalence of *T. trichiura*, however, was higher by 11 percent. The prevalence of *E. histolytica* was higher by a margin of 17.5 percent. Coyoweteri, an intermediate village, exhibited no such trend (Hurtado et al. 1997), nor did the acculturated mission villages of Parima B, Ocamo, and Mavaca.

The results of these comparisons are not revealing, but one may still draw certain conclusions. For example, in both comparisons, rates of *G. lamblia* were lower in the lighly contacted villages, suggesting that it (as well other infections contracted through the water supply) may be of greater concern for the Yanomamö in the future. For parasites that travel through the soil, results are not at all certain. This may be due to differences in sanitation in more missionized villages, or perhaps the buildup of parasites in the soil is mitigated by having greater and timelier access to vermicidal medications. The differences may also reflect dissimilarity in sampling techniques from one study to another. Perhaps a more controlled study of a similar nature could provide a more accurate comparison, and thus prescriptive value for treatment programs among the Yanomamö.

Our comparisons of lightly contacted and mission Yanomamö villages on one hand and heavily acculturated non-Yanomamö Amerindian and Venezuelan peasants living in the Upper Orinoco show few clear patterns.

Nevertheless, it seems that the variety of parasites and the mean number of parasites per person may be slightly greater in lighly contacted and mission Yanomamö villages than in Venezuelan peasant villages. Over the short term, it seems that increased settlement around missions will have little effect on Yanomamö health even though the potential for infection may be greater. We must stress that this will be true only if missionaries and governmental agencies continue to provide care and closely monitor epidemiological trends.

Yanomamö Demography

Mortality statistics provide critical information on the role that diseases play in a population. In tribal populations, as in most others, age-specific mortality rates commonly present themselves in a U-shaped or J-shaped distribution in relation to age: rates start high in the early years, decline steadily to the teen years, and then begin a slow but accelerating climb thereafter. Two excellent demographic studies (Melancon 1982; Early and Peters 2000) provide important information on mortality rates, life expectancy at various ages, and causes of death among the Yanomamö.

Understanding the causes of death will enable government health authorities, missionaries, and anthropologists to be in a better position to monitor health problems, design preventive programs, and treat the ill. Both of the demographic studies mentioned here tabulate causes of death, but some obvious problems are common to most ethnographic and retrospective investigations in establishing actual causes even within broad categories. The ethnographers had to rely on an informant's recollections of causes of death and then translate these causes to a Western typology. Infectious diseases such as malaria, influenza, and measles are probably reliably diagnosed by the Yanomamö, who are quite familiar with the symptoms. However, an illness that began as influenza could have led to pneumonia, which was the actual cause of death. More problematically, when the cause of death is unknown, this seriously distorts rates of reliably identified causes of death. In some studies (Melancon 1982: 42, his table 3.1), the percent of deaths due to unknown causes is 6 percent (figure 7.6), whereas in others, (Early and Peters 2000: 201), this percent can vary between 18 to 50 percent (figure 7.7) of all deaths, depending on the era studied. The difference largely reflects the recent four-year time span of Melancon's investigation compared with the sixty-six-year period covered by Early and Peters.

Aside from a large difference in unknown causes of death, comparing the two studies is problematic for two other reasons. Melancon does not

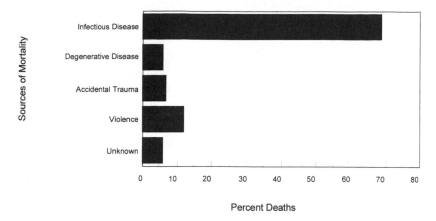

FIGURE 7.6   Causes of mortality among the Mavaca Yanomamö (Source of data: Melancon 1982).

list infanticide as a cause of death, not because it was absent in his area of study but because he decided not to classify such births as live births. This is not unreasonable, since the decision to commit infanticide is almost always made before an infant is born (unless the infant is born with a congenital anomaly), and therefore one can regard it as a kind of postpartum abortion. In contrast, Early and Peters count infanticide as a cause of death, and it constitutes from 5 to 20 percent of all deaths. Second,

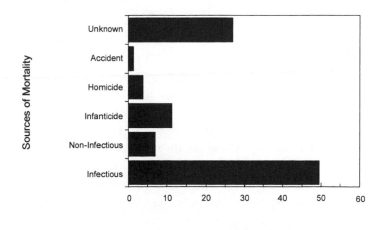

FIGURE 7.7   Causes of mortality among the Xiliana Yanomamö (Source of data: Early and Peters 2000).

although both studies use the category "infectious disease," Melancon has a category called "degenerative disease," and Early and Peters have a corresponding "non-infectious disease" category. Nevertheless, there is probably considerable overlap between these two categories. With these caveats in mind, we compare the two studies in the following.

Both studies indicate that infectious disease is the primary cause of death among the Yanomamö (although it is much higher for the Mavaca Yanomamö), and the rates of death from noninfectious and degenerative diseases are about the same. For the Mavaca Yanomamö, deaths from infectious diseases are 60 to 70 percent higher for children than for adults (Melancon 1982: 47, his table 3.2). The higher rate of infectious disease for the Mavaca Yanomamö (70 percent compared to 50 percent) to some extent is an artifact of Early and Peters classifying infanticide as a cause of death. If infanticide is removed as a cause of death, infectious disease as a cause of death for the Xiliana increases to 56 percent. And if the large number of unknown causes were known, death related to infectious diseases would be very similar for both populations.

Early and Peters's study spans a sixty-six-year period from 1930 to 1996, with their investigation divided into a time series based on degree and kind of contact with outsiders. Consequently, it, more than any other demographic study of which we are aware, allows us to understand how contact affects patterns of mortality and disease patterns in a previously uncontacted tribal population. They divide the demographic history of the Xiliana into precontact (1930–1957), contact (1958–1960), linkage (1961–1981), and Brazil (1982–1996) stages, which measure the degree to which interaction with Brazilians has increased through time. Causes of mortality through these periods are displayed in figure 7.8. Bearing in mind that "unknown" as a cause of death looms large in every period (especially precontact), the immediately recognizable trend is that death from infectious diseases increases dramatically from precontact to contact and changes little thereafter. During the contact period and thereafter, Early and Peters (2000) note, malaria and tuberculosis introduced by miners where the main causes for the increased force of infectious diseases as a source of Yanomamö mortality.

There seems to be little difference in survivorship between the two populations. Life expectancy at birth ranges between twenty-nine and forty-six years, depending on contact period, among the Xiliana (Early and Peters 2000: 199, their table 19.5) and is thirty-seven years for the Mavaca Yanomamö (Melancon 1982: 65, his table 3.6).[3] Significantly, the lowest life expectancy for the Xiliana is at first contact; life expectancy

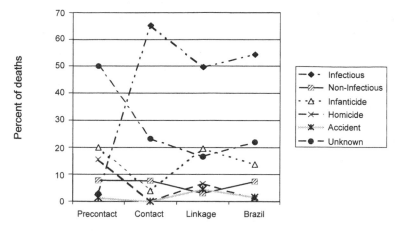

FIGURE 7.8   Variability in causes of mortality among the Xiliana Yanomamö
in four periods of their history (Source of data: Early and Peters 2000).

reaches the high point immediately after contact, during the linkage phase,
and declines to thirty-five years during the Brazil stage of sustained contact.

Crude birth and mortality rates and their relationship are fundamental measures of how well a population is adapted to the environment. If
a population increases through time, then by definition it is able to overcome various sources of environmental resistance (disease and resource
insufficiency) and has not reached carrying capacity (when fertility equals
mortality, and the population ceases to grow). Crude death rates for the
Xiliana Yanomamö (Early and Peters 2000: 194, their table 19.2a) range
from 17 to 56 per thousand, and for Melancon's study (1982: 89), 46 per
thousand, which places them in the moderate to high range (Early and
Peters 2000: 96) by world standards. Crude birth rates range from 28 to
52 per thousand for the Xiliana (Early and Peters 2000: 194, their table
19.2a) and 59 per thousand for the Mavaca (Melancon 1982: 89). The
natural rate of increase is estimated to be 1.25 percent for the Mavaca
Yanomamö and 1.12 percent for the Xiliana (derived from Early and
Peters 2000: their table 19.2c for all periods). These figures accord well
with early estimates by Neel and Weiss (1975: 38). It is important to realize that these demonstrations of Yanomamö population increase are probably not characteristic of growth patterns elsewhere among the Yanomamö
tribal distribution, as explained in the following discussion.

Where the Yanomamö come into chronic contact with outsiders and
where medical intervention is absent or ineffective, there is evidence of
population decline. In Brazil, military takeover of the Surucucu area

through the Calha Norte initiative and the construction of the BR 210 road provide dramatic examples of this process. In 1987, the Brazilian military took control of the Surucucu and Paapiú regions as part of the infamous Calha Norte project. They then permitted tens of thousands of gold miners to enter the area and expelled missionaries, health officials, and researchers. In 1989 it was estimated that "23 percent of the Yanomami had been killed by malaria or by *garimpeiro* bullets," (Ramos 1995: 277). Ramos also presents data on infectious disease in the area that show astounding increases (400 percent and more) in malaria, malaria-related illnesses (e.g., anemia), respiratory infections, tuberculosis, and malnutrition (Ramos 1995: 278, her figure 11.1). There is no indication of how many individuals or villages these figure applies to.

Earlier, in 1974, the construction of BR 210, a spur of the Transamazon Highway, in Brazil had a devastating impact on the Yanomamö living nearby. Ramos and Taylor (1979) report that medical treatments by local Catholic missionaries (Consolata Order) for viral diseases and their complications, diarrhea, skin diseases, and malaria, increased from 2,485 three years prior to the beginning of road construction to 12,529 three years after the road was completed. It is difficult to know whether this is a consequence of greater access to medical care, a real increase in disease, or a combination of both. A detailed investigation on the mortal consequences of road construction on three villages located within a few days' walk from BR 210 is particularly disturbing. Many Yanomamö died as a result of a measles epidemic that occurred from February to March 1977: in Iropitheri, 35 of the 69 inhabitants died (51 percent); in Uxiutheri, 15 of the 32 inhabitants died (46 percent); in Maxikopiutheri, 10 of the 33 inhabitants died (30 percent) (Saffirio and Hames, 1983: 12).

Colchester (1985: 29) claims that in Venezuela and Brazil, although some Yanomamö populations are holding steady or increasing, other groups are losing population. Citing Migliazza (1982), Colchester (1985: 64–65) suggests that the Ninam (a small ethnolinguistic division of the Yanomamö) in Venezuela and Brazil lost about 25 percent of their population (from a base of 125) as a consequence of introduced diseases from 1963 to 1978. In 1981 this same group was struck by a measles epidemic (Colchester 1985: 65) that caused the death of forty-one persons.

Finally Chagnon (1997) describes mortality rates (actually, percent of people who died from 1987 to 1991) in three types of villages and concludes that health practices of the Mavaca Salesian mission and Yanomamö visiting patterns to missions are responsible for a dramatic spike in mortality rates in villages that have intermediate contact.

Chagnon classified seventeen villages as belonging to one of three categories: mission villages that had "maximum" contact with missionaries, "intermediate" villages that had irregular contact with missions, and "minimum" or distant villages that had little or no contact with missions. Over that period, Chagnon shows, mission villages and distant villages suffered death rates of 5 percent and 6.5 percent, respectively but the intermediate villages suffered a rate of 20 percent. In addition, he compares age distribution data in distant and intermediate villages and finds a severe constriction in the one- to ten-year age cohort among the intermediate villages. This elevated rate for intermediate villages is attributed to an active campaign by Salesian missionaries to draw Yanomamö villages nearer to the mission and to inadequate health monitoring and treatment by missionaries in the context of an unnamed epidemic (or epidemics, Chagnon 1997: 249) that swept through the area. Although this demonstration is superficially persuasive, it presents several problems. There are no statistical tests of significance to demonstrate that the death rate differences are other than random. As mentioned, the epidemic is not named or even characterized, its source is unknown, and what fraction such deaths contributed to the differences between death rates is not mentioned. Finally, the locations of the villages are not specified, nor is the factor of degree of contact clearly operationalized.

Independently of these problems, the study demonstrates, at least in microcosm, the devastating effects of epidemics caused by direct or indirect contact by outsiders and is consistent with findings elsewhere on the Yanomamö, such as Neel et al.'s (1970) account of the 1968 measles epidemic. It also demonstrates the inherent dangers of attracting native peoples to the outposts of civilization even if it is believed to be in their best interests (Cowell 1973).

Conclusion

The Yanomamö suffer from extraordinary high disease loads as demonstrated by high mortality rates and short stature. This leads us to suspect that there is a synergetic relationship between high parasite loads (e.g., malaria) and chronic infections (e.g., hepatitis) that slows growth and ultimately reduces stature in adults. Short adults produce short children who are unable to mount adequate immune responses without compromising growth. It is also possible that chronic illness reduces adult economic productivity, leading to lowered nutritional intake, which increases mortality and slows growth.

There seems to be sufficient variation among Yanomamö in regard to stature and weight differences to allow researchers to attempt to untangle the relationship between disease, diet, and growth. For example, some lowland groups are approximately eight centimeters taller (see table 7.1, Kedi-Washawä Yanomamö villages) than highland groups. If we were to compare the tallest Yanomamö lowland groups with other Amazonian ethnic groups in table 7.1, we find that they are of average height for Amazonian peoples. Our review of the literature on parasite load and disease incidence in highland and lowland groups does not indicate any clear differences. Even if such differences were detected, they might not be revealing without additional data on intensity of infection, age and sex distributions, and season in which the measures were made. We would also need to know the degree to which a disease is likely to reduce growth and how diseases interact in this process.

Dietary differences between highland and lowland groups may also be implicated, as indicated by anthropometric and economic research. As discussed earlier, research by Hagen et al. (2001) showed that skinfolds of children in a lowland group at the village of Cejal were similar to those found by Holmes (1985) in her highland research, but they presented lower skinfold measurements than those taken in other lowland villages studied in 1987. The lowland village of Cejal had just suffered food shortages as a consequence of an El Niño–related weather condition. Other lowland villages where skinfold measurements were made in 1987 operated under normal economic and dietary conditions (Hagen et al. 2001), but their skinfold measurements were significantly greater than those of food-stressed Cejal or the highland measurements made by Holmes (1985). A reasonable interpretation of these findings suggests that highland groups are food stressed. Comparative ecological and economic research on highland and lowland groups elaborates on this possible dietary connection. Hames (1993) summarizes important contrasts between highland and lowland groups. Highland groups rely much more heavily on cultivated crops, whereas lowland groups rely more heavily on food resources foraged through hunting, gathering, and fishing. In fact, lowland groups expend twice as much labor time in foraging activities as they do in horticulture. Plantains and manioc, staples of the Yanomamö diet, are notoriously deficient in protein and micronutrients (Gross 1974), even though they provide adequate calories. It may be the case that lowland groups have a superior diet, especially protein and fatty acid intake, which may account for their greater stature. There are at least two ways in which dietary factors may affect growth: on one hand, it may simply be that a better diet leads directly to enhanced growth; more complexly, it may be that a better diet may counteract the stunting effects of chronic illness.

Regardless of the possible role of dietary differences in Yanomamö growth, we believe we have amply documented that disease is a major problem that affects all Yanomamö. Many of the most mortal and debilitating illnesses are spread as a consequence of contact with non-Yanomamö people. Some diseases such as measles and influenza periodically sweep through the Yanomamö and then disappear. Clearly, regulation of outside contact and health monitoring can deter these diseases. But extremely serious diseases such as hepatitis, tuberculosis, and malaria are now embedded in the Yanomamö. Their persistence as a chronic feature of Yanomamö life no longer depends on reintroduction from outside sources.

It is clear that the governments of Brazil and Venezuela, along with nongovernmental organizations, face a daunting task. Many of the parasitic illness can be treated simply with ivermectin, but without environmental sanitation practices, reinfection is guaranteed. Although there is a vaccine against hepatitis B virus infection, there is no cure for those already infected, and treatment to reduce its effects is expensive. At the same time, embedded cultural practices such a long-term breast-feeding, premastication of food, and the sharing of body piercing objects enhance its spread. The widely used BCG vaccine for tuberculosis, for unknown reasons, appears to have limited efficacy for the Yanomamö. For these reasons and many others, any attempt to develop appropriate campaigns to reduce disease among the Yanomamö must be accompanied by scientific biomedical and anthropological research to provide health care workers with accurate knowledge to apply the most effective treatments and interventions possible.

NOTES

1. In this comparison we ignore Spielman, da Rocha, and Weitkamp's (1972) eighteen-village study because it contains a mixture of highland and lowland groups. Nevertheless, this study's mean stature measures are greater than those of any of the highland groups.

2. Hetrazan is a medication that kills the microfilariae infecting the host. As it does so, however, the allergic response elicited by the dead parasites can be extreme; many persons receiving treatment may experience extreme itching and discomfort. In a few cases, anaphylaxis can result.

3. Melancon (1982), using a stable population model, arrives at a life expectancy at birth of 20.5 years for males and 22.9 years for females. We

use his empirical life expectancy at birth to make it consistent with that of Early and Peters (2000), who do not use stable population models.

REFERENCES

Black, F. L., W. H. Hierholzer, J. F. Lian-Chen, L. L. Berman, Y. Gabbai, and F. P. Pinheiro. 1982. Genetic correlates of enhanced measles susceptibility in Amazon Indians. *Medical Anthropology* 6: 37–46.

Bogin, B. 1999. *Patterns of Human Growth*. Cambridge University Press, Cambridge.

Centers for Disease Control. 2002. Division of Viral Hepatitis. Viral Hepatitis Fact Sheet. Available at http://www.cdc.gov/ncidod/diseases/hepatitis/b/fact.htm)

Chagnon, N. 1997. *Yanomamö*. 5th ed. Harcourt Brace Jovanovich, New York.

Chagnon, N., and R. Hames. 1979. Protein deficiency and tribal warfare in Amazonia: New data. *Science* 203: 910–913.

Coco, L. 1973. *Iyawei-teri: Quince anos entre los Yanomamos*. Editorial Salesiana, Caracas.

Colchester, M. 1985. The health and survival of the Venezuelan Yanomama. *International Workgroup for Indigenous Affairs* 53: 1–105.

Confalonieri, U. 1991. Intestinal helminths in lowland South American Indians: Some evolutionary interpretations. *Human Biology* 63: 863–873.

Confalonieri, U. E., A. J. Araujo, and L. F. Ferreira. 1989. Intestinal parasites among Yanomami Indians. *Memorias do Instituto Oswaldo Cruz* 84 (suppl. 4): 111–114.

Cowell, A. 1973. *The Tribe That Hides from Man*. Stein and Day, New York.

Crews, D. E., and J. Mancilha-Carvalho. 1991. Correlates of blood pressure in Yanomami Indians of northwestern Brazil. *Ethnicity and Disease* 3: 362–371.

Dufour, D. 1994. Diet and nutritional status of Amazonian peoples. In *Amazonian Indians*, edited by A. Roosevelt, pp. 151–176. University of Arizona Press, Tucson.

Early, J., and J. Peters. 2000. *The Xiliana Yanomami of the Amazon*. University Press of Florida, Gainesville.

Garn, S. 1980. Human growth. *Annual Review of Anthropology* 9: 275–292.

Grillet, M. E., M. G. Basanez, M. S. Vivas, N. Villamizar, H. Frontado, J. Cortez, P. Coronel, and C. Botto. 2001. Human onchocerciasis in the Amazonian area of southern Venezuela: Spatial and temporal variations in biting and parity rates of black fly (Diptera: Simuliidae) vectors. *Journal of Medical Entomology* 38: 520–530.

Gross, D. 1974. Protein capture and cultural development in the Amazon. *American Anthropologist* 77: 526–549.

Hagen, E., R. Hames, N. Craig, M. Lauer, and M. Price. 2001. Parental investment and child health in a Yanomamö village suffering short-term food stress. *Journal of Biosocial Science* 99: 1–33.

Hames, R. 1989. Time, efficiency, and fitness in the Amazonian protein quest. *Research in Economic Anthropology* 11: 43–85.

———. 1993. Foraging horticulturalists in Amazonia: Why do horticulturalists forage? Paper presented at the Fourth World Academic Conference on Human Ecology, Centro de Investigación y Estudios Avanzados, Merida, Mexico.

Harris, M. 1977. *Cannibals and Kings*. Vintage Books, New York.

Hodge, L., and D. Dufour. 1991. Cross-sectional growth of young Shipibo Indian children in eastern Peru. *American Journal of Physical Anthropology* 84: 35–41.

Holmes, R. 1984. Non-dietary modifiers of nutritional status in tropical forest populations of Venezuela. *Interciencia* 9: 386–391.

———. 1985. Nutritional status and cultural change in Venezuela's Amazon territory. In *Change in the Amazon Basin*. Vol. 2, *The Frontier after a Decade of Colonisation*, edited by J. Hemming, pp. 237–255. Manchester University Press, Manchester.

———. 1995. Small is adaptive: Nutritional anthropometry of native Amazonians. In *Indigenous Peoples and the Future of Amazonia*, edited by L. Sponsel, pp. 121–148. University of Arizona Press, Tucson.

Hurtado, A. M., I. Hurtado, K. Hill, and S. Rodriguez. 1997. The evolutionary context of chronic allergic conditions. *Human Nature* 8: 51–75.

Huss-Ashmore, R., and F. Johnston. 1985. Bioanthropological research in developing countries. *Annual Review of Anthropology* 14: 475–528.

Jenkins, C. 1981. Patterns of growth and malnutrition among preschoolers in Belize. *American Journal of Physical Anthropology* 56: 159–171.

Kent, S., and E. Weinberg. 1989. Hypoferremia: Adaptation to disease? *New England Journal of Medicine* 320: 670.

Laserson, K. F., I. Petralanda, R. Almera, R. H. Barker, Jr., A. Spielman, J. H. Maguire, and D. F. Wirth. 1999. Genetic characterization of an epidemic of *Plasmodium falciparum* malaria among Yanomami Amerindians. *Journal of Infectious Diseases* 180: 2081–2085.

Lawrence, D. N, J. V. Neel, S. H. Abadi, L. L. Moore, G. Adams, G. Healy, and I. Kagan. 1980. Epidemiologic studies among Amerindian populations of Amazonia. III. Intestinal parasitoses in newly contacted and acculturating villages. *American Journal of Tropical Medicine and Hygiene* 29: 530–537.

Lizot, J. 1977. Population, resources, et guerre chez les Yanomami. *Libre* 2:111–145.

Low, B. 1990. Marriage systems and pathogen stress in human societies. *American Zoology* 30: 325–339.

Mackintosh, J. 2001. The antimicrobial properties of melanocytes, melanosomes, and melanin and the evolution of black skin. *Journal of Theoretical Biology* 211: 101–113.

Martorell, R. 1989. Body size, adaptation, and function. *Human Organization* 48: 15–20.

Melancon, T. 1982. Marriage and reproduction among the Yanomamö of Venezuela. Ph.D. diss., Pennsylvania State University.

Migliazza, E. 1982. Linguistic prehistory and the linguistic model in Amazonia. In *Biological Diversification in the Tropics*, edited by G. Prance, pp. 479–519. Columbia University Press, New York.

Neel, J. V. 1979. Health in Amerindians. In *Health and Disease in Tribal Societies*, Ciba Foundation Symposium 49 (new series), pp. 155–178. Elsevier, Amsterdam.

Neel, J. V., W. Centerwall, N. Chagnon, and H. Casey. 1970. Notes on the effect of measles and measles vaccine in a virgin soil population of South American Indians. *American Journal of Epidemiology* 91: 418–429.

Neel, J. V., M. Layrisse, and F. M. Salzano. 1977. Man in the tropics: The Yanomama Indians. In *Population Structure and Human Variation*, edited by G. A. Harrison, pp. 109–142. Cambridge University Press, Cambridge.

Neel, J. V., and K. M. Weiss. 1975. The genetic structure of a tribal population: The Yanomamö Indians. XII. Biodemographic studies. *American Journal of Physical Anthropology* 42: 25–51.

Perez Mato, S. 1998. Anemia and malaria in a Yanomami Amerindian population from the southern Venezuelan Amazon. *American Journal of Tropical Medicine and Hygiene* 59: 998–1001.

Peters, J. F. 1980. The Shirishana of the Yanomami: A demographic study. *Social Biology* 27: 272–285.

Ramos, A. R. 1995. *Sanuma Memories*. University of Wisconsin Press, Madison.

Ramos, A. R., and K. Taylor. 1979. The Yanomama in Brazil 1979. *International Workgroup for Indigenous Affairs* 37: 1–157.

Rassi, E. B., N. Lacerda, and J. A. Guimarães. 1976. Study of the area affected by onchocerciasis in Brazil: Survey of local residents. *Bulletin of the Pan American Health Organization* 10: 33–45.

Saffirio, G., and R. Hames. 1983. *The Forest and the Highway*. Working Papers on South American Indians no. 6 and Cultural Survival Occasional Paper no. 11 (joint publication), edited by K. Kensinger and J. Clay. Cultural Survival, Cambridge.

Salzano, F. M., and S. M. Callegari-Jacques. 1988. *South American Indians: A Case Study in Evolution*. Clarendon Press, Oxford.

Santos, R. V., and C. E. A. Coimbra Jr. 1996. Socioeconomic differentiation and body morphology in the Surui of southwestern Amazonia. *Current Anthropology* 37: 851–856.

Seckler, D. 1982. "Malnutrition": An intellectual odyssey. *Western Journal of Agricultural Economy* 5: 219–227.

Sousa, A. O., J. I. Salem, F. K. Lee, M. C. Vercosa, P. Cruaud, B. R. Bloom, P. H. Lagrange, and H. L. David. 1997. An epidemic of tuberculosis with a high rate of tuberculin anergy among a population previously unexposed to tuberculosis, the Yanomami Indians of the Brazilian Amazon. *Proceedings of the National Academy of Sciences, USA* 94: 13227–13232.

Spielman, R. S., F. J. da Rocha, and L. R. Weitkamp. 1972. The genetic structure of a tribal population, the Yanomama Indians. VII. Anthropometric differences among Yanomama villages. *American Journal of Physical Anthropology* 37: 345–356.

Stini, W. A. 1971. Evolutionary implications of changing nutritional patterns in human populations. *American Anthropologist* 73: 1019–1030.

Tierney, P. 2000. *Darkness in El Dorado: How Scientists and Journalists Devastated the Amazon*. Norton, New York.

Torres, J. R., M. Magris, L. Villegas, M. Torres, B. Gomez, L. Suarez, H. Rivera, R. Ramirez, and C. Vivas. 1997. Epidemiologia de al infección malárica en poblacions Yanomami de la Cuenca del Alto Orinoco. In *Del Microscopio a La Maraca*, edited by J. Chiappino and C. Ales, pp. 387–396. Editorial Ex Libris, Caracas.

Torres, J. R., M. Magris, L. Villegas, V. M. A. Torres, and G. Dominguez. 2000. Spur cell anemia and acute haemolysis in patients with hyperreactive malarious splenomegaly: Experience in an isolated Yanomamö population of Venezuela. *Acta Tropica* 77: 257–262.

Torres, J. R., and A. Mondolfi. 1991. Protracted outbreak of severe delta hepatitis experience in an isolated Amerindian population of the Upper Orinoco Basin, Venezuela. *Reviews of Infectious Diseases* 13: 52–55.

Torres, J. R., G. O. Noya, G. A. Mondolfi, C. Peceno, and A. C. Botto. 1988. Hyperreactive malarial splenomegaly in Venezuela. *American Journal of Tropical Medicine and Hygiene* 39: 11–14.

8

DISEASE SUSCEPTIBILITY AMONG NEW WORLD PEOPLES

Francis L. Black

New World peoples, those who were isolated from most other humans prior to the age of European exploration, had to a large extent developed a modus vivendi with parasitic microbes. A few microbes, such as the agent of tuberculosis, may have continued to cause problems (Rothschild and Hobling 2002), and some viruses that primarily infect animals, such as yellow fever (Causey et al. 1961), retained virulence for these people. However, the vast majority of infectious agents that New World people encountered in their new homes were relatively innocuous. There would have been a selection process by which agents that were preadapted and tended to cause persistent infection without debilitation would have been those carried into the new land. There may have been some selection of the host for tolerance and virus innocuity after arrival, but we are not sure how much of this reflected strains from which the agent came and how much occurred later. Strains of agents encountered in New World tend to be distinctive, such as JC, a small papillomavirus (Fernandez-Cabo et al. 2002); human T-cell lymphotropic virus type II (HTLV-II), a relative of the much-feared virus of AIDS (Biggar et al. 1998); several viruses from the herpes group (Black et al. 1974; de Freitas et al. 1994; Biggar et al. 2000); and DNA viruses. All these typically cause infection in infancy and persist throughout life.

Of particular concern here are infectious agents introduced to these people by outsiders, especially the virus measles. Like any New World people experiencing a new infection, the Yanomamö must have been unusually susceptible to the virus of measles in 1967. There is no good estimate of the toll measles took on them, but it is unusually virulent in New World peoples in general. Before vaccine became available, measles killed 27 percent of the population of Fiji in a virgin-soil epidemic (Cliff and Haggett 1985). In contrast, among a population long exposed to measles, the people of the United States before the vaccine, death ensued in only 0.1 percent of 4 million cases occurring each year (Black 1997). Many other virgin-soil epidemics attest to an unusual susceptibility in populations experiencing a new infection (Black 1994). Measles virus evolved after the Americas had been settled and cut off by flooding Beringia (Black 1997), so it was doubtless novel to the Yanomamö. Because of Yanomamö's special susceptibility, J. V. Neel and N. Chagnon were right in trying to protect them from this disease.

Tierney (2000) implies that Neel made a mistake in choosing the Edmonston B vaccine over further attenuated vaccine. Both were available at the time of Neel's study, but Edmonston B has since been completely displaced by several further attenuated strains. However, at the time of Neel's vaccinations, further attenuated vaccine had only been used in adults in studies in Iceland (Gudnadottir and Black 1966) and in the Tiriyo, a tribe 1,000 kilometers from the Yanomamö (Black et al. 1969). Reports of these studies may not have been available to Neel when he laid his plans. More to the point, when Neel planned his trip, little experience was available on the durability of immunity offered by the further attenuated vaccines, but we had eight years of experience with Edmonston B. Further attenuated vaccines were deliberately selected to have a level of attenuation equivalent to Edmonston B plus gamma globulin (Schwartz et al. 1960). Tierney (2000) suggests that Neel did not always use gamma globulin with his vaccine; in fact, while he gave excess vaccine without gamma globulin to Brazilians for use in Yanomamö on their side of the border, and to missionaries in Guyana for use in the Wai Wai, it seems that all vaccinations he himself carried out were accompanied by gamma globulin and hence were equivalent, in reaction induced, to further attenuated vaccine.

The level of success achieved by Neel's team cannot be known because there had been no census of the tribe, and because the vaccinators were under such pressure to move along that they did not collect adequate follow-up data. Clearly, Tierney's (2000) estimates of vaccine-caused deaths are wrong. He ignored the incubation period and included deaths that occurred when the vaccine would have had no effect. Measles vaccine causes its reaction between seven and fourteen days after injection; any illness outside that period must have been caused by something else. Also, Tierney uses the wrong reasons for his assumption of Yanomamö susceptibility. In part he attributes it to the older age of susceptible persons, but mostly to a poor immunological response. Reactions to the vaccine at different ages do not vary dramatically. Reactions of diverse age-groups to wild virus are dealt with later in this chapter. After considering the effect of age on severity of reaction to wild measles virus, I will define the factors associated with excess risk of new diseases in virgin-soil populations and fit these reasons to an alternative explanation.

The Effect of Age on Susceptibility to Wild Virus

It is true that there is a difference in the ages attacked in virgin and endemic situations. All ages are susceptible in a virgin population, whereas in a cosmopolitan population, measles and other "children's diseases" are essentially confined to children aged one to fifteen. Mortality, relative to age, must be considered individually for each disease. For some, such as diphtheria (Nelson 1996) and croup (Glezen and Denny 1997), mortality is highest in young children; for others, such as paralytic poliomyelitis (Peart and Nagler 1954) and influenza (Osborn 1977), it is higher in adults. For measles, age-specific mortality has been determined in several epidemics (figure 8.1). High mortality rates occur in persons under one year of age, and from ten years onward, the rates trend higher. In a cosmopolitan population most babies under one year are protected by maternal antibody. As a proportion of all Yanomamö, these would be few. Tribal populations are also heavily weighted toward children, with few people living more than fifty years. Thus, the effect of age on excess mortality in New World people from wild measles virus is less than might be expected.

Measles encephalitis does become more frequent with age (Greenberg et al. 1955), and extrapolation of its frequency into adulthood might seem to infer an enhanced susceptibility of adults to measles. In fact, measles encephalitis is rare and the number of its cases small compared with direct effects of the virus. Vitamin A deficiency is a major factor in the mortality rates observed in many less developed populations, with its effects seen mostly in newly weaned children (Barclay et al. 1997). It is prevalent in parts of Africa and the Indian subcontinent, but there is nothing to suggest that this nutritional deficiency was common among the Yanomamö. Measles mortality rates are higher in virgin-soil popula-

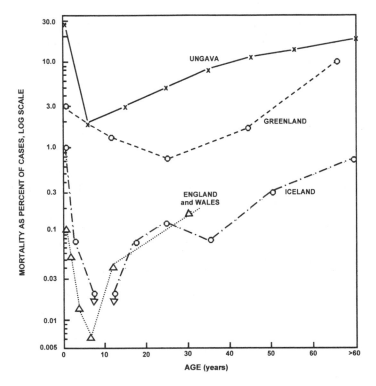

FIGURE 8.1   Age-specific mortality rates from measles in virgin-soil areas (Ungava and Greenland) and endemic countries (England and Wales, Iceland). Adapted from Black (1997).

tions than in groups among which measles has occurred before, but it is higher at all ages (see figure 8.1).

Determinants of Excessive Susceptibility to Infection

The Khoi-San of southern Africa, the Melanesians and Polynesians of the Pacific, the Aboriginals of Australia, the Amerinds of North and South America, and many other less well known indigenous groups have all suffered major population declines when they first had contact with people of the Old World. These declines have been variously ascribed to warfare, enslavement, expropriation of food sources, and the ravages of infectious diseases. Warfare was commonly associated with enslavement, and even where neither enslavement nor food expropriation was a major factor, as in the Pacific, dramatic death rates occurred. Enslavement did not prevent sub-Saharan African people from remaining one of the world's main ethnic groups. Warfare, enslavement, and food depletion were not insignificant elements in the decline of New World people, but introduced infections were the chief reason these groups failed to thrive when brought into contact with people from the Old World.

Specific figures on the extent of this historic decline are not available. There can be no good estimate of the size of precontact populations because diagnoses were often vague, and because the ultimate survivors are genetically mixed with the contacting people. Thus, the Khoi-San originally occupied most of Cape Province and much of Namibia and Botswana, but after a series of epidemics most of their descendants are classified as "colored" and of mixed ancestry. Stannard (1989) intensively analyzed data for the population of the Hawaiian Islands before contact to come up with a number between 850,000 and 1 million, although many doubt his high figure. Now only a few thousand Hawaiians claim pure Polynesian ancestry. Connecticut was well populated by Amerinds before contact, but the indigenous people were affected by several devastating epidemics, as well as warfare, and now those who still claim native parentage are clearly of mixed ancestry. Any explanation of the susceptibility of virgin-soil populations to introduced disease must be applicable to a wide variety of New World populations.

An explanation for excess mortality should also be applicable to a wide variety of infections. Smallpox was the most readily identifiable infection and certainly one of the most devastating. Disruption caused by smallpox prevented the Aztecs from finishing off Cortés when he was driven from Tenochtitlán, and the fact that it had preceded Pizarro into the Peruvian highlands and killed the reigning Inca and his heir permitted the Spaniards to conquer that realm (McNeill 1976). Fenn (1999) has analyzed a long series of smallpox outbreaks that extended from Mexico into the Canadian north during the late 1700s. Mortality reached 90 percent in those epidemics. In later years, smallpox was controlled in developed countries by vaccination, and isolated populations were protected indirectly. Measles and smallpox were only the most easily identified of myriad diseases that were introduced with Old World contact; New World people were often killed by infections we usually consider minor. The number of Southern Kayapo declined steadily from about 7000 at the time of first contact in 1903 to only 2 or 3 in the 1950s as a result of mostly unidentified diseases (Ribeiro 1956). The Xikrin declined from 164 to 80 in just two years because of *resfriados*, or common colds (Frikel 1963). Of course, what appeared to be common cold to an outside observer may actually have been influenza or another virus with greater potential, but it was neither smallpox nor measles, as evidenced by lack of antibody to these viruses in survivors.

Cholera, malaria, and tuberculosis were also important, but all of these cause high mortality rates in Old World people, and rates in both New World and Old World populations are dependent on environmental conditions and disease-specific responses. Furthermore, tuberculosis and malaria were not entirely novel. Related, but in the case of malaria, probably (Dunn 1965), and tuberculosis, possibly (Salo et al. 1994), less lethal strains of pathogens preceded the introduced strains to the Americas. If, indeed, these diseases were preexistent in the Americas, the high mortality they, particularly tuberculosis (Nutels 1965; Sousa et al. 1997; Hurtado et al. 2002), exacted from Amerind people must at least have been associated with a novel strain. Any theory as to why New World people are unusually susceptible to measles virus cannot be specific to this agent but must apply to a broad spectrum of pathogens.

One would dearly like to know whether disease agents passing in the reverse direction, from the New World to the Old World, posed similar threats. They would have the same novelty to Old World people as did Old World diseases to people in the New World. This possibility is always of concern to persons entering a newly contacted group for the first time. As noted at the outset of this chapter, many infections that are indigenous to New World people are not novel to us. Papovavirus (Brown et al. 1975), HTLV (Black et al. 1996), several hepatitis viruses (Black and Jacobson 1986; Black et al. 1986; Hadler et al. 1989), and several herpes group viruses (de Freitas et al. 1994; Biggar et al. 2000; Robinson et al. 2002) are familiar, although possibly of a distinctive strain. Others, the agent of Chagas' disease, *Trypanosoma cruzi*, the complex that causes cutaneous leishmeniasis, the togavirus Mayaro, the flavivirus Ilheus, the arenaviruses Junin and Machupo, and the bunyavirus Oropouche have not caused epidemics except where environmental conditions like those of South America occur. No one cares to test these agents elsewhere, but it seems they depend on locally occurring insects. Personal experience suggests that Caucasians entering the Amazon forest are more likely to be troubled by leishmania than are Amerinds, who seldom bear its scar. However, the age at initial infection may be important, and no data on this exist.

The best bet for an agent that may have gone from the Amerinds to the Old World is that of syphilis, *Treponema pallidum* (Zimmer 2001). Amerind populations are frequently infected with an organism that cross-reacts with *T. pallidum* in both VDRL and fluorescent antibody tests (Lee et al. 1978). This treponeme is well tolerated by the Indians, who seldom

experience the direct effects of syphilis when carrying it or exhibit congenital disease in serologically positive children. The syphilis that appeared
in Europe shortly after Colombus's return from the New World was unusually virulent (McNeill 1976). This virulence fits the pattern of transfer
from an experienced to an inexperienced population, but the organism
must have become partially attenuated to form the modern strain. If it
could go from high to moderate virulence in the European, the transition from the nonpathogenic Amerindian strain to the pathogenic European one could have been caused by mutation of the parasite, not
susceptibility of the host. Alternatively, syphilis may derive from another
treponeme: pinta, yaws, or bejel. Sequence data are inadequate to link it
to one or another. Thus, there is no good example of a disease that is well
managed by isolated people but that affects the major ethnic groups severely. It would be advantageous if any theory on why New World populations are susceptible to introduced disease agents permitted this effect
to work in one direction only.

One also wishes for better data on the effect of repeated epidemics of
the same disease. Cliff and Haggett (1985) give mortality figures for a series of epidemics in Fiji between the initial one in 1875 and 1978 that
show progressively decreasing death rates. It is not clear, however, what
proportion of the population exposed to each outbreak was already immune, nor what proportion derived from immigrants from India. Newson
(1991) cites numerous epidemics with high mortality in Andean countries, but it is not clear which epidemics were caused by the same agent,
and the highest mortality seems often to have occurred when two diseases followed closely on one another. In essence, New World populations
become less susceptible to Old World diseases as time passes, but one
cannot say what part of this is due to immunity in the most susceptible
age-groups, what to improved nursing care, what to introduction of resistance genes from outside, and what to mutation or selection of the
population. Only if these factors could be sorted out would it be possible
to determine whether mutation of some hypermutable locus is a major
determinant. The effect occurs too rapidly to be explicable by conventional mutation of typical nuclear genes.

Evidence of a reduction over time of mortality caused by introduced
diseases in New World populations comes from the Amerinds of the Eastern Cordillera. Throughout the Western Hemisphere, from Mexico to
Bolivia, are areas where indigenous people had attained urban assemblages
with substantial population mixing before the advent of Old World contact. After being hit hard by the initial epidemics (Newson 1991), these

populations have revived. One cannot now say what proportion of this population is mestizo and what of unmixed Amerind ancestry, but substantial numbers of genetically indigenous people seem to persist. Any theory that explains New World people were so susceptible to introduced diseases would fit more easily if it allowed for an increased survival potential of unusually large indigenous populations.

Theories of Immune Responsiveness

Tierney (2000) seems to believe that the immune system only recognizes and protects against antigens for which positive selection has occurred in the past, an idea that contradicts the basic theory for generation of antibody diversity. The generally accepted theory holds that the array of antigens against which both B and T cells react is derived from random rearrangements of a hypermutable portion of the genome of lymphocyte precursors. A second step specifically eliminates those cells whose immune products react to circulating host components. This process leaves cells reactive with essentially every imaginable amino acid sequence, carbohydrate, and many other chemicals, except those self-antigens that are exposed to the immune system (Janeway and Travers 2001). To generate protection when a new antigen is encountered, a mammal has only to stimulate lymphocytes capable of the appropriate immune response and wait about a week for them to multiply to a level that produces a significant manifestation of that response. There is no need to acquire, by genetic change, a new mechanism to defend against the new pathogen.

If defenses against new pathogens had to be acquired de novo, one would expect those developed first to be of limited effectiveness and low titer. In fact, titers of measles hemagglutinin-inhibiting antibodies in a virgin-soil group of Amerinds increased at the same time and to the same level as those of children in the nearest Brazilian city (figure 8.2; Black et al. 1969). This antibody in Amerinds was effective in protecting against measles (van Mazijk et al. 1982). Not only measles antibody but also antibody to rubella, mumps, meningococci, pneumococci, and others, all novel to Amerinds, are produced in normal titer and at the usual time after vaccination. To suppose that New World populations are at greater risk from introduced diseases because they lack an ability to mount a good immune defense is contrary to practical experience and to the prevailing theory of immunity.

The genetics of the South Amerindian population have been analyzed extensively and shown to be less variable than those of cosmopolitan

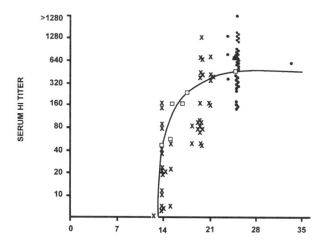

FIGURE 8.2   Measles serum antibody titers after vaccination in a virgin-soil and a neighboring urban measles-experienced population. Individual values are given for each virgin-soil vaccinee (x or o) and daily means, coupled with the curve for the urban vaccinees.

•, x Titers in individuals of a population experiencing measles virus for the first time.

❑ Mean titer for that day in previously nonimmune persons of a measles-experienced population (Marajó). The line is drawn through the latter points. Adapted from Black et al. (1969).

groups (Salzano and Callegari-Jacques 1988). There is no unusual number of deleterious genes that might make Amerinds more susceptible. Some private polymorphisms occur, that is, mutations that have not spread widely either within or beyond the population of their origin, but not more than might be expected to result from normal mutability (Neel 1973). However, there is a distinct paucity of variability in normally polymorphic genes. All South Amerinds seem to have only one of the four ABO blood types that are dominant elsewhere, namely, 0. There is nothing wrong with having the allele *ABO*0* as an individual; many of us have it, often in homozygous form, without ill effect. The unusual fact is that the South Amerinds as a population have nothing else. Neither do South Amerinds have polymorphic variability in Kell, albumin, transferrin, or several enzymic variants that commonly occur in multiple forms in Old World populations. Amerinds have only two KM and three GM alleles (Black and Pandey 1997). In the mitochondria, Amerinds have only four lineages (Bonatto and Salzano 1997), whereas cosmopolitan populations have many. This homogeneity is a normal effect of the bottlenecks through which South Amerinds have passed when they crossed the Bering Strait and the Isthmus of Panama. There has not been enough time in the 11,500 or more years that have elapsed since passage for diversity to have been regenerated by evolutionary processes. Most individual Amerind groups derive from a small number of founders and have only some of the alleles carried by the whole population.

The limited diversity exhibited by South Amerinds has not been caused only by bottlenecks. Diversity is also limited by inbreeding within a tribe and selected for by reduction of autoimmune reactions in populations that do not need a broad range of responses to fight diverse infectious agents. A new tribe is usually formed by fission of an older group along lines of kinship, or simply by a family wandering off. For some, a level of diversity is maintained by acquiring sexual partners by capture, but this process increases intertribal hostility and limits voluntary exchange. Many tribes are too small or insufficiently warlike to capture spouses. Within a tribe, inbreeding is also enhanced by a preference for uncle-niece (Wagley and Galvão 1946) and cross-cousin marriages (Riviere 1969).

With regard to the selective advantage of limited diversity, the absence of "d" from the Rh system of Amerinds means that newborn anemia is rare and seldom severe, and the restriction on immune responses imposed by limiting HLA diversity (Bhatia et al. 1995) reduces other autoimmune reactions. Asthma is one of the chief causes of death before reproductive age in developed societies, yet both it and skin sensitivities are rare in the Amerind even though IgE, an essential component of both reactions, is present at high levels (Kantor et al. 1979; Hurtado et al. 1999). South Amerinds have been able to eliminate many HLA reactions that permit production of antibody against self, such as B27 in ankylosing spondylitis, because they have not had to maintain the ability to fight the same spectrum of pathogens.

Lack of diversity in the HLA system seems to be an especially important part of the reason for susceptibility of Amerindians to introduced disease. Similar reductions of HLA diversity have been seen in other New World populations (Bhatia et al. 1995) and seems to be a distinctive feature of them. Each of the several HLA alleles is able to bind a specific amino acid sequence, and antigens attached to this sequence are then presented to either T or B lymphocytes. The spectrum of HLA types limits the spectra of antigens recognized. When the diversity of types in a village is limited, that village is also limited in the responses it can mount, even if each person individually has a normal range of responses. South Amerinds have

4 of 22 known serotypic alleles at HLA class 1 A; 6 or 7 of 34 at B; and 5 of 15 at C. Thus they only recognize 15 or 16 of the 71 serologically determined class 1 sequences, or less than one in four (Hedrick and Black 1997; Bodmer et al. 1999). Cosmopolitan populations have most of, but not all, the 71 known alleles.

Serologically determined HLA types are not the only source of variation at these loci. Sequence analyses of the genes involved indicate that several sequences may occur within one serological type (Bellich et al. 1992; Watkins et al. 1992; Marcos et al. 1999). Amerind sequences are often different from more canonical ones and react with distinct peptides, but usually only one sequence is found per serologically determined allele per tribe. Thus, sequence uniformity further decreases the number of peptides recognized. The tribes studied in this way were relatively small, and, because sequence variation is determined by recombination within a hypervariable region, the larger populations of Mexico and Peru may have greater diversity even though they have no novel serological alleles. With this diversity, larger groups would be able to recognize a greater variety of antigens, broadening, somewhat, their response capability and increasing their chance of survival.

As with other markers of heterogeneity, individual tribes have less HLA diversity than do South Amerinds as a group. The Yanomamö lack B15, a serological type common in other Amerinds (Layrisse et al. 1973). They also have a 51 percent frequency of HLA2, meaning that fully a quarter of the Yanomamö conceived have no other antigen at this locus. An extreme case of tribal restriction at HLA is represented by the Araweté, a tribe of South Pará, whose members have only three alleles at the A locus and only two at each of the B and C loci (Salzano et al. 1991). Any one person can carry two antigens at each locus, so even among the Araweté most individuals can be equipped with a normal complement of responses. A problem occurs because the spectrum of response will be the same for many other members of this tribe; thus, although individual capabilities may be normal, the tribe as a whole has a limited range of responses to microbial antigens.

Pathogen Mutability

The genetics of humans represents only one side of the coin. Infectious disease involves interaction between two genetic elements. Measles virus and most of the *resfriados* that halved the Xikrin population have RNA genomes. There is no proofreading mechanism in the replication of these viruses, and mutations occur with very high frequency. Steinauer and Holland (1987) estimated that poliovirus, another virus with an RNA genome, makes 10^{-4} changes per base per replication, an extraordinarily high rate. Some microbial sequences are essential to the organism, and microbes that have modifications in these sequences would not survive, but assuming that serologically dominant sequences are exposed to the immune system and may be mutable, it would not take many replications for any RNA virus to develop a population that avoided those sequences that are recognized by the limited HLA spectrum in an Amerind village. Such a microbial population would have a selective advantage.

Although the incoming agent may be recognized by the immune system and immunity turned on in the first infected person, its progeny will have mutations that avoid the immune response. These modified agents will soon predominate in transfer to new hosts. If these secondary hosts have the same limited capacities to respond as the first, the microbe will be preadapted, able to replicate faster and to cause more serious disease. In a virgin-soil epidemic, many people are sick at once, and new cases are likely to receive virus from several sources. If any one of these viruses is preadapted to avoid the immune response of the recipient, that virus will take off and dominate. In a cosmopolitan population, on the other hand, there are roughly a million HLA haplotypes, and it is likely that any progeny will have to adjust to a new set of immune responses when it moves from one host to an unrelated one.

The importance of this phenomenon was demonstrated in a study of measles mortality in Senegal by Garenne and Aaby (1990), who found that a person was almost four times as likely to die of measles if the virus came from a sibling than if it came off the street. Many HLA haplotypes would be represented in the village, and the chances of getting a preadapted virus off the street would be slim. A virus coming from within the family will have at least a 75 percent chance of being preadapted to one haplotype and a 25 percent chance of being adapted to both. If the parents are related, as often occurs in Africa, the chances would be higher. In terms of genetic homogeneity, a New World tribe is much more like a family than like an Old World village.

Only about half of all viruses have RNA genomes, and many infections are caused by bacteria or protozoa that use DNA as their genetic material. It has been pointed out that the increased susceptibility to imported disease is broad and includes DNA-based microbes such as smallpox. There is some proofreading of DNA genomes, whose rate of mutation is much lower than that of RNA viruses. Nevertheless, a virus with a DNA genome, or any DNA-based microbe, will multiply many times in the course of infecting a single person, and each replication brings a chance for mutation. Some more complex microorganisms have special mechanisms for avoiding the immune response, such as multiple copies of genes producing different coat antigens. The chance that DNA pathogens will be pre-adapted by their first passage in a member of a tribe to avoid a limited range of immune responses, like the RNA viruses, will be high.

The Problem of Tribal Survival

In essence, then, New World populations, whatever their location, exhibit unusual susceptibility to Old World diseases of diverse genetic composition. The explanation offered here—the ability of microorganisms to adapt to a limited immune response—would cover all New World people and diverse infectious diseases and would exclude Old World people with New World diseases. An explanation that is dependent on the novelty of the infecting agent would work in both directions; members of Old World populations would be unusually susceptible to New World diseases, but there is little evidence of that. The novelty theory is also incompatible with the resurgence of initially large New World populations, whereas, with certain assumptions, the genetic homogeneity theory becomes relevant. Most important, the novelty theory conflicts with our knowledge of the mechanism of the immune response. Genetic homogeneity of New World people makes them susceptible to a wide variety of diseases. The fact that this theory is capable of explaining most observed susceptibility does not imply that it is the only mechanism. The lack of specific genetic traits in New World people, such as the Duffy antigens and hemoglobin S that would confer specific resistance to *vivax* and *falciparum* malaria, respectively, certainly plays an additional role.

General aspects of the ethics of this understanding of Amerindian susceptibility to new diseases have been elaborated. Sentimentally, and ethically, one wants to preserve these unique people and their cultures. The theory presented here implies that acquisition, by a New World population, of Old World levels of resistance to disease still depends on mutation, a slow process, or on miscegenation, a process with serious cultural implications. One way to avoid high rates of contact-related deaths is to maintain tribal isolation and thus maintain the status quo. This would provide short-term amelioration but would block both avenues by which resistance might be gained. True isolation is also difficult to maintain in part because new diseases need not be introduced by direct contact and in part because many isolated people themselves may want to make contact. Poliomyelitis can be carried into otherwise isolated tribes by drinking water and malaria by mosquitoes. Even if such agents were controlled, it would be paternalistic to restrict the desire of tribal members for the benefits of civilization. Vaccination offers a partial solution, but the process of its delivery entails breaching isolation. Vaccines exist against many of the diseases that cause dramatic mortality in newly contacted tribes, but many other diseases that kill them are not of sufficient importance to cosmopolitan people to warrant vaccine development. To protect against these diseases, medical care would have to be provided; our repertoire of drugs can ameliorate many infections, but delivery of the drugs would further breach isolation.

North America offers a less than ideal model for solution of the problems of South America, in that most natives who survive on the northern continent have developed a reasonable level of resistance to new infections, but at a cost of high mortality and loss of cultural continuity. This resistance has been achieved largely by miscegenation, partly between tribes but especially with people from other continents. Perhaps the word "miscegenation" could be avoided and a compromise struck by mimicking the advantages of the large populations of the Andes and Central America and encouraging intermarriage between smaller South Amerindian tribes. Obviously, one cannot force two people to marry, but increasing opportunities for intertribal mixing through intertribal councils and increased use of intertribal hostels—"casas do Indio"—would further this goal. Such a process would still be accompanied by a loss of tribally distinct culture, but at least those elements common to a whole ethnic group could be maintained.

REFERENCES

Barclay, A. J. G., A. Foster, and A. Sommer. 1997. Vitamin A supplements and mortality related to measles: A randomized clinical trial. *British Medical Journal* 294: 294–296.

Bellich, M. P., J. A. Madrigal, W. H. Hildebrand, J. Zemmour, R. C. Williams, R. Luz, M. L. Petzl-Erler, and P. Parham. 1992. Unusual HLA-B alleles in two tribes of Brazilian Indians. *Nature* 357: 326–329.

Bhatia, K. K., F. L. Black, T. A. Smith, M. L. Prasad, and G. N. Koki. 1995. Class I HLA antigens in two long-separated populations, Melanesians and South Amerinds. *American Journal of Physical Anthropology* 97: 291–305.

Biggar, R .J., M. E. Taylor, J. V. Neel, B. Hjelle, P. H. Levine, F. L. Black, G. M. Shaw, P. H. Sharp, and B. H. Hahn. 1998. Genetic variants of human T-lymphotropic virus type II in American Indian groups. *Virology* 216: 165–173.

Biggar, R. J., D. Whitby, V. Marshall, A. C. Linhares, and F. L. Black. 2000. Human herpesvirus 8 in Brazilian Amerindians: A hyperendemic population with a new serotype. *Journal of Infectious Diseases* 181: 1562–1568.

Black, F. L. 1994. An explanation of the high death rates among New World peoples when in contact with Old World diseases. *Perspectives in Biology and Medicine* 37: 292–307.

———. 1997. Measles. In *Viral Infections of Humans*, 4th ed., edited by A. S. Evans and R. A. Kaslow, pp. 507–529, Plenum, New York.

Black, F. L., R. J. Biggar, R. B. Lal, A. A. Gabbai, and J. P. B. Vieira-Filho. 1996. Twenty-five years of HTLV type II follow-up with a possible case of tropical spastic paraparesis in the Kayapo, a Brazilian Indian tribe. *AIDS Research and Human Retroviruses* 12: 1623–1627.

Black, F. L., W. J. Hierholzer, F. P. Pinheiro, A. S. Evans, J. P. Woodall, E. M. Opton, J. E. Emmons, B. S. West, G. Edsall, W. G. Downs, and G. D. Wallace. 1974. Evidence for persistence of infectious agents in isolated human populations. *American Journal of Epidemiology* 100: 230–250.

Black, F. L., and D. L. Jacobson. 1986. Hepatitis A antibody in an isolated Amerindian tribe 50 years after exposure. *Journal of Medical Virology* 19: 19–22.

Black, F. L., and J. P. Pandey. 1997. Evidence for balancing at KM but not GM alleles by heterotic advantage in South Amerinds. *Human Genetics* 100: 240–244.

Black, F. L., J. P. Pandey, and R. A. Capper. 1986. Hepatitis B epidemiology and its relation to immunogenetic traits in South American Indians. *American Journal of Epidemiology* 89: 168–175.

Black, F. L., J. P. Woodall, and F. P. Pinheiro. 1969. Measles vaccine reactions in a virgin population. *American Journal of Epidemiology* 89: 168–175.

Bodmer, J. D., S. G. E. Marsh, E. D. Albert, W. F. Bodmer, R. E. Bontrop, B. Dupont, H. A. Erlich, J. A. Hansen, B. Mach, P. Parham, E. W. Petersdorf, I. Sasazuki, G. M. T. Schreuder, J. L. Strominger, A. Svejgaard, and P. Terasaki. 1999. Nomenclature for factors of the HLA system. *Tissue Antigens* 53: 407–446.

Bonatto, S. L., and F. M. Salzano. 1997. Diversity and age of the four major mtDNA haplogroups and their implication for the peopling of the New World. *American Journal of Human Genetics* 61: 1413–1423.

Brown, P., T. Tsai, and D. C. Gadjusek. 1975. Soroepidemiology of human papovaviruses: Discovery of virgin populations and some unusual patterns of antibody prevalence among remote peoples of the world. *American Journal of Epidemiology* 102: 331–340.

Causey, O. R., C. E. Causey, O. M. Maroja, and D. G. Macedo. 1961. The isolation of arboviruses, including members of two hitherto undescribed serological groups, in the Amazon region of Brazil. *American Journal of Tropical Medicine and Hygiene* 18: 227–249.

Cliff, A. D., and P. Haggett. 1985. *The Spread of Measles in Fiji and the Pacific*. Australian National University Press, Canberra.

De Freitas, R. B., M. I. S. Linhares, and A. C. Linhares. 1994. Prevalence of human herpesvirus 6 antibodies among isolated Amerindian communities in Brazil. *Transactions of the Royal Society of Tropical Medicine and Hygiene* 88: 167–169.

Dunn, F. L. 1965. On the antiquity of malaria in the Western Hemisphere. *Human Biology* 37: 385–393.

Fenn, E. A. 1999. "Pox Americana: The great North American smallpox epidemic of 1775–1783." Ph.D. diss., Yale University.

Fernandez-Cabo, M., H. T. Agostini, G. Britez, C. F. Ryschkewitsch, and G. L. Stoner. 2002. Strains of JC virus in Amerind-speakers of North America (Salish) and South America (Guarani), Na-Dene-speakers of New Mexico (Navajo) and modern Japanese suggest links through an ancestral Asian population. *American Journal of Physical Anthropology* 118: 154–168.

Frikel, P. 1963. Notas sobre a situação atual dos índios Xikrin do rio Caeteté. *Revista do Museu Paulista* 14: 145–148.

Garenne, M., and P. Aaby. 1990. Pattern of exposure and measles mortality in Senegal. *Journal of Infectious Diseases* 161: 1088–1094.

Glezen, W. P., and F. W. Denny. 1997. Parainfluenza viruses. In *Viral Infections of Humans*, 4th ed., edited by A. S. Evans and R. A. Kaslow, pp. 551–567. Plenum, New York.

Greenberg, M., O. Pelliteri, and D. T. Eisenstein. 1955. Measles encephalitis. I. Prophylactic effect of gamma globulin. *Journal of Pediatrics* 46: 642–647.

Gudnadottir, M., and F. L. Black. 1966. Measles vaccination of adults in Iceland: Response to further attenuated vaccine. *Bulletin of the World Health Organization* 35: 961–965.

Hadler, S. C., M. A. de Monzon, G. Bensabath, M. M. Duran, G. Schatz, and H. A. Fields. 1989. Epidemiology of hepatitis delta virus in less developed countries. In *Hepatitis Delta Virus*, edited by J. L. Gerin, R. H. Purcell, and M. Rizetto, pp. 21–31. Wiley-Liss, New York.

Hedrick, P., and F. L. Black. 1997. Random mating and selection in families against homozygotes for HLA in South American Indians. *Hereditas* 127: 51–58.

Hurtado, A. M., K. R. Hill, W. Rosenblatt, J. Bender, and T. Scharmen. 2002. A longitudinal study of tuberculosis outcomes among immunologically naive Ache natives of Paraguay (submitted).

Hurtado, A. M., I. A. Hurtado, R. Sapier, and K. Hill. 1999. The evolutionary ecology of childhood asthma. In *Evolutionary Medicine*, edited by W. Trevathan, E. Smith, and J. McKenna, pp. 99–134. Oxford University Press, New York.

Janeway, C. A. Jr., and P. Travers. 2001. *Immunobiology*, 5th ed. Garland, New York.

Kantor, F., F. L. Black, R. V. Lee, and F. P. Pinheiro. 1979. Active and passive wheal and flair immunity in genetically restricted Indians of the Amazon. *Federation Proceedings* 38: 931.

Layrisse, Z., M. Layrisse, T. Malavé, P. Terasaki, R. H. Ward, and J. V. Neel. 1973. Histocompatibility antigens in a genetically isolated American Indian tribe. *American Journal of Human Genetics* 25: 493–509.

Lee, R. V., F. L. Black, W. H. Hierholzer, and B. S. West. 1978. A novel pattern of treponemal antibody in isolated South American Indian populations. *American Journal of Epidemiology* 107: 47–53.

Marcos, C. Y., M. A. Fernandez-Viña, A. M. Lazaro, M. E. Moraes, and P. Stastny. 1999. Novel HLA A and B alleles in South American Indians. *Tissue Antigens* 53: 456–485.

McNeill, W. H. 1976. *Plagues and Peoples*. Doubleday, Garden City, N.Y.

Neel, J. V. 1973. "Private" genetic variants and the frequency of mutation among South American Indians. *Proceedings of the National Academy of Sciences, USA* 70: 3311–3315.

Nelson, J. D. 1996. Diphtheria. In: *Rudolf's Pediatrics*, 20th ed., edited by A. M. Rudolf, J. I. E. Hoffman, and C. D. Rudolf, pp. 567–570, Appleton and Lange, Philadelphia.

Newson, L. A. 1991. Old World epidemics in early colonial Ecuador. In *Secret Judgments of God: Old World Disease in Colonial Spanish America*, edited by N. D. Cook and W. G. Lovell, pp. 567–570. University of Oklahoma Press, Norman.

Nutels, N. 1965. Medical problems of newly contacted Indian groups. *Pan American Health Organization Scientific Publication* 165: 68–76.

Osborn, J. 1977. *Influenza in America, 1918–1976*. Prodist, New York.

Peart, A. W. F., and F. P. Nagler. 1954. Measles in the Canadian arctic. *Canadian Journal of Public Health* 45: 146–157.

Ribeiro, D. 1956. Convívio e contaminação: Efeitos dissociativos da depopulação provocada por epidemias em grupos indígenas. *Sociologia* (São Paulo) 18: 3–50.

Riviere, P. 1969. *Marriage among the Trio*. Clarendon Press, Oxford.

Robinson, L. G., F. L. Black, F. L. Lee, A. O. Sousa, S. L. Henderson, D. Danielsson, and A. J. Nahmias. 2003. Sero-anthropological patterns of herpes simplex viruses 1 and 2 in Amazon Indians (in preparation).

Rothschild, M., and H. Hobling. 2002. Pandemic TB or not TB. *American Journal of Physical Anthropology* Suppl. 34: 134.

Salo, W. L., A. C. Aufderheide, J. Buikstra, and T. A. Holcomb. 1994. Identification of *Mycobacterium tuberculosis* DNA in a pre-Columbian mummy. *Proceedings of the National Academy of Sciences, USA* 91: 2091–2094.

Salzano, F. M., F. L. Black, S. M. Callegari-Jacques, S. E. B. Santos, T. A. Weimer, M. A. Mestriner, R. R. Kubo, J. P. Pandey, and M. H. Hutz. 1991. Blood genetic systems in four Amazonian tribes. *American Journal of Physical Anthropology* 85: 51–60.

Salzano, F. M., and S. M. Callegari-Jacques. 1988. *South American Indians: A Case Study in Evolution.* Clarendon Press, Oxford.

Schwartz, A. J. F., P. A. Boyer, A. W. Zirbel, and C. J. York. 1960. Experimental vaccination against measles. I. Tests of live measles and distemper vaccine in monkeys and two human volunteers under laboratory conditions. *Journal of the American Medical Association* 173: 861–867.

Sousa, A. O., J. L. Salem, and F. K. Lee. 1997. An epidemic of tuberculosis with a high rate of tuberculin anergy among a population previously unexposed to tuberculosis, the Yanomami Indians of the Brazilian Amazon. *Proceedings of the National Academy of Sciences, USA* 94: 13227–13232.

Stannard, D. E. 1989. *Before the Horror: The Population of Hawai'i on the Eve of Western Contact.* Social Science Research Institute, University of Hawaii, Oahu.

Steinauer, D. A., and J. J. Holland. 1987. Rapid evolution of RNA viruses. *Annual Review of Microbiology* 41: 409–434.

Tierney, P. 2000. *Darkness in Eldorado: How Scientists and Journalists Devastated the Amazon.* Norton, New York.

van Mazijk, J., F. P. Pinheiro, and F. L. Black. 1982. Measles and measles vaccine in isolated Amerindian tribes. I. The 1971 Trio (Tiriyo) epidemic. *Tropical and Geographical Medicine* 34: 3–6.

Wagley, C., and E. Galvão. 1946. O parentesco Tupi-Guarani (Tupi-Guarani kinship). *Boletim do Museu Nacional, Antropologia* 6, Rio de Janeiro.

Watkins, D. L., S. N. McAdam, X. Liu, C. B. Strang, E. L. Milford, C. G. Levine, T. L. Garber, A. L. Dogon, S. A. Ghim, G. A. Troup, A. L. Hughes, and N. L. Letvin. 1992. New recombinant HLA-B alleles in a tribe of South American Indians. *Nature* 357: 329–333.

Zimmer, C. 2001. Can genes solve the syphilis mystery? *Science* 292: 1091.

9

PUBLIC HEALTH AND ADAPTIVE IMMUNITY AMONG NATIVES OF SOUTH AMERICA

A. Magdalena Hurtado, Inés Hurtado & Kim Hill

In 1977, Francis Black and colleagues wrote that "if . . . homozygosity of the HLA region is associated with enhanced susceptibility to certain infectious diseases, [South American natives] will continue to require special medical consideration by comparison with more diversified populations" (Black et al. 1977). Over two decades later we still do not know why natives tend to be more susceptible to disease than nonnatives, and in the meantime very little has been done to increase medical attention (as was suggested by Black) to those at-risk populations. To solve this problem we suggest that biomedical researchers should not just continue to study native health problems and publish numerous papers without becoming actively involved in the development and implementation of effective public health programs. They must engage in both simultaneously. There has always been a pressing need for the translation of biomedical research findings into action, but it was easily overlooked for as long as native communities did not question the activities of researchers. More recently, however, native communities have realized that after many years of research, they are still at least as bad off as they were before frequent visits from researchers, and they are now refusing to participate in research projects. It is unfortunate that most biomedical institutions and their researchers, in spite of having extensive knowledge of health problems among natives, failed to respond sooner.

In this chapter, we hypothesize that native susceptibility to infectious diseases is a multifactorial phenomenon. An explanation of that susceptibility must take into account environmental effects mediated by the immune system. More specifically, we hypothesize that the mix of T-helper cells (mainly T-helper 1 and T-helper 2 cells) that is activated among natives and nonnatives at birth, and maintained throughout life, is an essential determinant of differences in infectious disease susceptibility between these two populations. A discussion of the combined effects of genotype and environment on the differential proliferation of T-helper 1 versus 2 cells in hosts follows. After presenting these hypotheses, we discuss the epidemiology and the public health implications of this differential proliferation, which, if ignored, will continue to promote health disadvantages among natives that have persisted since the conquest. We then expand on epidemiological and public health implications with analyses of a tuberculosis epidemic among Aché foragers of eastern Paraguay within a decade of contact and the potentially disastrous effects the epidemic could have had if public health officials and researchers had not intervened quickly. Then we suggest how research on the causes of native susceptibility to infectious diseases such as tuberculosis is essential to sound public health intervention and prevention programs in native communities of South America. Finally, we conclude that the success of these types of efforts depends entirely on active community participation.

Disease Susceptibility in Native Populations

Health in Indians and Non-Indians

The biomedical literature on natives of South America is extensive. Most research has focused on genetics, to a lesser extent on social and cultural aspects of health, and to a minimal extent on immunology and public health interventions (Hurtado 2002). Although authors focus on one or another type of factor, most would probably agree that the problem of natives being more susceptible to many diseases than nonnatives is multifactorial and that applied solutions must be multifactorial as well.

In many studies, researchers report higher susceptibility to infectious (see chapter 8, this volume) and chronic (Crews and Bindon 1994, Young 1997) diseases among natives as compared with nonnatives. In addition, the few studies that rely on very large survey samples ($n > 10,000$) show that urban and rural natives report worse health than nonnatives (Psacharopoulos and Patrinos 1994). These include indicators such as having been ill in the last four weeks, a higher number of days ill or incapacitated in the last four weeks, having been sick or injured in the past thirty days, and having been kept from work over seven days because of illness (table 9.1). These statistics are particularly disturbing in light of the large number of indigenous inhabitants throughout Latin America (table 9.2), and the consistently higher levels of poverty among natives than among nonnatives in every Latin America country where this comparison has been studied (Psacharopoulos and Patrinos 1994).

The Immunology of Native Susceptibility

In the literature on South American natives, susceptibility to disease refers to a lack of resistance to communicable pathogens that are novel to these populations. Communicable pathogens are infectious agents that, along with their toxins, cause illnesses, which arise through transmission of the pathogen or its products. The transmission occurs via an infected person, animal, or inanimate reservoir to a susceptible host, either directly or indirectly through an intermediate plant or animal host, vector, or the inanimate environment (Centers for Disease Control 1994). Lack of resis-

TABLE 9.1   General Health Condition by Ethnicity

	Urban Bolivia[1]		
	Indigenous		
Characteristics	Monolingual	Bilingual	NonIndigenous
Sick or injured (in past 30 days) (percent)	38.8	20.7	14.3
Kept from work over 7 days (percent)	10.7	7	4.5

	Peru[2]	
Characteristics	Indigenous	Nonindigenous
Ill in past 4 weeks (percent)	34.1	31.4
Days ill in last 4 weeks	9.4	8.7
Days incapacitated in last 4 weeks	2.9	2.1

[1]Characteristics of the sample: $n = 37,864$; survey, Encuesta Integrada de Hogares; survey question: What language do you speak most often?; urban centers, >10,000 people.
[2]Characteristics of the sample: $n = 11,500$; survey, Encuesta Nacional de Niveles de Vida; survey question: What is your mother tongue? What language do you speak?; rural and urban populations.

Source: Patrinos and Psacharopoulos (1996).

TABLE 9.2   Estimates of Latin America's Indigenous
Population, 1980s

Country	Number of Indigenous People	Percent of Total Population
Brazil	225,000	0.2
Venezuela	150,000	0.8
Colombia	300,000	0.9
Costa Rica	29,000	0.9
Argentina	360,000	1.1
Nicaragua	48,000	1.2
Paraguay	80,000	1.9
Honduras	110,000	2.1
Panama	99,000	4.1
Chile	550,000	4.2
Mexico	12,000,000	14.2
Belize	27,000	14.7
Peru	9,100,000	40.8
Ecuador	3,100,000	43.8
Bolivia	4,150,000	56.8
Total	30,328,000	3.3

Source: Patrinos and Psacharopoulos (1996).

tance is usually measured in terms of clinical symptoms and the presence of antibodies or cells having a response to specific antigens of pathogenic agents that cause a particular infectious disease. When antibodies are present in sera, and hosts have severe clinical symptoms or die, then hosts are said to lack resistance to that pathogen.

In remote native villages of South America, without access to laboratories or medical personnel, researchers must make inferences about levels of resistance from observational data. Thus, epidemics, or the occurrence of cases of an illness or outbreak at rates higher than an expected level, are the main indicators used to assess susceptibility to disease in South American native communities (Black et al. 1977). Populations with frequent epidemics that are characterized by high attack rates, that is, many new cases of illness over a short period of time, are considered susceptible to the pathogen responsible for the illness (Centers for Disease Control 1994).

Most questions about why natives are susceptible to diseases refer exclusively to intracellular pathogens to which they became exposed at some recent time in their history (Nutels 1968; Neel 1977). This, however, should not be interpreted to mean that natives are free of diseases, or that diseases endemic to their populations do not exact important biological costs.

Hyperendemic diseases are ones that are persistently transmitted from vectors to hosts and between hosts, whereas holoendemic diseases occur early in life and affect most of the population (Centers for Disease Control 1994). The latter can be a subset of the former, but not vice versa. Native populations of South America have historically experienced both types. Some examples of hyper- and holoendemic exposure to *intracellular* pathogens identified through serological and skin test techniques include herpesvirus, Epstein-Barr virus, cytomegalovirus, treponema, streptococcus, yellow fever, Mayaro virus, *Toxoplasma*, *Leptospira*, and human T-cell lymphotropic virus type-III (HTLV-III), a retrovirus closely related to the human immunodeficiency virus (HIV) (Salzano and Callegari-Jacques 1988: 103). Multiple ectoparasites and *extracellular* pathogens of the gastrointestinal tract are also hyper- and holoendemic in native communities (mainly ectoparasites: ticks, lice, sand fleas, and botflies; helminths: *Ascaris lumbricoides, Trichuris trichiura, Ancylostoma duodenale, Strongyloides stercoralis, Enterobius vermicularis, Taenia* sp., *Hymenolepis nana, Capillaria* sp.) (Salzano and Callegari-Jacques 1988).

Thus, all explanations of why natives tend to be more susceptible to novel pathogens at contact and beyond must minimally consider immunological adaptations to native disease ecologies that include diverse endemic pathogens. The received wisdom has not done so. Instead, most researchers propose that natives are susceptible to introduced diseases that cause sudden and lethal epidemics (e.g., measles, mumps, rubeola, influenza, rotavirus, Norwalk agent, hepatitis B, malaria, tuberculosis) for two primary reasons:

1. The immunological memory hypothesis. A lack of exposure to pathogens early in life leads to an increase in susceptibility to infectious diseases later in life. Without this exposure, the immune system is not primed to mount effective responses upon subsequent exposure throughout life (Neel 1977). This "immunological memory" hypothesis suggests that after adequate exposure, natives' ability to mount an effective immune response should be equivalent to that of nonnatives; or

2. The HLA heterozygosity hypothesis. Low HLA-related heterozygosity among natives leads to a lower diversity of disease-resistant immunological phenotypes than among nonindigenous hosts (Black et al. 1977). HLA refers to the

human leukocyte antigens found in high concentrations on different types of immune cells such as T cells. These antigens are molecules on the T-cell membrane that function chiefly as binding sites for fragments of pathogenic proteins. The major histocompatibility complex (MHC) is a closely linked complex of genes that governs the production of these HLA antigens. The MHC molecules bind fragments of intracellular pathogenic proteins and display them on the cell surface for recognition by T cells (Hyde 1995). Thus, the higher the genetic heterozygosity of MHC genes, the higher the diversity that can bind to diverse proteins produced by pathogens. When compared with individuals of Caucasian descent, natives have much lower HLA heterozygosity and thus, in principle, can recognize a smaller repertoire of proteins derived from pathogens.

The HLA hypothesis suggests that even after adequate exposure to pathogens early in life, the native response will never be equivalent to that of more genetically diverse populations.

But the present literature appears to be missing a third hypothesis. Native susceptibility to infectious diseases may also be due to native adaptations to health insults that are characteristic of their social and physical ecologies, mainly, large holoendemic loads of helminths and ecto-parasites, and physical trauma and injury throughout life. These health insults are generally absent from the ecologies of Caucasian populations. Recent advances in immunology provide insight into how these two very disparate types of health insults that are prevalent in native communities shape the immune system throughout development and render it ineffective when exposed to Western, introduced pathogens.

The Th1/Th2 Hypothesis

Recent work on the interplay of T-helper 1 (Th1) and T-helper 2 (Th2) cells suggests that the balance between these two types of cells in hosts is critical to understanding the variation in resistance to a wide range of intracellular infectious pathogens between individuals and across populations (Borkow et al. 2001). We hypothesize that differences in disease susceptibility between natives and nonnatives is partly the result of large differences in the mix of Th1 and Th2 cells across these populations. The evidence suggests that natives are Th2 cell dominant, whereas nonnatives are Th1 cell dominant (Kaplan et al. 1980; Sousa et al. 1997), and Th2 cell dominance is associated with lower resistance to introduced intracellular bacteria and viruses (Borkow et al. 2001). Importantly, the mix of Th1 and Th2 cells is set in part by environmental exposures during infancy and childhood (Erb 1999). *More specifically, we propose that helminth and ecto-parasitic infection, trauma, and genetics are the three major factors responsible for a skewed Th2 response among South American natives.*

Thus, we focus not on a general view of immunological memory but on specific types of immunological memory, their relative effectiveness, and the point at which they are activated during the hosts' development, in different environments, and in populations with different T-cell-specific genotypes. Consequently, the problem of native susceptibility to disease is concerned with susceptibility at contact and susceptibility that is transmitted across generations through cultural, environmental, or genetic mechanisms. Are the mechanisms responsible for high death rates at contact the same mechanisms that keep South American native populations at a health disadvantage for many subsequent generations (Psacharopoulos and Patrinos 1994)? Here we propose a parsimonious immunological explanation that, if correct, might contribute to the efficacy of future basic and applied research models of public health interventions in native communities.

T Cells and Adaptive Immunity

T cells play an essential role in the process of adaptive immunity, which is specific to pathogens and improves through time with subsequent exposures to the same pathogens (i.e., there is immunological memory). In contrast, innate immune responses that do not involve T cells are non-specific and do not improve upon repeated exposure to infectious agents or their toxins. There are two types of adaptive immunity: humoral, which refers to immune responses to helminths and ectoparasites that are mediated primarily by antibodies with the help of T cells, and cell-mediated, which refers to responses to intracellular pathogens mediated primarily by T cells (Janeway et al. 1999).

T-cell function is regulated by highly complex genes, mainly class I and class II genes that encode the HLA-A through HLA-D transmembrane α and β chains. These chains give rise to receptors on T-cell membranes that serve as antigen recognition sites. Antigen-presenting cells process and present antigen to T cells on their cell surface in association with MHC class I or II molecules (Janeway et al. 1999).

There are at least six types of T cells: cytotoxic, enducer (Tc), suppressor (Ts), delayed-type hypersensitivity (Tdth), memory (Tm), and helper (Th). Helper-T cells are CD4+ lymphocytes that include two subsets: Th1 and Th2 cells with important humoral and cell-mediated functions (Hyde 1995).

Helper-T cells can exert their humoral and cell-mediated functions only with the assistance of cytokines. Cytokines are small proteins that act on the cell that produced them or on other nearby cells. Along with hormones and neurotransmitters, they serve as messenger protein that regulates development, tissue repair, and the immune response in all multicellular organisms. Cytokines exert their effects by activating genes in the nucleus. They do so by binding to specific receptors at the cell membrane, setting off a cascade that leads to the expression of genes that induce, enhance, or inhibit intracellular signaling pathways.

Different cytokines induce pathways that enhance some genes but not others. This difference in the effects that cytokines exert on the genes of cells determines the differentiation of Th0 cells into Th1 or Th2 cells. Th0 cells differentiate into Th1 cells through the action of interleukin-12 (IL-12), interferon gamma (IFN-γ), tumor necrosis factor beta (TNF-β), and IL-3; they differentiate into Th2 cells through the action of IL-4, IL-5, IL-6, IL-9, IL-10, and IL-13 (Janeway et al. 1999).

The cytokine profile that is evoked during an adaptive immune response is determined by (1) the types of pathogenic antigens that infect the host; for example, IFN-γ is produced early during viral infection, and IL-10 is produced early in helminth and ectoparasitic infections (Janeway et al. 1999; see figure 9.1); and (2) the amount of antigen (*antigen dose*) that a host is exposed to during a single infectious event; the larger the dose, the greater the tendency for hosts to evoke a Th2 rather than a Th1 cytokine profile (Janeway et al. 1999).

Th1/Th2 Balance and Its Ontogeny

One of the most fascinating aspects of Th1 versus Th2 differentiation is that the cytokines of each type of helper-T cell inhibit the proliferation of the other type of cell. This may be due to energetic or morbidity trade-offs, or both. The immune response is energetically constrained such that, if left unchecked, the proliferation of both types of T cells would exert considerable energetic costs on the host. Alternatively, or complementarily, simultaneous proliferation may greatly increase the risk of

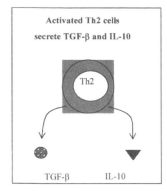
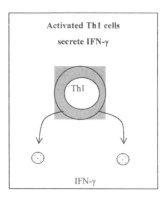
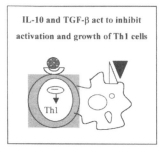
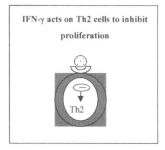

FIGURE 9.1   The two subsets of CD4+ T cells each produce cytokines that can negatively regulate the other subset. Th2 cells make IL-10, which acts on macrophages to inhibit Th1 activation, perhaps by blocking macrophage IL-12 synthesis, and TGF-β, which acts directly on the Th1 cells to inhibit their growth (left panels). Th1 cells make IFN-γ, which blocks the growth of Th2 cells (right panels). These effects allow either subset to dominate a response by suppressing outgrowth of cells of the other subset (Janeway et al. 1999: 395).

injury to the host's tissue, and possibly autoimmunity (when immune cells attack healthy host cells rather than nonself proteins, toxins, or damaged host cells).

Th2 cells release IL-10, which acts on macrophages to inhibit Th1 activation, perhaps by blocking macrophage IL-12 synthesis, and transforming growth factor beta (TGF-β) acts directly on the Th1 cells to inhibit their growth. TGF-β is a cytokine that is produced by Th2 cells. Th1 cells make IFN-γ, which blocks Th2 cell growth (Janeway et al. 1999) (see figure 9.1).

In Caucasian populations, where neonatal immune responses have been studied extensively, neonates have immune responses that are biased toward Th2 (Wilson et al. 1986) and then shifts toward Th1 responses around the age of five. This means that infants should be more susceptible to intracellular pathogens than are children. Those children who fail to make this switch produce insufficient amounts of IFN-γ when compared with children who do (Warner et al. 1994; Prescott et al. 1999). Overall, infants and young children have a much lower IFN-γ producing capacity than do adults (Holt et al. 1992). Interestingly, Th2-skewed responses comprising IL-4, IL-5, IL-6, IL-9, and IL-13 are present in almost all newborns, and IL-10 dominates their production.

Thus, it appears that a fetal immune deviation response is designed for skewness to Th2 (Prescott et al. 1998). During pregnancy, a Th2-type cytokine response is associated with improved fetal survival through inhibition of the action of Th1 or cell-mediated responses. However, a Th2-dominant response during pregnancy comes at a cost to pregnant women who although able to save the fetus, simultaneously become more susceptible to intracellular pathogens (Wegmann et al. 1993).

Tipping the Balance Later in Life

In many non-Caucasian populations, the switch from Th2 to Th1 dominance does not appear to take place early in childhood, and if it does, it is reversed later in life. Africans (Borkow et al. 2001), African-Americans (Gold et al. 1993; VonBehren et al. 1999), and South American natives tend to be more Th2 dominant than Th1 dominant (Kaplan et al. 1980; Sousa et al. 1997). In these studies, indicators used to assess humoral immunity dominance (Th2) over cell-mediated immunity (Th1) include impaired responses to delayed-type hypersensitivity tests against infectious agents, and extraordinarily high levels of antibody, mainly immunoglobulin E (IgE). Th2 cells stimulate the production of IgE more so than they do any other immunoglobulin. Thus, high IgE levels are a measure of Th2 dominance.

Here we propose that helminth and ectoparasitic infection, trauma, and genetics are the three main factors responsible for a skewed Th2 response among South American natives. The latter are hyperinfested with helminths (Salzano and Callegari-Jacques 1988) and ectoparasites (Hurtado 2002). Th2 cells are essential in defense against helminths and ectoparasites because they are responsible for the recruitment of antibodies that destroy them through various mechanisms that involve other immune cells such as macrophages, eosinophils, and mast cells. Antibodies then attack helminths and their toxins through neutralization, opsonization, or complement activation (Janeway et al. 1999). Thus, it is not surprising that populations with high parasite loads also tend to be Th2 dominant (Cooper et al. 2000).

Several studies suggest that a Th2-type cytokine response protects hosts against helminth and ectoparasitic infestation (Finkelman and Urban 2001). Among inhabitants of endemic areas who have been cured of *Schistosoma mansoni* infection, researchers found an inverse association between serum IgE levels (an indicator of IL-4 and IL-3 activity, as well as of Th2 dominance) and severity of infection (Butterworth 1998; Demeure et al. 1993). Moreover, Atkins et al. (1999) observed an inverse association between serum IgE levels and number of parasite larvae in stools, while McSharry et al. (1999) found that as IgE antibody to *Ascaris lumbricoides* antigen increased, susceptibility to *Ascaris* infection decreased. Finally, infection with human T lymphocyte virus-1, which causes an increase in IFN-γ production, a Th1 cytokine, and decreases in IL-4 and IgE levels, salient features of Th2 responses, was associated with exacerbation of *Strongyloides* infection (Robinson et al. 1994; Neva et al. 1998).

Information on the effects of a Th2-type cytokine response to ectoparasites is less extensive. However, studies on protection against ticks suggests that mast cells and IgE are actively involved. Mast-cell degranulation may increase vascular permeability, making it more difficult for ticks to locate host blood vessels (Matsuda et al. 1990).

To date, most research has focused on the effect of helminths and ectoparasites on Th2 dominance. However, a growing body of literature now suggests that physically traumatic events also raise the population of Th2 relative to Th1 cells in hosts. For example, among patients who undergo open surgery, Th1-type cytokines such as IFN-γ, TNF-α and IL-12 production decrease (Decker et al. 1996; Brune et al. 1999). Moreover, IgE levels, the main humoral component of the Th2 response, increase significantly among patients who undergo surgery, and the levels of IgE also increase significantly with surgical trauma intensity (Navarro-Zorraquino et al. 2001). In addition, other studies show that seven days after severe injury, mice shift to a Th2-type cytokine response (Mack et al. 1996), with a concomitant increased risk of death from *Candida* infection (Mack et al. 1997). This suggests that Th2 cell activity does not protect hosts from some infectious agents. As a result of burns and severe injuries, human patients, like rats, are at higher risk of infection, a major source of concern among emergency medicine surgeons (O'Sullivan et al. 1995). Apparently this is due not only to exposure of tissue to infectious agents in the environment but also to a compromised Th1-type immune response.

The mechanisms through which injury and trauma exert an influence on the differentiation of T cells are complex. Neuroendocrine mediators and prostaglandin E2 (PGE2) are two powerful endogenous suppressors of the Th1 response during healing from trauma and injury. Recent evidence show that cortisol, norepinephrine, epinephrine, histamine, and adenosine inhibit the production of IL-12 and TNF-α, that is, Th1-type cytokines, but do not dampen the production of IL-10, a Th2-type cytokine. Since a Th1 response is essential protection against intracellular infections, susceptibility increases among patients with injuries and burns. Along with neurotransmitters, PGE2 is also secreted in large quantities in response to injuries, and it too inhibits Th1-type cytokines and activates Th2 cells (Faist et al. 1996).

Taken together, the evidence leads to the conclusion that the inherent ability to overcome the complications of trauma and injury is insufficient and requires a great deal of exogenous support (Faist et al. 1996). This is also true of pregnancy in humans (see earlier text), throughout human history a time period in which women have required substantial support from spouses, family, and friends (Hurtado et al. 1992).

In spite of this endogenous insufficiency, some studies suggest that the Th2 response may be essential to the restoration of injured tissues. That is, without a Th2 response, endogenous insufficiency would be still greater. Research on mice shows that during the course of brain injury, more neurotrophic substances are secreted by astrocytes. While IL-10, a Th2-type cytokine, increased the secretion of nerve growth factor (NGF), IFN-γ and IL-2, or Th1-type cytokines, did not induce such synthesis. In fact, IFN-γ completely inhibited NGF secretion. The researchers concluded that IL-10, along with IL-4 and IL-5, provides neurotrophic support to injured tissues (Awatsuji et al. 1993; Brodie 1996). Th2-type cytokines may provide similar benefits in other tissues, which would help explain why they are favored in response to trauma and injury.

We hypothesize that trauma and injury are the main causes of morbidity and mortality among South American indigenous populations. However, relatively little is known about this aspect of native epidemiology. Through our work among Aché natives of eastern Paraguay, we have learned that before contact with outsiders, accidents and physical trauma were important causes of death. Events like being hit by lightning, snake bites, drownings, being smothered by falling trees, jaguar attacks, and falls from trees were responsible for 3, 11, 29, and 7 percent of all deaths, respectively, at ages 0–3, 4–14, 15–59, and over 60 (Hill and Hurtado 1996). These statistics underestimate the true overall level of trauma- and injury-related deaths because some deaths attributed to infection may have been caused initially by injuries resulting from an accident or intraspecific violence (e.g., club fights or domestic contests). In addition, after contact, the Aché have maintained a lifestyle that is associated with frequent injuries to tissue. They still hunt and gather, experiencing numerous cuts, large and small, on forest treks. They are also physically very active and playful in the forest or in agricultural settlements, and these activities often result in falls and injuries. Moreover, the Aché have high infestations with parasites such as lice, ticks (*Haemaphysalis longicornis*), fleas, and sand fleas, which constantly bite or burrow in the skin. Recent surveys show that injuries and skin infections caused by ectoparasites, along with helminth infestations, are some of the most frequent causes of health complaints in Aché health care posts (Hurtado 2002).

Finally, immune shifts in favor of Th2 over Th1 responses are influenced in part by genetic differences between hosts and populations. Individuals with Th2-type cytokine response are more likely to have genetic variants in the IL-4 region (C-589T) and in the IL-4 receptor gene ll-50 than are other individuals (Burchard et al. 1999; Pillary et al. 1999; Zhu et al. 2000). These genetic variants and Th2 dominant immune responses are more frequent in African-Americans than in other populations, presumably because their ancestors evolved in tropical environments with high levels of helminthic and ectoparasitic infestation (LeSoeuf et al. 2000).

In summary, there appears to be a universal tendency for Th2 dominance during infancy that is quickly reversed in some environments, and in hosts with certain genetic tendencies. We suggest that among South American natives, two environmental factors maintain Th2 dominance throughout life: helminths and/or ectoparasites, and trauma. Although breastfeeding may protect infants from helminth and ectoparasitic infestation early in life, during the weaning period between two and five years of age, exposure to helminths and ectoparasites increases manifold. In addition, during the weaning period, at which time children are walking and exploring their physical environment, they are at higher risk of frequent trauma and injuries—cuts, wounds, falls, accidents, biting insects, and ectoparasites (biting insects of all sorts). If helminths, ectoparasites, and injuries have been consistent aspects of disease ecology throughout South American history and prehistory, and Th2 cells increase survival under such circumstances, then we should expect to find a high prevalence of genes that favor the Th2 response among natives. The implication of this Th2 dominance would be decreased Th1 activity and greater susceptibility to disease than that experienced by

European populations. To adequately test this hypothesis, a great deal of research still needs to be done.

Epidemiological Implications

A Graphical Analysis

The epidemiological implications of the effects of environmental and genetic factors on the predominance of Th2- versus Th1-type cytokine responses in native versus nonnative populations are summarized in figures 9.2a. As the prevalence of macroparasites and trauma decreases, the number of Th2 cells relative to Th1 cells decreases in both populations. Similarly, as Th1 cells increase, so does resistance to infectious disease in both populations.

The figure also illustrates the hypothesized genetic interaction with this response. If the prehistorical and historical disease ecologies of nonnative and native populations differ considerably, leaving their mark on genetic selection for Th2 versus Th1 dominance (LeSouef et al. 2000), then we should expect to find that the shape and magnitude of the relationship between environmental exposure and disease-resistant phenotypes should differ between them. Thus, as the graphs show, nonnative, or populations of Caucasian descent, at all levels of exposure to macro-

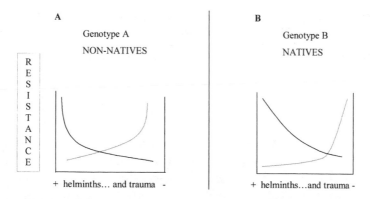

FIGURE 9.2   Graphical description of qualitative relationships between exposure to helminths, ectoparasites, and trauma and resistance to infectious diseases. The dashed line represents number of Th1 cells, an indicator of resistance to infectious disease, and the solid line represents number of Th2 cells, an indicator of diminished resistance to infectious diseases but increased resistance to helminths and ectoparasites.

parasites and trauma are at lower risk of infectious diseases because the ratio of Th1 to Th2 cells is higher. Second, the decrease in resistance to infectious diseases per unit of macroparasitic or past traumatic exposure is greater in natives than in nonnatives.

This model suggests that, even when natives are exposed to Western pathogens early in life, they would still fail to attain the same level of resistance to intracellular infection that nonnatives can mount, including intracellular agents that are endemic to the native population. This lower disease resistance is due to genetic difference in combination with greater exposure to parasites and trauma during childhood. The implications of this model are inconsistent with those derived from the immunological memory hypothesis, but they are consistent with the HLA-heterozygosity hypothesis. However, the HLA hypothesis attributes lack of resistance to low heterozygosity, whereas the Th2 hypothesis identifies other regions of immune system genes as essential determinants of resistance to infectious disease. It also points to environmental agents as essential to the expression of genetic endowment. The HLA and Th2 hypotheses could both be correct, and if so, HLA homozygosity and selection for strong Th2 responses put natives at an even greater disadvantage in their daily battle against infectious diseases.

The Example of Tuberculosis

Tuberculosis can cause the rapid demise of South American native populations as they come into contact with carriers of milder, chronic forms of the infection. There are many examples from Lowland South American groups that were never exposed to *Mycobacterium tuberculosis* until recently and that suffered tragic consequences (Chiappino 1975; Coimbra and Santos 1994; Sousa et al. 1997).

During a twenty-year-long study of demography and life history (Hill and Hurtado 1996), tuberculosis emerged as a major source of mortality and morbidity in two Aché communities of eastern Paraguay whose inhabitants had been full-time hunter-gatherers with no peaceful contact with outsiders until the late 1970s (Hurtado et al. 2002). The epidemic required urgent medical relief interventions and documentation by anthropologists and international, local, and national health officials (Hurtado et al. 2002). According to informants, the sources of tuberculosis infection in Aché communities were Avá Guaraní indigenous neighbors (contacted by Europeans in the sixteenth century) with active disease (Reed 1995).

Over the course of ten years, the Aché learned very quickly about tuberculosis, as they watched friends and relatives either die or become very ill. They had never seen tuberculosis before and had no word for the illness in their language. In 1986, they had seen a 31-year-old woman die of pulmonary tuberculosis and had watched a 60-year-old-man grow increasingly weaker and thinner as symptoms of active pulmonary disease became more severe. In 1993, a 47-year-old woman died of tuberculosis in the same community. Her death was followed in 1995 by that of a 59-year-old and a 71-year-old man, and finally, in 1996, by the deaths of two young women who were only 26 and 31 years of age. These six patients died either because they were diagnosed and treated too late or because they refused to take treatment.

In 1992, physicians working for public health nongovernmental organizations and the Ministry of Health of Paraguay diagnosed 78 cases of active tuberculosis in the two communities that we studied. The lifetime prevalence rate of active tuberculosis at that time was 18.2 percent (78 cases out of 429 individuals at risk), that is, a cumulative incidence rate of 3.7 percent per year over a period of five years (1987–1992). By 1997, six individuals with active tuberculosis had died, a case fatality rate of 7.7 percent. The treatment failure rate among those patients treated in 1992 was 34.6 percent (27 out of 78 individuals). These 27 patients remained disease free for several years but had to be treated again when they developed anew the clinical signs and symptoms of severe pulmonary tuberculosis. If these patients had not been treated again, it is very likely that most of them would have died. Thus, it is possible that close to 20 percent of the Aché population would have died of tuberculosis within a decade of first exposure if they had not been treated with antimicrobial agents.

In 1997, 31 new active cases of tuberculosis were diagnosed (6.5 percent or 31 cases out of 474 individuals who had never been diagnosed with tuberculosis). According to these population figures, the tuberculosis epidemic reached a peak in 1992, followed by a reduction in the number of new cases, probably due to prompt medical relief. In contrast, rates of infection increased from 47.7 percent (52 out of 109) in 1992 to 64.6 percent (106 of 164) in 1997. Thus, over the sample period, infection rates increased.

The rate of extrapulmonary tuberculosis was only 1.8 percent, mainly two cases of Mal de Potts (tuberculosis of the bone) out of 109 cases diagnosed between 1992 and 1997. This is probably an underestimate of the true rate, since in nonimmunocompromised individuals extrapulmonary tuberculosis is diagnosed in about 15 percent of cases in some European populations (Thornton 1995; Escobar et al. 2001) and in 9 percent of new cases in Paraguay in 1999 (Ministerio de Salud y Bienestar Social 1999). Paraguayan rural clinics and most urban hospitals are ill equipped to diagnose adequately extrapulmonary cases of tuberculosis. Thus, it is possible that extrapulmonary tuberculosis caused some deaths during the period of observation.

The study of tuberculosis in two Aché communities of eastern Paraguay (Hurtado et al. 2002) is the first to track longitudinally the inception and course of an epidemic in a group of Lowland South American natives. In fewer than fifteen years after first contact, 18 percent of the population had been diagnosed with active tuberculosis. This rate is almost twice as high as the 10 percent rate of active disease that is expected among individuals of Caucasian descent who have been infected with *M. tuberculosis*. Caucasians are expected to develop disease late in life and many years after initial infection. In addition, during the initial five years of the epidemic from 1987 to 1992, the annual cumulative incidence rate of active tuberculosis of 3.7 percent (3,700 per 100,000 individuals) observed among the Aché was eighteen-fold higher than that observed in Paraguay in 1999 (826 cases for a population of 4,585,652, or 206 active cases of tuberculosis per 100,000; Ministerio de Salud y Bienestar Social 1999). The rate observed among the Aché is also almost tenfold higher than that observed in 1993 in indigenous areas of the Paraguayan Chaco (400 cases per 100,000; Galeano Jimenez 1995), where tuberculosis has been a public health menace for decades. The true difference between rates observed among the Aché and regional or national rates is probably lower, however, because surveillance of tuberculosis cases in other native groups (population size 49,487 in 1992 [Meliá 1997: 92]) is inadequate, and these groups have the highest rates of tuberculosis in the country (Galeano Jimenez 1995).

Clearly, the Aché of Paraguay are extremely susceptible to intracellular pathogens such as *M. tuberculosis*. As has been found in other studies (Miranda 1985), more-acculturated Aché who have stronger economic and social ties to Paraguayan peasants are at higher risk of tuberculosis infection and disease than are less-acculturated Aché. In addition, susceptibility to infectious disease in general is extraordinary among the Aché. At contact, virgin-soil respiratory diseases that were never adequately diagnosed killed about 37 percent of the Aché population within two years (Hill and Hurtado 1996). Because deaths occurred within weeks or months of exposure, and within days of onset of illness, it is unlikely that the pathogenic agent that caused these contact-related respiratory illnesses was *M. tuberculosis*. However, if individuals who are susceptible to acute respiratory infections are more likely to be susceptible to tuberculosis, a survivor bias would occur and would affect the interpretation of our findings. If this bias is expressed in the current surviving study population, then the true rate of tuberculosis would have been much higher had previous respiratory epidemics failed to kill so many Aché at contact.

The observed rate of tuberculosis is nevertheless extraordinarily high. In fewer than twenty years after contact, tuberculosis could have taken the lives of close to 20 percent of the population, mostly adults of reproductive age. Medical interventions prevented what could have been an even higher death rate during the early stages of the epidemic and saved many lives among those afflicted with tuberculosis several years later. The case fatality rate among persons with active disease would have probably been much higher without medical intervention (47.4 percent; 31 recurrent cases plus 6 deaths divided by 78 cases diagnosed in 1992) than that observed (7.7 percent) if recurrent cases of tuberculosis had not been promptly treated a second time with rifampicin, isoniazid, pirazinamide or etambutol.

Humoral Immunity and Susceptibility among the Aché and the Yanomamö

A closer look at responsiveness to tuberculin challenge (i.e., whether or not an individual has a positive reaction to purified protein derivative [PPD] injection) provides insights into the uniqueness of South American Indian immune responses. Given that an individual has been exposed to tuberculosis, poor responsiveness to tuberculin challenge, measured as negative tuberculin reaction rate, indicates that the host's response to *M. tuberculosis* is ineffective. The negative tuberculin reaction rate observed among the Aché is slightly lower (68.3 percent) than is the rate reported for the Yanomamö of Brazil (76 percent; Sousa et al. 1997; Hurtado et al. 2002) and for the Chippewa of Wisconsin in the 1930s (73 percent; Indian Health Service 1930).

Because these population statistics may include individuals who may not be at risk of infection, it is useful to examine rates of responsiveness among individuals who have had active disease. Based on the principle of immunological memory (Janeway et al. 1999), those with active disease at any point in their lives should always test positive for tuberculosis infection. However, among the Aché and the Yanomamö, we find that

39 percent of individuals who currently have active disease, or who had it in the past, had negative reactions in response to PPD injection, whereas only 12 percent of Brazilian descendants of Europeans and Africans with active disease had negative reactions. In addition, whereas 59 percent of nonindigenous Brazilians have wheal sizes over fifteen millimeters, only 33 percent of the Aché and 24 percent of the Yanomamö have wheal sizes this large. This suggests that the Amerindian immune response to tuberculosis may be different from that of populations of Caucasian admixture.

High susceptibility to tuberculosis is probably common in most South American native communities. The median percentage of positive responses to tuberculin tests among adults of indigenous South American communities that have not been vaccinated with BCG at the time of the studies is 18.5 percent (range: 0–71, $n = 24$ communities; Salzano and Callegari-Jacques 1988: 93), a lower prevalence than that observed among the Aché (64.6 percent). However, several communities in the sample have prevalences close to those documented in this study, mainly the Ona and Yámana (62 percent), Alacaluf (50 percent), Oajana (42 percent), and Aymara (46 percent). These studies took place from the 1940s until the 1960s. Tragically, and possibly due to tuberculosis, the Ona became extinct in the 1940s, and the Alacaluf are close to extinction. If public health agencies have not intervened in these communities, rates of infection are likely to be much higher today.

Finally, another study from the state of Rondonia of Brazil shows that the difference in tuberculosis rates between natives and nonnatives is tenfold. The annual incidence of active tuberculosis is 1 percent per year (1,000 per 100,000 individuals) versus 0.1 percent (100 per 100,000 individuals), respectively (Escobar et al. 2001).

In summary, it is possible that high helminth and ectoparasite loads, in combination with high rates of injuries, are important environmental determinants of lack of resistance to introduced intracellular pathogens such as tuberculosis among South American natives. According to informants, helminth infection has increased, whereas trauma and injuries have decreased among the Aché since contact.

Other evidence suggests that genetic differences may interact with these environmental exposures to produce the levels of susceptibility to infectious diseases that are observed among natives. In the study conducted among the Yanomamö, Brazilians with Caucasian admixture mounted a stronger Th1 response to *M. tuberculosis*, as indicated by wheal size, than did their native neighbors (Sousa et al. 1997). Other epidemiological observations suggest that this pattern may be pervasive throughout South

America. According to a local physician, Paraguayan peasants whose settlements are contiguous to Aché villages, and who interact with the Aché frequently, had very few, if any, cases of active tuberculosis throughout the course of the epidemic described here. In the meantime, Avá (Guarani) natives, who also live close by, continue to experience extraordinarily high rates of active tuberculosis.

Without adequate studies, it is not possible to determine to what extent these differences are due to genetic predisposition or to environmental exposures. However, physicians who service native and nonnative rural populations of Paraguay report that peasants tend to have lower helminth and ectoparasite loads, as well as lower levels of injury, than do natives residing in the same region. They also report that it is puzzling that few nonnatives are diagnosed with active tuberculosis, although their exposure to natives with active disease is considerable. Both genetics and environment probably play an important role.

Public Health Implications and Conclusions

If genetic predisposition and phenotypic expression of Th2 dominance are major contributors to health problems among South American natives, then, as Black et al. (1977) have suggested, natives will continue to require different medical consideration than populations with strong Th1-type cytokine response. This is the case not only because the native HLA region is more homozygous than that of nonnatives but also because interaction effects between environmental exposures and T-cell-specific genetic tendencies produce bleak results. In order to improve native health, environmental exposures must be modified, and genetic differences must be taken into account.

In the case of the tuberculosis epidemic among the Aché, the research team was not aware of the significance of differential T-cell expression for understanding the levels of susceptibility that we observed. We were faced with a medical emergency and responded accordingly. What worked, and what was critical to Aché survival, involved an immediate response to the crisis, along with sustained surveillance and follow-up of each active case in collaboration with Aché health care workers. Moreover, in response to treatment failures, a system for daily or weekly monitoring of medication intake was implemented and was accompanied by community-wide education efforts (Hurtado et al 2002).

However, many other aspects of this intervention were, and continue to be, very deficient. Involvement of public health officials at the regional or national level proved nearly impossible, and in the few instances in which officials did become involved, they had outdated information on treatment protocols. Not a single health post in the area had sufficient tuberculosis medications to treat active cases, and natives were required to travel once a month to fill their prescriptions, although they lacked the means to do so at such regular intervals. The reason for these problems is simple: the National Commission for Tuberculosis Control of Paraguay is severely underfunded.

Given these constraints, natives cannot count on governmental agencies to take care of their health problems. Instead, community participation and commitment are essential to the effectiveness and sustainability of public health interventions. To obtain this commitment, natives need to be presented with the scientific evidence that indicates they have special health needs. Representatives of native communities should be actively involved in the implementation and evaluation of public health interventions, and in the critical assessment of the validity of the scientific evidence as new information is generated, in their own communities, nationally, or internationally. Thus, effective programs require active and ongoing collaboration between scientists and native communities.

Some of the implications of what is known about native disease patterns need to be carefully evaluated. Although Th2-type cytokine response puts individuals at risk of infectious diseases, it also protects hosts against macroparasites and against damage to tissue after injury. Consequently, the use of novel and efficacious therapies developed in Western countries that are designed to neutralize Th2 cytokines could have detrimental effects in native populations. In principle these therapies should potentiate a Th1 response. In spite of this benefit, they should not be used in populations at risk of helminth infection and ectoparasitic infestation (Finkelman and Urban 2001), or until the frequency of trauma and injuries is greatly reduced. Such therapies would increase the risk of lethal helminth infection, as well as the likelihood of development of Th1 cytokine-related inflammatory disorders, such as type 1 diabetes mellitus, multiple sclerosis, Crohn's disease, rheumatoid arthritis, and sarcoidosis (Finkelman and Urban 2001).

This raises an important problem that native communities may face in the near future. As natives spend more time in housing with permanent walls, floor, roofs, and windows that close, the rates of asthma and allergies are likely to increase (Hurtado et al. 1999). At the same time, as new treatments for asthma and allergies that involve the blockade of Th2-cytokine receptors (Zhou et al. 2001) prove to be efficacious, they will be exported to developing countries. They may eventually reach remote rural communities of South America, where the recipients of these treatments will be unaware of the potential dangers associated with their use.

These considerations raise two concerns. First, although it would appear that a decrease in Th2-type responses would be beneficial to natives, the way that this public health goal is achieved has important epidemiological consequences. If this outcome is attained primarily through sanitation and through changes in lifestyle that reduce injury and trauma, then natives can find a natural way to attain a Th2/Th1 balance that boosts the immune system's ability to fight viruses and bacterial pathogens. However, if this outcome is attained through the administration of therapeutic agents that block Th2 cytokine receptors, the consequences could be disastrous.

In evaluating their options as to which public health intervention strategies may be most beneficial to communities, natives also need to be aware of the potential costs associated with Th1 dominance. A recent study on Type I diabetes in Latin American countries found that Th1 dominance is an important risk factor, and that Amerindian genes protect against Th1 proliferation (Gorodezky et al. 1997). Many complex trade-offs will need to be assessed before an optimal path to increased native disease resistance can be found.

In summary, just as citizens of Western European nations consume information on health in order to learn about prevention and intervention options, native peoples, if given the option, are equally interested in the public health options that are available to them. Biomedical researchers and anthropologists who are knowledgeable about these options are in an excellent position to translate scientific evidence into pedagogical materials that can be understood by natives. The work is best done in collaboration with local health officials and health care workers. Perhaps then we will not have to conclude that scientific research has done little to ameliorate native health problems, while doing a great deal to improve the health of other populations around the world.

References

Atkins, N. S., D. J. Conway, J. F. Lindo, J. W. Bailey, and D. A. Bundy. 1999. L3 antigen-specific antibody isotype responses in human strongyloidiasis: Correlations with larval output. *Parasite Immunology* 21: 517–526.

Awatsuji, H., Y. Furukawa, M. Hirota, Y. Murakami, S. Nii, S. Furukawa, and K. Hayashi. 1993. Interleukin-4 and interleukin-5 as modulators of nerve-growth factor synthesis secretion in astrocytes. *Journal of Neuroscience Research* 190: 539–545.

Black, F. L., F. Pinheiro, W. Hierholzer, and R. V. Lee. 1977. Epidemiology of infectious disease: The example of measles. In *Health and Disease in Tribal Societies*, Ciba Foundation Symposium 49 (new series), pp. 115–136. Elsevier, Amsterdam.

Borkow, G., Z. Weisman, Q. Leng, M. Stein, A. Kalinkovich, D. Wolday, and Z. Bentwich, 2001. Helminth, human immunodeficiency virus and tuberculosis. *Scandinavian Journal of Infectious Diseases* 33: 568–571.

Brodie, C. 1996. Differential effects of Th1 and Th2 derived cytokines on NGF synthesis by mouse astrocytes. *FEBS Letters* 394: 117–120.

Brune, I. B., W. Wilke, T. Hensler, B. Holzmann, and J. R. Siewert. 1999. Downregulation of T helper type 1 immune response and altered pro-inflammatory and anti-inflammatory T cell cytokine balance following conventional but not laparoscopic surgery. *American Journal of Surgery* 177: 55–60.

Burchard, E. G., E. K. Silverman, L. J. Rosenwasser, C. Yandava, A. Pillari, S. T. Weiss, J. Hasday, C. M. Lilly, J. G. Ford, and J. M. Drazen. 1999. Polymorphisms of the IL-4, TNF-alpha, and Fc epsilon RI beta genes and the risk of allergic disorders in at-risk infants. *American Journal of Respiratory and Critical Care Medicine* 160: 919–922.

Butterworth, A. E. 1998. Immunological aspects of human schistosomiasis. *British Medical Bulletin* 54: 357–368.

Centers for Disease Control. 1994. *Communicable Diseases of Man.* American Public Health Association, Atlanta.

Chiappino, J. 1975. *The Brazilian Indigenous Problem and Policy: The Aripuanã Park.* International Work Group for Indigenous Affairs, Amazind/Geneva, Copenhagen.

Coimbra, C. E. A. Jr., and R. V. Santos. 1994. *Epidemiological Profile of Amazon Amerindians from Brazil, with Special Emphasis on the Xavante from Mato Grosso and on Groups from Rondonia: A Report for the World Bank.* World Bank, Washington, D.C.

Cooper, P. J., M. E. Chico, C. Sandoval, I. Espinel, A. Guevara, M. W. Kennedy, J. F. Urban Jr., G. E. Griffin, and T. B. Nutman. 2000. Human infection with *Ascaris lumbricoides* is associated with a polarized cytokine response. *Journal of Infectious Diseases* 182: 1207–1213.

Crews, D. E., and J. R. Bindon. 1994. Correlates of plasma-glucose diabetes and associated risk factors among Brazilian Yanomami, Mississippi Choctaw, and Samoan Americans. *American Journal of Human Biology* 6: 119–120.

Decker, D., M. Schondorf, F. Bidlingmaier, A. Hirner, and A. A. von Ruecker. 1996. Surgical stress induces a shift in the type-1/type-2

T-helper cell balance, suggesting down-regulation of cell-mediated and up-regulation of antibody-mediated immunity commensurate to the trauma. *Surgery* 119: 316–325.

Demeure, C. E., P. Rihet, L. Abel, M. Ouattara, A. Bourgois, and A. J. Dessein. 1993. Resistance to *Schistosoma mansoni* in humans: Influence of the IgE/IgG4 balance and IgG2 in immunity to reinfection after chemotherapy. *Journal of Infectious Diseases* 168: 1000–1008.

Erb, K. J. 1999. Atopic disorders: A default pathway in the absence of infection? *Immunology Today* 20: 317–321.

Escobar, A. L., C. E. A. Coimbra Jr., L. A. Camacho, and M. C. Portela. 2001. Tuberculose em populações indígenas de Rondônia, Amazônia, Brazil. *Cadernos de Saúde Pública* 17: 285–298.

Faist, E., C. Schinkel, and S. Zimmer. 1996. Update on the mechanisms of immune suppression of injury and immune modulation. *World Journal of Surgery* 20: 454–459.

Finkelman, F. D., and J. F. Urban Jr. 2001. The other side of the coin: The protective role of the TH2 cytokines. *Journal of Allergy and Clinical Immunology* 107: 772–780.

Galeano Jimenez, A. 1995. Tuberculosis y SIDA en el Paraguay. *Boletin de la Oficina Sanitaria del Panamá* 188: 248–253.

Gold, D. R., A. Rotnizky, A. I. Damokosh, J. H. Ware, F. E. Speizer, B. G. Ferris Jr., and D. W. Dockerv. 1993. Race and gender differences in respiratory illness prevalence and their relationship to environmental exposures in children 7 to 14 years of age. *American Review of Respiratory Disease* 203: 10–18.

Gorodezky, C., A. Olivo, C. Alaez, M. N. Vázquez, G. de la Rosa, H. Debaz, C. Robles, N. Altamirano, Z. Layrisse, P. L. Balducci, E. Domínguez, F. Herrera, S. Montagnani, B. Esparza, O. Balbas, P. Gunczler, R. Lanes, R. Amaro, R. Zaro, V. Fuenmayor, F. Montoya, C. I. Bedoya, M. C. Restrepo, A. Villegas, and J. L. Vicario. 1997. Secuencias moleculares de alto y bajo riesgo en enfermedades autoinmunes: Un análisis de la diabetes tipo I en Latinoamérica. *Gaceta Médica de México* 133: 125–132.

Hill, K., and A. M. Hurtado. 1996. *Aché Life History: The Ecology and Demography of a Foraging People.* Aldine de Gruyter, New York.

Holt, P. G., J. B. Clough, B. J. Holt, M. J. Baronhay, A. H. Rose, B. W. Robinson, and W. R. Thomas. 1992. Genetic risk for atopy is associated with delayed postnatal maturation of T-cell competence. *Clinical and Experimental Allergy* 22: 1093–1099.

Hurtado, A. M. 2002. The health status of South American natives. *American Review of Anthropology* (in preparation).

Hurtado, A., K. Hill, H. Kaplan, and I. Hurtado. 1992. Tradeoffs between female food acquisition and child care among Hiwi and Ache foragers. *Human Nature* 3: 185–216.

Hurtado, A., K. Hill, W. Rosenblatt, J. Bender, and T. Scharmen. 2003. A longitudinal study of tuberculosis outcomes among immunologically naive Aché natives of Paraguay. *American Journal of Physical Anthropology* (in press).

Hurtado, A. M., I. Hurtado, R. Sapien, and K. Hill. 1999. The evolutionary ecology of childhood asthma. In *Evolutionary Medicine*, edited by W. R. Trevathan, E. O. Smith, and J. J. McKenna, pp. 101–134. Oxford University Press, New York.

Hyde, R. M. 1995. *Immunology*. Williams and Wilkins, Media, Pa.

Indian Health Service. 1930. *Wisconsin, Indian Health Survey, Chippewa*. Wisconsin State Board of Health, Madison.

Janeway, C. A., P. Travers, M. Walport, and J. D. Capra. 1999. *Immunobiology: The Immune System in Health and Disease*. Garland, New York.

Kaplan, J. E., J. W. Larrick, J. Yost, L. Farrell, H. B. Greenberg, K. L. Hermann, A. J. Sulzer, K. W. Walls, and L. Pederson. 1980. Infectious disease patterns in the Waorani, an isolated Amerindian population. *American Journal of Tropical Medicine and Hygiene* 29: 298–312.

LeSouef, P. N., J. Goldblatt, and N. R. Lynch. 2000. Evolutionary Adaptation of Inflammatory Immune Responses in Humans. *Lancet* 356: 242–244.

Mack, V. E., M. D. McCarter, H. A. Naama, S. E. Calvano, and J. M. Daly. 1996. Dominance of T-helper 2-type cytokines after severe injury. *Archives of Surgery* 131: 1303–1308.

Mack, V. E., M. D. McCarter, H. A. Naama, S. E. Calvano, and J. M. Daly. 1997. *Candida* infection following severe trauma exacerbates Th2 cytokines and increases mortality. *Journal of Surgical Research* 69: 399–407.

Matsuda, H., N. Watanabe, Y. Kiso, S. Hirota, H. Ushio, Y. Kannan, M. Azuma, H. Koyama, and Y. Kitamura. 1990. Necessity of IgE-antibodies and mast cells for manifestation of resistance against larval *Haemaphysalis longicornis* ticks in mice. *Journal of Immunology* 144: 259–262.

McSharry, C., Y. Xia, C. V. Holland, and M. W. Kennedy. 1999. Natural immunity to *Ascaris lumbricoides* associated with immunoglobulin E antibody to ABA-1 allergen and inflammation indicators in children. *Infectious Immunology* 67: 484–489.

Meliá, B. 1997. *Demografia Histórica y Análisis de los Resultados del Censo Nacional de Población y Viviendas*. Official de Estadisticar y Censo, Gobierno del Paraguay, Asunción, Paraguay.

Ministerio de Salud y Bienestar Social. 1999. Casos nuevos de tuberculosis por grupos de edad y diagnóstico, Paraguay 1999. Asunción, Paraguay.

Miranda, J. A. N. 1985. Trabalho que vem sendo realizado pela Unidade de Atendimento Especial da Divisão Nacional de Pneumologia Sanitária nas comunidades indígenas. Communication, Symposium Alternativa para a Saúde Indígena, Rio de Janeiro, February 12–14.

Moreira-Silva, S. F., and F. E. Pereira. 2000. Intestinal nematodes, *Toxocara* infection, and pyogenic liver abscess in children: A possible association. *Journal of Tropical Pediatrics* 46: 167–172.

Navarro-Zorraquino, M., R. Lozano, J. Deus, C. Pastor, L. Larrad, E. Tejero, J. Roman, M. J. Palacios, J. Torcal, and J. C. Salinas. 2001. Determination of the immunoglobulin E postoperative variation as a measure of surgical injury. *World Journal of Surgery* 25: 585–591.

Neel, J. V. 1977. Health and disease in unacculturated Amerindian populations. In *Health in Tribal Societies*, Ciba Foundation Symposium 41 (new series), pp. 155–177. Elsevier, Amsterdam.

Neva, F. A., J. O. Filho, A. A. Gam, R. Thompson, V. Freitas, A. Melo, and E. M. Carvalho. 1998. Interferon-gamma and interleukin-4 responses in relation to serum IgE levels in persons infected with human T lymphotropic virus type I and *Strongyloides stercoralis*. *Journal of Infectious Diseases* 178: 1856–1859.

Nutels, N. 1968. Medical problems of newly contacted Indian groups. In *Biomedical Challenges Presented by the American Indian*, Pan American Health Organization Scientific Publication 165, pp. 68–76. Pan American Health Organization, Washington, D.C.

O'Sullivan, S. T., J. A. Lederer, A. F. Horgan, D. H. Chin, J. A. Mannick, and M. L. Rodrick. 1995. Major injury leads to predominance of the T helper-2 lymphocyte phenotype and diminished interleukin-12 production associated with decreased resistance to infection. *Annals of Surgery* 222: 482–490.

Patrinos, G., and H. Psacharapoulos. 1996. *Indigenous People and Poverty in Latin America*. World Bank, Washington, D.C.

Pillary, A., C. M. Lilly, C. N. Yandava, and M. J. Drazen. 1999. Association of interleukin-4 receptor alpha gene mutations and asthma (abstract). *American Journal of Respiratory and Critical Care Medicine* 159: A645.

Prescott, S. L., C. Macaubas, B. J. Holt, T. Smallacombe, R. Loh, P. D. Sly, and P. G. Holt. 1998. Transplacental priming of the human immune system to environmental allergens: Universal skewing of initial T cell responses toward the Th2 cytokine profile. *Journal of Immunology* 160: 4730–4737.

Prescott, S. L., C. Macaubas, T. Smallacombe, B. J. Holt, P. D. Sly, and P. G. Holt. 1999. Atopic children are unable to produce sufficient amounts of IFN-gamma as neonates. *Lancet* 353: 196–200.

Reed, R. K. 1995. *Prophets of Agroforestry: Guarani Communities and Commercial Gathering*. University of Texas, Austin.

Robinson, R. D., J. F. Lindo, F.A. Neva, A. A. Gam, P. Vogel, S. I. Terry, and E. S. Cooper. 1994. Immunoepidemiologic studies of *Strongyloides stercoralis* and human T lymphotropic virus type I infections in Jamaica. *Journal of Infectious Diseases* 169: 692–696.

Salzano, F. M., and S. M. Callegari-Jacques. 1988. *South American Indians: A Case Study in Evolution*. Clarendon Press, Oxford.

Sousa, A. O., J. L. Salem, and F. K. Lee. 1997. An epidemic of tuberculosis with a high rate of tuberculin anergy among a population previously unexposed to tuberculosis, the Yanomami Indians of the Brazilian Amazon. *Proceedings of the National Academy of Sciences, USA* 94: 13227–13232.

Thornton, G. F. 1995. Extra-pulmonary tuberculosis, excluding the central nervous system. In *Tuberculosis: Clinical Management and New Challenges*, edited by M. D. Rossman and R. R. MacGregor, pp. 173–184. McGraw-Hill, New York.

VonBehren, J., R. Kreutzer, and D. Smith. 1999. Asthma hospitalization trends in California, 1983–1996. *Journal of Asthma* 36: 575–582.

Warner, J. A., E. A. Miles, A. C. Jones, D. J. Quint, B. M. Colwell, and J. O. Warner. 1994. Is deficiency of interferon-gamma production by allergen triggered cord-blood cells a predictor of atopic eczema? *Clinical and Experimental Allergy* 24: 423–430.

Wegmann, T. G., H. Lin, L. Guilbert, and T. R. Mosmann. 1993. Bidirectional cytokine interactions in the maternal-fetal relationship: Is successful pregnancy a Th2 phenomenon? *Immunology Today* 14: 353–356.

Wilson, C. B., J. Westall, L. Johnston, D. B. Lewis, S. K. Dower, and A. R. Alpert. 1986. Decreased production of interferon-gamma by human neonatal cells: Intrinsic and regulatory deficiencies. *Journal of Clinical Investigation* 77: 860–867.

Young, T. K. 1997. Recent health trends in the Native American population. *Population Research and Policy Review* 16: 147–167.

Zhou, Y., M. McLane, and R. Levitt. 2001. *Th2 Cytokines and Asthma: IL-9 as a Therapeutic Target*. Magainin Pharmaceuticals, Plymouth, Pa.

Zhu, S. K., M. Chan Yeung, A. B. Becker, H. D. Ward, A. C. Ferguson, J. Manfreda, W. T. A. Watson, P. D. Pare, and A. J. Sanford. 2000. Polymorphisms of IL-4 genes. *American Journal of Respiratory and Critical Care Medicine* 161: 1655–1659.

Part IV

The Future

10

THE ETHICS OF ANTHROPOLOGICAL RESEARCH WITH REMOTE TRIBAL POPULATIONS

Kim Hill & A. Magdalena Hurtado

Fieldwork with Tribal Groups

Anthropologists have been conducting fieldwork with remote tribal populations around the world for a century and a half. Such work is critical for achieving the major goals of anthropology: the documentation of human variation and human universals and the investigation of those patterns. But the character of such research presents unique problems that are not encountered in any other kind of academic research. Specifically, we anthropologists are well educated and informed outsiders who must procure collaboration from study subjects in order to obtain useful information. Such study subjects are virtually always underinformed about the basic goals of the anthropological research conducted upon them. They are also usually underinformed about the likely economic and career gains of visiting researchers, the ethical values of the researchers' societies, and the options for recourse available to them if they are unhappy with the character of the research relationship.

In short, study subjects are unaware of their own economic bargaining position based on potential career gain to researchers, they are unaware of a commonly accepted code of human rights among Western societies that engage in anthropological research, and they do not know how to guarantee that they receive just treatment in either realm. These

conditions mean that study subjects can be easily exploited by researchers who know the limitations of their knowledge and also understand the
difficulties subjects would face if they attempted to report exploitation
to an audience of the researcher's peers. In this chapter, we address these
issues in the context of Patrick Tierney's recently published book (2000),
which examines James Neel and Napolean Chagnon's anthropological
research with the Yanomamö from the 1960s to the 1990s. Specific examples are drawn from that book to illustrate principles of modern anthropological ethics.

Principle 1: The Well-Being of the Study Population Is Our Top Priority

First and foremost, anthropologists should be aware that while we may
have multiple intellectual goals, we should all share a single priority: the
health and welfare of the study population must always take precedence
over any academic goal. And when native health and welfare are at risk,
academic goals must be temporarily or permanently abandoned.

In the book *Darkness in El Dorado*, Tierney charges that Neel and
Chagnon allowed many Yanomamö to die from a measles epidemic because they were more focused on completing a research protocol than on
treating sick people. Chagnon is additionally described as teaching his
graduate students to callously collect observational data while refusing
to intervene in health emergencies. Likewise, Tierney reports that during
the making of the Nova film *Warriors of the Amazon*, four Yanomamö in
a village of ninety people died who could have easily been saved by intervention from the film production crew. Another woman was deathly
ill and was filmed extensively while suffering, but she recovered without
assistance from the filmmakers. Although the film crew expended exor-
bitant resources on their production, they did nothing of significance to
save the Yanomamö lives that were slowly vanishing before their eyes.
They did, however, fly in an extra camera from London and stick around
long enough to film a climax to their project, the funeral pyre of a dead
women who could have been saved by their intervention. All these events,
if true, seem to represent a callous prioritizing of career gain over the lives
of the native population.

Although we believe that all field anthropologists should unwaveringly
offer critical emergency medical intervention when it can save the life of a
member of the study population, consideration of the responsibility to
safeguard the study population beyond life-and-death emergencies raises

some very complex issues. Should we expect people who visit indigenous populations to do a job (whether it be collecting data or carrying out a geological survey) to also provide free medical services to all local people they encounter when such medical service should be the responsibility of national and local government agencies? Very infrequently have field anthropologists done *everything* possible to ensure the health and welfare of their study population. Instead, we find people encompassing the entire range of assistance behavior from heroes to slackers. This is true in all different areas and theoretical camps of anthropology. Some of the fiercest critics of Chagnon cited in the Tierney book provided no medical services themselves during times when we observed them in the field with the Yanomamö (they claimed they lacked proper training). And some anthropologists have even attacked others who provide medical services, suggesting that they are meddling in traditional societies that have their own health practices. Many anthropologists make no pretense about their lack of qualifications to engage in providing medical services to their study population. Some cultural anthropologists' discussions of this issue invokes a strange double standard. They believe that it is appropriate for them to go to the field for years and provide no medical services for their study population (because they are often unqualified and have no medical skills—a conscious choice that they make before embarking for the field) but that biomedical researchers should be obligated to donate their time and resources to provide help at whatever cost to them personally. Clearly, all persons who intend to enter indigenous regions have a responsibility to get some medical training and provide whatever assistance they can.

Tierney implies that Neel should have abandoned his research (and his ethical commitment to the U.S. taxpayers who contracted him to do that research) and made vaccination of Yanomamö communities his top priority. Sometimes such action will be required in the case of extreme medical emergencies. We and our colleagues completely abandoned our research for several weeks in Manu Park in 1986 when a respiratory epidemic hit the isolated Yaminahua and Matsiguenga populations with whom we were working. We also flew in medical supplies at our own expense and against the wishes of a Peruvian anthropologist who threatened to revoke our research permit if we did so (because the supplies came from Summer Institute of Linguistics missionaries and because they "interfered with the natural population regulation mechanisms of the tribal peoples"—i.e., high death rates). In the case of the Yanomamö measles epidemic, however, it is ironic that Tierney seems prepared to attack the one person in the world who did the most to save Yanomamö lives. James Neel's actions during this epidemic saved more Yanomamö lives than those of any other person on the planet, yet he was severely criticized for not doing more. Strangely, Tierney does not lay much blame on the Catholic missionaries who had been present in the area for some time without vaccinating the Yanomamö or the Venezuelan government, which could have prevented the epidemic.

James Neel was a researcher. His job in 1968 was to collect information on human genetic diversity, mutation rates, and genetic load. He had to weigh the benefits of his research to the world community against the benefits of abandoning his research to help the Yanomamö. There are some common standards for researchers caught in such dilemmas. For example, when physicians from the U.S. Centers for Disease Control are called into a country to research an outbreak of disease, they do their job as *researchers, not clinical practitioners*. They do not and cannot get involved in treating every sick person they encounter in the field; that is the job of local and national government agencies. Most scientific researchers studying a human population or any other phenomenon (weather, geology, ecology, air pollution, cosmic radiation, etc.) would never accept the proposition that it is their responsibility to provide medical care to a population that happens to become ill in proximity to their research. Likewise, very few people believe that they are morally obligated to donate their time and resources to help every needy human group just because they receive information about the suffering of those groups (many will, however, volunteer help, just as Neel did). Why should Neel have been obligated to donate his valuable time to provide medical care to the Yanomamö but anthropologists (and anthropology students) who know today that the Yanomamö are still suffering from serious health problems are not "obligated" to give up part of their yearly income to help the Yanomamö? The health problems of South American Indians have been widely publicized in the debate about the Tierney book. Each anthropology student who bought a music CD this year despite knowing about Yanomamö suffering has essentially made the same decision of which Neel is accused, namely, placing his or her own needs over those of the Yanomamö. We think that such prioritization is human, and that to highlight such difficult human decisions uniquely in Dr. Neel's case smacks of hypocrisy.

Thus, we cannot expect that all anthropologists will give up their entire income and all their time to work unendingly to improve the health situation of remote populations. If such practices were adopted by field anthropologists, funding agencies would no longer provide research funds because no research would ever be carried out. On the other hand, basic human decency provides some guidelines for ethical behavior in times of need. It is not ethical to observe another person dying over a period of time when one has the means to save him. It is not ethical to justify a lack of intervention by claiming that "traditional outcomes" (such as high death rates from disease and accident) are favorable to "acculturation" or "modernization." And it is not ethical for a researcher to withhold assistance from an individual who has hosted and collaborated with the researcher just because that assistance might cost a little money and take up a bit of time. There are things in the world that are more valuable than a few dollars, and priorities more important than a lost day of work.

Principle 2: Research with Native Populations Requires Informed Consent

In some cases anthropological research is designed specifically to provide information that could help the study subjects themselves. In other cases the results may be important for the entire study population or ethnic group. But in most cases anthropological research is not intended to provide direct help either to the individuals studied or to their ethnic populations. Some anthropologists assert that all research done on indigenous populations that is not designed to help *those same populations* is unethical. We disagree. Research done on native peoples that can be used to help the world community at large (e.g., basic medical research) or other indigenous populations (e.g., Neel's studies on virgin-soil epidemics in Amerindians) is indeed ethical as long as (1) there is informed consent by the study subjects as to the dangers of the data collection procedures; (2) the subjects clearly understand that the research is not being carried out just to help them; (3) there is fair remuneration for the subjects' cooperation; and (4) the procedures are not potentially dangerous.

Thus, for example, we see nothing unethical about recruiting the Yanomamö as study subjects for research into childhood asthma, which is a major killer in the United States but is not present among the Yanomamö. Indeed, the lack of this medical condition among the Yanomamö is the very reason they represent a good study population for research. Likewise, contrary to Tierney's assertions, Marcel Roche's research on goiter with Yanomamö study subjects using small amounts of radioactive iodine was not unethical per se. It did, however, lack adequate informed consent and should not be repeated again under the same conditions. Roche's logic at the time was that much could be learned about goiter that would benefit numerous Venezuelans with the disease, as well as indigenous populations and probably the Yanomamö themselves in the future. His research protocol was not dangerous, but it was too complicated to be understood by the Yanomamö participants and thus was not explained to study subjects (the Yanomamö couldn't possibly understand radioactive tracers at that time). Such research should always be voluntary, informed, and appropriately rewarded. Roche's lack of informed consent was an error by today's standards, but it did not represent a callous disregard for Yanomamö welfare that would constitute blatantly unethical research behavior.

Indigenous peoples should not be indoctrinated to believe that all research done with them should benefit *only* them. They are members of a larger world community, and they should cooperate with that community for the common good, just as they expect to receive the benefits from research done on other communities (all the modern medicine they receive is based on prior research with other groups). Most natives with whom we have discussed this issue are proud to be able to contribute to the world community in this way.

Informed consent, in theory, should include not only information about the potential dangers of the research methodology but also some information concerning the larger goals of the research. While biomedical researchers sometimes fail to carry out this step adequately because of gaps in the educational background of the study population, this oversight is just as common in cultural anthropology. Explanations of cultural anthropology research goals are often totally lacking. Do cultural anthropologists fully inform subjects, for example, that their research into oppression is primarily intended to provide ammunition for ideological battles at a national or international level which may lead to political systems that the native population finds distasteful? Do they explain that research into male and female activities, or political power, may be used to advocate the imposition of sex roles that native peoples find incongruent with their own cultural values? Did Claude Lévi-Strauss fully explain to the Brazilian Indians he studied how he intended to use data on them to advocate a theory of duality about their social organization, and did his study subjects give informed consent for him to forward such a view? Yes, standards of informed consent need to be developed in anthropology, but they should be consistent across subfields and theoretical camps and regardless of whether the research is scientific or nonscientific in goals and methodology. There was no justification for Tierney singling out Neel and Chagnon as violators of modern standards of informed consent. The vast majority of anthropologists working with tribal peoples in the twentieth century have done so.

But it is also important to consider the levels of information required in order to label consent as truly "informed." We suggest that a *perfectly* informed opinion about the implications and significance of any particular research project requires one to be a specialist in that research area—something unrealistic for Yanomamö or even American populations. Instead, "informed consent" should include a complete understanding of the potential risks of a research protocol and a more general understanding of the purpose of the research. We do not believe that the Yanomamö have a full understanding of the implications of any of the anthropological or medical research conducted among them, but we do think that the general research goals can be adequately explained to them, and that perhaps knowing that is sufficient for "informed" consent.

When we consider biomedical research ethics, we must acknowledge that there is a long tradition of protective regulation in biomedical research with native subjects. Interested readers might consult such documents as the Belmont Report (1979), which has been the basis for subsequent biomedical and behavioral research protections developed in the United States (and heavily influential on institutional review board regulations), or the Australian National Guidelines for research on aboriginal populations (NHMRC 1991) and the Canadian Tri-Council Working Group on Ethics (1996), both of which concern specifically protections that should be implemented when carrying out biomedical research with native groups. These documents and the numerous discussions generated from them during recent years are far more comprehensive than the Nuremberg guidelines cited by Tierney in his criticism of scientists who did research on the Yanomamö. The Nuremberg code, which was highly restricted to deal with human experimentation, does not attempt to regulate observational research and is not relevant to epidemiological surveillance required in public health emergencies.

Basic moral principles should guide all protective measures that form a part of informed consent. First, politically vulnerable groups should not be subjected to dangerous research against their will or through the exploitation of their lack of understanding about the potential dangers of any research. Second, individual and community consent is required for most research among native populations unless that consent is withheld as a tactic to perpetuate oppression (e.g., male leaders refusing to allow research on spousal abuse). And, third, when public health is at stake, the need for informed consent and the rights of individuals to refuse to cooperate with research are balanced against the interests of a larger world community.

There is a fundamental difference between experimentation, observational research, and epidemiological surveillance in health research. Experiments require interventions on study populations and can carry some risk to the individual participant. Such research should be thoroughly regulated, with fully informed consent as the cornerstone of any protection policy. Observational research by its very nature does not put study subjects in danger because it includes no intervention (although some methods, such as blood sampling, may include a slight potential for harm). Observational biomedical research includes activities such as taking blood pressure and body temperature, recording skin lesions, collecting blood and fecal samples, and so on. It is important to realize that all advanced health treatment centers immediately begin observational research on any patient admitted to their facility, and the request for treatment at such a facility automatically implies informed consent. The same may be implied when native populations in the field approach researchers for health care.

Observational research that is not intended to provide information for clinical treatment is indeed regulated in most cases but can be conceptualized as a business agreement between those who sell information (the study subjects) and those who buy it (the researchers). As such, study populations should be allowed to decide if they want to sell their product (allow the research) and at what price. They must clearly be informed about the dangers of collaboration, but it is not clear that we should expect them to fully understand how their product (data about them) will be used. A Yanomamö artisan does not need to know what will be done with a basket she sells in order to decide whether or not to sell it. Likewise, Yanomamö study subjects do not need to understand the long-term goals of a study on salt intake and blood pressure in order to decide whether they want to "sell" data on their diet and blood pressure values. There are, of course, some commonsense limits here—buying a basket to use it in a museum display that mocks the Yanomamö people would likely change the seller's mind about whether or not to offer the product. Likewise, using Yanomamö blood pressure data to argue that they are mentally inferior would probably influence whether or not Yanomamö study subjects are willing to allow such data collection. Thus, something about *how* scientific data are used can be expected to influence native decisions about whether or not to participate in research, and this is the logic for providing basic information about the purpose of the study.

Finally, however, when data collection constitutes epidemiological surveillance critical to the public health of a wider community, there is no requirement of informed consent in most countries. For example, in the United States no informed consent is required to collect data on HIV prevalence among patients who are treated in U.S. hospitals. There is a critical public interest at stake in knowing what percentage of the population is infected with HIV, and informed consent would invalidate the accuracy of that estimate (if infected groups were more likely to refuse permission). In such cases where research represents a vital public interest, public health officials often supersede the authority of local police and military. We bring this up because some anthropologists seem unaware, for example, that under special circumstances the Yanomamö could be *required* to provide blood samples whether or not they give consent (e.g., in a hypothetical scenario where they are the seed population of an extremely infectious type of drug-resistant tuberculosis).

In between experimentation (which clearly requires informed consent) and critical public health surveillance (which does not require informed consent), there is a wide range of public health research that is more or less critical to the well-being of the world community. Indigenous populations should have a strong voice in research protocols brought to their communities and make final decisions about whether they wish to participate in any particular study. But they should also be better informed about the potential benefits of such research by people who understand them. Frankly, many anthropological activists who have attempted to sway indigenous opinion on these matters are not qualified to assess potential benefits of such research. Tierney, for example, sees little value in Roche's study of goiter and insists that such research could not foreseeably benefit the Yanomamö. We disagree. Although the Yanomamö did not have a high prevalence of goiter at the time Roche conducted his iodine tracer studies, there were indications that this problem could become more serious for them in the future. Some populations in Venezuela have a very high prevalence of goiter, and one of Roche's goals was to determine why the Yanomamö were generally unaffected by goiter in the 1960s despite having a diet with no marine source of iodine. This research carries the obvious implication that such research could later help to explain why the Yanomamö might begin to develop this health problem. The same analogy could be drawn for the study of any "disease of modern society" (asthma, cardiovascular disease, anxiety, depression, etc.) that was carried out among the Yanomamö, who may not yet be afflicted by such a condition.

Likewise, some anthropologists see little practical value to the Yanomamö of research into human genetic variation and suggest that the

Yanomamö should consider having their blood samples destroyed rather than allow them to become integrated into the human genome project. We cannot imagine more counterproductive advice. First, the samples already exist, and thus the beneficiaries do not have to undergo any new procedure in order to reap future benefits. Although some anthropologists report that the Yanomamö have a special cultural aversion to allowing their blood to be possessed by strangers, we suspect that most well-informed Yanomamö would quickly make an exception, for example, if they arrived at a hospital with a massive infection and were told that medical personnel must draw blood to measure their white blood cell count. Cultural aversions can quickly adapt when important benefits are at stake (another example might be gynecological exams, which are probably culturally inappropriate in every traditional society in the world but often later accepted because of their potential value).

The study of human genetic variation has enormous implications for understanding human disease and pathology, and this is likely to be much more critical for small inbred populations than for members of large Western state societies. This is why groups like the Ashkenazi Jews and the inhabitants of Iceland have been very proactive in encouraging genetic research on their populations. Indeed, as we move into the era of a completely mapped human genome, one of the clearest patterns to emerge is that human genetic diversity is more related to disease adaptation than any other environmental factor. The world community stands to benefit from the analyses of Yanomamö genes, but the Yanomamö themselves are likely to benefit even more. Unfortunately, Tierney and many of his most vocal allies are completely unqualified to assess the benefits to native populations of genetic research. What possible benefit could the Yanomamö gain from the destruction of this material that is already archived? We believe that the Yanomamö, instead of insisting that previously collected blood samples be destroyed, should write to the guardians of those samples, requesting that research be initiated with them that could benefit the Yanomamö community. Scientists should be co-opted as allies rather than alienated and attacked. But we must add one strong qualification to this postition: any commercial use of Yanomamö genetic material must be approved by the Yanomamö beforehand and must include fair compensation and a share of profits. Unauthorized commercial use of Yanomamö genes should immediately lead to a lawsuit.

Because of oversights in obtaining clear "informed consent" for earlier research, some anthropologists suggest that the Yanomamö should con-

sider filing lawsuits against a variety of institutions that supported previous biomedical research. We believe that such action is not in the best
interests of the Yanomamö. In these modern times of escalating tendencies to litigation over every imaginable issue, there should be commonsense moral guidelines that provide the criteria for justifiable lawsuits. They
should be filed to compensate for real damages or to punish reckless lack
of concern for potential damage caused by research procedures. We do
not believe previous Yanomamö research meets either criteria. If it does
not, such lawsuits are frivolous and send the wrong moral message to the
Yanomamö (that they should be willing to extract resources from anybody they can if they can get away with it regardless of the ethics of doing
so). Filing frivolous lawsuits against researchers or research agencies will
only lead to scientists being unwilling to return to the Yanomamö communities, something that would be disastrously counterproductive given
their growing health problems.

The Ethics of Field Methods

In his book, Tierney makes numerous additional allegations against Napoleon Chagnon that address important ethical issues. Most notable
among these are claims that Chagnon's portrayals of the Yanomamö have
harmed them, that Chagnon's gifts caused conflict, that he used unethical methods to obtain data from the Yanomamö, that he allied himself
with people who intended to harm the Yanomamö, and that he did little
to help the Yanomamö during his many years working with them. These
charges should cause all anthropologists to reflect on their own fieldwork
(even if the charges against Chagnon are false). First, it is true that anthropologists should demonstrate concern about how the information
they publish could harm or embarrass a study population. This is true even
if the ethnographic portrayals are accurate and based on scientific data.
Such concern for our study subjects does not imply that we should falsify
results to make study populations look flawless, but simply that we must
be sensitive to potential damage that can come from some types of information. For example, when we published a book about Aché demography (Hill and Hurtado 1996), we were careful not to overemphasize high
infanticide rates and promiscuity in Aché society, even though such patterns were evident in the data we collected. We did not call the Aché "the
baby killers" or "the lovemakers" on the jacket of our book, nor did we
emphasize exotic behavioral patterns in the media that might draw attention to ourselves or our book. Instead, we put the data in scientific

papers and books where they belong, and where they can be discussed by appropriately qualified scholars. Indeed, we were so concerned about the potential damage of our results that we met with several community leaders before publishing our book. Those meetings led to an agreement that we would not publish our findings in Spanish. This meant that our work was unlikely to be cited by local news media and made available to the close neighbors of the Aché, who might use it against them. Instead, the information would be read primarily by a well-educated segment of the world population that was more likely to be sympathetic to the contingencies associated with these behaviors in the first place. This is an example of the type of compromise between scientific findings and image concern that should be a part of modern anthropology.

The same commonsense rule applies to embarrassing portrayals in film, photos, or text. Nobody wants photos published of them picking their nose or engaging in many other aspects of personal hygiene, even if such activities are common behaviors that can be readily caught on camera. Drug-induced dazes and filthy faces are not "cute" to the people being portrayed even if they are "good copy" in some circles and are encouraged by book editors. Anthropologists have a responsibility to be sensitive to the feelings of their study population as well as being true to their research results. Candid photos should not be published if the subjects in such photos are offended by their publication.

Another important issue raised by Tierney's book is the extent to which gifts from anthropologists cause conflicts in the study population. Despite Tierney's assertions to the contrary, Chagnon's gifts were typical of field anthropologists at the time and not particularly excessive given the rewards that he gained from his research (it would be unethical not to share such economic success). While it is possible to exercise bad judgment in this realm, and to induce social conflict (e.g., giving massive support to one faction in a village and nothing to others), Tierney provides no compelling evidence that Chagnon made such errors. Indeed, there is no evidence that Chagnon's gift giving was any more or less destructive than Tierney's own gift giving. The solution that Tierney implies (but then later ignores when he travels in the field) is that anthropologists should provide no material goods to study populations so as not to introduce potential conflict. This solution is paternalistic and would surely be opposed by all native groups.

Tierney also asserts that Chagnon was culturally insensitive in obtaining names and genealogies and frequently tricked informants into providing information or exploited existing conflicts to get sensitive information from enemies about each other. These charges, if true, seem to imply unethical behavior. But many anthropologists use a variety of tricks to obtain desired sensitive information, and journalists are much worse. Cultural anthropologists routinely ask for information from children or neighbors and show no reluctance to delve into local gossip networks, opportunistically exploiting social divisions as a way of getting information that would not be obtained from certain individuals voluntarily. The ethics of such techniques should indeed be carefully considered by professional anthropologists. Is obtaining the dirt on an individual from his or her neighbor unethical? Is obtaining information on sexual activities through secret inquiry a legitimate activity? Does it matter whether the anthropologist has lived with the study population for one week or twenty years? Many anthropologists explicitly practice a moral double standard here. Any techniques are acceptable when they help to expose the activities of certain politically incorrect groups (e.g., oppressors) but the same methods become unethical when used to gather information on politically correct groups (e.g., the oppressed). This may seem like a reasonable moral position until we consider who decides which groups can acceptably be deceived by the investigator. Should we conclude, for example, that feminist anthropologists can lie and deceive male informants (whom they view as oppressors) to collect data, but that the same tactics of collecting data on women would be unethical?

One guideline to such issues might be that if an anthropologist angers his or her study population through the employed data collection methods, then those methods are unacceptable. Tierney asserts that Chagnon infuriated the Yanomamö by the mere act of obtaining the names of adults and dead people. But John Peters and Bruce Alberts also obtained names and genealogies of hundreds of living and dead Yanomamö, and all available evidence suggests that their study populations were quite accepting of these activities. Thus, there is little doubt that there are appropriate ways to obtain this information and that Yanomamö names are not unconditionally taboo, as Tierney asserts. The only question here is whether Chagnon employed methods unacceptable to a large fraction of the study population. Certainly any data collection can potentially anger a small faction of any study group (usually those who want to hide certain truths). But anthropologists routinely collect information that has the potential of upsetting some individuals (often those in power who do not want some of their behaviors revealed). In light of this, we need to develop specific guidelines about what kinds of data collection are acceptable and how this changes depending on who is being studied and what the relationship is between the anthropologist and the study population.

Tierney also alleges that Chagnon allied himself with disreputable characters (e.g., Cecilia Matos and Charles Brewer) who intended harm to the Yanomamö through mining activities or expropriation of native lands. It is important to remember, however, that both of these individuals were "legitimate" Venezuelan government officials at the time. And there was no evidence available to Chagnon at the time that either of these two intended to dispossess the Yanomamö of their land or carry out illegal mining on their lands. Instead, it appears that Chagnon simply associated with these people because they were powerful Venezuelans who could help him gain access to the Yanomamö at a time when it was being denied. Associating with unsavory characters seems like unwise behavior by a scientist who very badly wanted to continue his research, but no obvious ethical violations are apparent. Are anthropologists to be held responsible for all interaction with individuals in a foreign country who later on turn out to be corrupt government officials? If so, very few anthropologists who have done long-term fieldwork would ever be innocent of such misjudgment. We work with government officials because we have to, and we have no input into who those officials are. We often know little about their official activities and less about their personal lives. The alternative to "association" with such people would be a failure to obtain required permits and the subsequent inability to do anything at all to assist native populations in large areas of the world. Anthropologists should be held responsible for such "associations" only when they constitute true collaboration with individuals who knowingly carry out actions harmful to the study population.

Anthropological fieldwork ethics should also include a strong concern for the truth even when advocating native causes. Deception rarely works to help secure native rights in the long run. It is disturbing to see some anthropologists get carried away in the spirit of well-meaning action and exaggerate or distort the truth about indigenous rights issues in an attempt to stimulate more public support for their cause. We believe that such tactics are always doomed to backfire. One of the most frequent anthropological deceptions in the past has been an exaggeration of population size in census estimates. In virtually every country in South America, it is easy to find examples where the size of specific populations has been intentionally distorted by anthropologists hoping to gain more support (land, resources, etc.) for groups that are deemed worthier when they are larger. Likewise, exaggerations of indigenous suffering are not uncommon, and they cheapen the information that we have on true indigenous suffering.

In the 1980s we were extremely distressed to be forced to contradict reports about "genocide" in Paraguay because they contained blatant distortions and flat-out fabrications about the Aché situation. Photos of Aché children swimming in a river, supplied by a German anthropologist, were published in a German magazine along with a caption claiming that they were "floating corpses from a massacre." A photo of an Aché man with traditional charcoal and feather decorations was published in an edited volume on human rights with a caption claiming that it showed the torture of an Aché chief. Both of these cases involved intentional deception by well-meaning anthropologists. Our demographic research at the time revealed that earlier reports of Aché "genocide" were based on gross errors of fact. When we published accurate accounts of the Aché situation, we were visited by the director of a European indigenous rights organization, who implored me to retract the data analyses and then later threatened that we might be sued if we did not. He stated that the issue was not indigenous rights so much as the important campaign to destabilize the Stroessner military dictatorship that ruled Paraguay at the time. The Indians were just props in a larger political battle. He told us that insistence on publishing the truth was the stance of innocent fools and that there was in fact no such thing as truth, only the question of "whose side are you on?"

This was our first exposure to a shockingly amoral brand of postmodernism, and we were indeed naïve. We adhered to the principle that any cause that is truly "just" can prevail through the use of truth as a weapon. If the cause requires lying to support it, it may not be "just" after all. The director of the indigenous rights organization took the position that the battle itself was so moral that the importance of truth was superseded by the importance of winning the battle. We are not so naïve as to believe that truth is the supreme morality in the universe, and we might also willingly distort factual information if it were required to save lives. But our gut feeling is that deception is a tactic that usually produces only short-term gains in any human rights battle. When the deception is discovered, the strength of a morally correct position is heavily undermined. Anthropologists must incorporate this reality in order to engage in truly ethical advocacy.

Sharing Economic Success

Another ethical issue in the Tierney book concerns our responsibilities to provide long-term assistance to study populations and what constitutes a fair redistribution of the economic gains that come from our collaboration with anthropological study populations. When we visited the Yanomamö, we heard complaints that Chagnon had made a great deal of money off them and had done next to nothing to help them or share his economic success with them. These charges may be true, but anthropologists should not be too quick to accept all complaints they hear against their colleagues. We have heard similar complaints expressed about ourselves at our own long-term field site, despite our having provided nearly a quarter million dollars in economic aid for that population during the past twenty years and at a time cost to both of us that has been enormous. This included providing long-term medical care, paying for emergency evacuation and hospital bills, building schools, clinics, housing, water, and electrical facilities, working to obtain land titles, providing long-term employment, and designing training programs for the study group. Some members of anthropological study populations have a short memory, and at times they simply get irked at something and make irresponsible statements.

It is rumored that Chagnon made a good deal of money from books and films about the Yanomamö, and in fact his entire lifetime academic earnings can be tied directly to the Yanomamö, since his scientific reputation was based solely on his work with them. Chagnon paid the Yanomamö for data when it was collected but apparently did not provide any other assistance to the tribe. Is this a fair distribution of the gains that came from the Chagnon-Yanomamö collaboration, or is it exploitation? Although Chagnon has been singled out here for criticism, this is an issue that applies to a great number of anthropologists. We have seen numerous field anthropologists over the years work in precisely the same way as Chagnon is alleged to have done. They provide a few gifts to informants and then never again return to share out any of the economic success that comes from a career that was built on that fieldwork. Few anthropologists could withstand the scrutiny of careful investigation into their own activities on this front, including most of the anthropologists working in the twentieth century who were as famous as Chagnon.

Some anthropologists have adopted a policy of donating all proceeds from books they write to the study populations described in those books. The logic here is that we all earn enough money from our academic salaries to maintain a decent lifestyle, and therefore additional income that is produced directly through the collaborative assistance of a study population should be redistributed back to that population. Likewise, many anthropologists donate the proceeds from photo publishing rights and film sales back to their study populations. But some anthropologists go much further in providing economic assistance to their collaborators. John Peters recently suggested[1] that ethnographers should be willing to share a continual percentage of their regular academic salaries with study populations. For those of us raising families on ever-shrinking academic incomes, this might seem like a great sacrifice indeed. But we can all use our skills to provide valuable services to study populations. Anthropologists are good writers who understand the world political and economic system. Native peoples need allies with such skills. Anthropologists can form nongovernmental organizations to provide assistance, and we can write proposals to larger organizations that fund small-scale development projects. In this way we can indeed build schools, clinics, sanitation facilities, and infrastructure by obtaining funds that are not easily accessible to illiterate native populations with no understanding of the bureaucratic procedures required by funding agencies. This type of work, often carried out in our spare time, can provide much greater resources than we are likely to be able to donate on an individual level. Such activities should become standard procedure for all future anthropologists whose own careers are enhanced by the hospitality offered by any small study population.

Conclusion

Anthropological fieldwork has evolved considerably in the past century and a half. It began as an extension of colonial conquest, where native populations were coerced into providing information (sometimes at gunpoint) that could be used to successfully dominate them and entertain the conquerors. The earliest ethnographic documents, such as the reports by the Lewis and Clark expedition, or Burton and Speke's descriptions of interior Africa, were useful tools in that colonial expansion. Later ethnographic reports include volumes on topics such as "the uncivilized races of man" and "the sexual life of savages" that served as entertainment for conquering populations. Many nineteenth-century ethnographies and early twentieth-century anthropological works became best-sellers, and those who provided exotic descriptions of far-off "savage peoples" became celebrities themselves (e.g., Margaret Mead). Slowly anthropology has morphed into a field that is concerned with describing and understanding human variation; however, an exploitative character has remained. Most studies, whether cultural or biomedical, are designed mainly to serve the interests of the Western societies that produce anthropologists. Native study populations have often been exploited because they were uninformed about our goals and the rights that they can demand in the research relationship. We need to be aware of this historical background and make every attempt to move anthropology into a new era of collaboration and respect between researchers and study populations. We have suggested in this chapter some important areas where anthropological procedures can be improved in order to constitute a truly ethical enterprise with which we can be proud to be associated. Above all, however, anthropological ethics must include a healthy dose of common sense and human decency. No procedures should ever be carried out on native study populations that we would not want our own friends and family exposed to as well. The best guide to appropriate action is the simple question, Would I want somebody to conduct research on me in this fashion? Let us hope that our students will help move us in the direction of a new era in which the answer to this question is always a resounding yes.

NOTE

1. See Peters's second essay in the discussion posted on the following Web site: http://www.publicanthropology.org/.

REFERENCES

Belmont Report. 1979. *Ethical Principles and Guidelines for the Protection of Human Subjects of Research.* National Commission for the Protection of Human Subjects of Biomedical and Behavioral Research, Department of Health, Education and Welfare, Washington, D.C.

Canadian Tri-Council Working Group on Ethics. 1996. *Code of Conduct for Research Involving Humans.* Ministry of Supply and Services, Ottawa.

Hill, K., and A. M. Hurtado. 1996. *Aché Life History: The Ecology and Demography of a Foraging People.* Aldine de Gruyter, New York.

NHMRC. 1991. *Guidelines on Ethical Matters in Aboriginal and Torres Strait Islander Research.* Australia's National Health and Medical Research Council, Canberra.

Tierney, P. 2000. *Darkness in El Dorado: How Scientists and Journalists Devastated the Amazon.* Norton, New York.

11

CONCLUSIONS

A. Magdalena Hurtado & Francisco M. Salzano

The publication of Patrick Tierney's book *Darkness in El Dorado* raised the following questions: Can anthropologists continue to conduct fieldwork in native populations as they have done in the past? If not, what must be done differently? Answers to these questions must take into account several institutional constraints. First, most academic institutions train researchers to do research among natives in order to publish, not to protect their societal welfare over the short or long term except for rare exceptions. Second, even if researchers decide to provide such protection, the networks and funding necessary to do so well are very limited. Third, senseless debates over the relative virtues of scientific versus humanistic approaches have become an important aspect of anthropology (chapter 4, this volume) at a time when many disciplines recognize that the combination of the two is essential to excellent basic and applied research. It will be difficult, but not impossible, to overcome these constraints. To do so, the implementation of new guidelines for research, publication, and native health initiatives must be grounded in research, and they must be well funded.

In Pursuit of Excellence

In their pursuit of knowledge and academic excellence, anthropologists since the early 1900s have written prolifically about native culture and biology. They look for answers in native populations that industrialized populations cannot give them. Some, like Neel, try to "reconstruct the experiences of people who had been long dead, the people who had experienced the forces shaping human evolution 10,000 or more years ago" in the blood, behavior, or social organization of natives (chapter 2, this volume). Others look for opportunities to study nation-state hegemony, dialectics, folklore, language, ethnobotany, shamanism, cognitive function, female prowess, and so forth.

This raises an ethical dilemma. Native groups, one of the populations with the greatest need for helpful interventions, are also the ones that many anthropologists hope will stay pristine the longest. Coupled with this interest in "primitive man," in order to keep these populations seemingly "untarnished," anthropologists unintentionally relied on the concept of cultural relativity—that is, all human experience is equally valid, and outsiders to those situations should not intervene. This left native groups without protection against an onslaught of newly acquired microbes and long-standing local maladies.

For decades, the argument that the study of native populations is essential to our understanding of humanity has been an unquestioned premise in anthropology. The field has thrived around this premise. Some still believe that the preservation of cultural diversity through native isolation is a primary goal of anthropology. But natives throughout the globe, and in South America, have not prospered under this perspective. Instead, in many communities, the situation is progressively deteriorating (see chapters 6, 7, and 9, this volume, and later discussion in this chapter).

Someone is to blame for such negligence in the early years of anthropology. But, ultimately, the collective action of those who followed and the institutions that they have created do the greatest harm. To this day, funding agencies and academic departments reward those who collect the most data, and they have little regard for the long-term welfare of native communities. Neel summarized this well: "The real medical pay dirt comes from careful and intensive study of blood, saliva, urine, and stool specimens which we collect in the field" (chapter 2, this volume). Cultural and social anthropologists and journalists might say that the real pay dirt comes from interviews, stories, films, photos, observations, and interpretations.

Several chapters in this book are the result of years of work by researchers who for decades have sought answers in remote native populations. Our objective now is to ask what are some of the things that we have learned from these efforts, and how this knowledge can be used to promote changes leading to better protection of native societal welfare. Less is known about the epidemiology of native than nonnative populations, and governments still do not invest in epidemiological surveillance in native communities (chapter 6, this volume); nevertheless, anthropologists have a great deal of information that they can start to act on. This book has shown that the health status of South American natives is quite disheartening, and in most places it is likely to get worse (tables 11.1 and 11.2).

Health Patterns

The decline in native populations since conquest has been the subject of many books and articles (see Cook 1998 and references therein). The authors of the present book report several examples (see table 11.1). The size

TABLE 11.1 Summary of Mortality Indicators for Native South American Populations Reported in This Volume

Mortality	Reported In
Native population decline	
In Brazil: from 6,000,000 in 1500s to 300,000 in 2000s	Coimbra
Southern Kayapo: 7,000 in 1903 to 2 in the 1950s	Black
Xikrin: 164 to 80 within the decade of the 1950s	Black
Yanomamö, Niman: 125 in 1963 to 94 in 1978	Hames and Kuzara
Life expectancy at birth (years)	
Sierra Leone (lowest life expectancy in the world): 48.5 in 2000	Hurtado and Salzano
All Brazilians: 59.1 in 2000	Hurtado and Salzano
All Brazilian natives: 48.2 in 1993; 45.6 in 1994	Hurtado and Salzano
Mato Grosso do Sul natives: 37.7 in 1994	Hurtado and Salzano
Yanomamö, Xiliana: 35 years in 1980 (lowest at first contact, and after contact)	Hames and Kuzara
Yanomamö, Mavaca: 37 years in 1980	Hames and Kuzara
Aché: 45.2 (females), 50.4 (males), 1978–1993	Hurtado and Salzano
Infant mortality rate	
Xavante: 87.1/1000, all Brazilians: 31.5/1000	Coimbra
Measles mortality	
Yanomamö: 17.7% of cases, 1960s	Hames and Kuzara
Yanomamö: 30, 47, and 51% of total populations, February–March 1977	Hames and Kuzara
USA: 0.1% of 4,000,000 cases of measles die per year, 1990s	Black
Smallpox mortality	
Native Americans (Mexico-Canada): 90% of the population, 1700s	Black

TABLE 11.2   Summary of Morbidity Indicators for Native South American Populations Reported in This Volume

Morbidity	Reported In
Low weight-for-age	
Various natives: 10.5%, infants and children up to 5 years of age, 1990s	Coimbra
Anemia	
Suruí: 71% of infants and children up to 9 years of age, 1990s	Coimbra
Xavante: 74% of children between 1 and 10 years of age, 1990s	Coimbra
Yanomamö, Ocamo and Mavaca: 82–99%, all ages, 1990s	Hames and Kuzara
Yanomamö: 91%, all ages, 1990s	Hames and Kuzara
Hepatitis	
Yanomamö: 84% infected in 1986; 30% with active disease, 1980s	Hames and Kuzara
Tuberculosis	
Yanomamö: 6.4% prevalence of active disease, 1990s	Hames and Kuzara
Yanomamö: 16% prevalence of suspect cases of active disease, 1960s	Hames and Kuzara
Aché: 18.2% prevalence of active disease (1987–1992)	Hurtado et al.
Onchocerciasis	
Yanomamö, highland: 24–80% of the population infected, 1990s	Hames and Kuzara
Yanomamö, lowland: 2.4% of the population infected, 1990s	
Yanomamö, Toototobi: 61% with the disease, 1970s	Hames and Kuzara
Yanomamö, Auris: 25% with the disease, 1970s	Hames and Kuzara
Yanomamö, Surucucu: 24% with the disease, 1970s	Hames and Kuzara
Malaria	
Yanomamö, Ocamo and Mavaca: 24–80% of the population is infected, 1990s	Hames and Kuzara
Yanomamö, Coyoweteri, Matoweteri: 4.4-45.2% active disease, 1990s	Hames and Kuzara
Yanomamö, Ocamo and Mavaca: 7% with severe hemolytic anemia in 1980s	Hames and Kuzara
Yanomamö, Ocamo and Mavaca: 45–77% splenomegaly, all ages	Hames and Kuzara
Yanomamö: 39–67% infection, 1980s	Hames and Kuzara
Yanomamö: 76–89% infection, 1970s	Hames and Kuzara
Macroparasites (various)	
Yanomamö:	
Prevalence and number of parasites similar in remote and acculturating villages	Hames and Kuzara
1–92% prevalence in 1980s	Hames and Kuzara
1–10 different intestinal parasites in those infested in 1980s	Hames and Kuzara
50% infested with 4 or more parasites in 1980s	Hames and Kuzara
Nonnative neighbors:	
5% infested with 4 or more parasites in 1980s	Hames and Kuzara

TABLE 11.2   (continued)

Morbidity	Reported In
Microparasites	
Yanomamö:	
Entomoeba histolytica: 28–77% prevalence	
in 1970s; 28.5–40% in 1990s	Hames and Kuzara
Giardia lamblia: 4.20% prevalence in 1970s and 1980s	Hames and Kuzara
Toxoplasma gondii: 39% prevalence in 1990s	Hames and Kuzara
Infectious disease–related hospital visits	
Yanomamö: 2,485 in 1971 to 1,2529 in 1977	

of the current native population in Brazil is only 5 percent of its estimated size in the 1500s. This decline is the consequence of loss of land and resources and acute and chronic ongoing infections that interact with fertility as living conditions change through time (Thornton 1997). In most instances, we can only guess why, hundreds of years after conquest, groups like the Southern Kayapo lost 99.9 percent of their original population in fifty years. Likewise, the Xikrin and Yanomamö within ten and fifteen years have declined almost 50 and 25 percent, respectively (see table 11.1).

Comparisons of life expectancies and infant mortality rates across regions suggest that native groups are one of the populations at highest risk of infectious disease morbidity and mortality in the world and in history. The calculation of life expectancies at birth is influenced in large part by infant mortality rates (Zopf 1992), which were almost three times higher among the Xavante than among other Brazilians in the 1990s (see table 11.1). Life expectancy at birth is often twenty or more years lower for natives than for their nonnative neighbors, and forty or more years lower than that for Americans today (76.9 years; Centers for Disease Control 2002). Compare, for example, the life expectancy of all Brazilians (59.1 years) and the Xiliana Yanomamö (35 years) (see table 11.1). More striking, however, is the observation that the life expectancy of natives in Brazil and Venezuela is lower than that for the United States in 1900 (47.3 years; Zopf 1992) and lower than in Sierra Leone, which has the lowest reported national life expectancy in the world today. (48.5)

Infectious diseases cause much of the dreadfulness in the lives of natives. The rates of mortality among individuals with measles (i.e., the case fatality rate) were close to 20 percent during Neel's expedition made famous by Tierney (see table 11.1). This is extraordinarily high, and intolerable by Western standards, in spite of Neel's attempts to thwart the epidemic. We will never know the true population death rate due to measles at that time because, as Black (chapter 8, this volume) points out, two types of data are missing: complete censuses of communities prior to the epidemic, and total number of deaths due to measles during the epidemic. However, as Black also notes, the high mortality that the Yanomamö experienced has been observed in other isolated populations without prior exposure to measles. Thus, we can only guess that Neel's vaccination campaign must have saved many lives, because it provided immunological protection that was absent in communities prior to the vaccination. We can also only guess that the death rate was never as high as it was in unvaccinated Yanomamö villages that, ten years later, lost 30 to 50 percent of their communities to measles in two months (see table 11.1).

There have probably been other epidemics within the past two decades that have gone unnoticed because Latin American governments do not have epidemiological surveillance systems in place in native communities (chapter 6, this volume). Although there is a body of scientific literature on virgin-soil epidemics among native peoples, as well as a long period of missionary and governmental experience, individuals and organizations making contact with isolated native groups in Brazil in recent years seem as uninformed as those from a hundred years earlier. In October 1996, the National Indian Foundation of Brazil (FUNAI) planned a contact of the Korubo, one of fifty groups that still live in isolation in Brazil, which included twenty-six individuals who were not screened or quarantined, including eight journalists and their assistants, but no medical personnel. When outsiders suggested that the original team may have infected the Korubo, government officials returned to the contact site for a few hours, but without qualified medical personnel (National Geographic Society 1996). The previously contacted group turned hostile and killed a FUNAI official. It is not clear if the anger was a reaction to deaths caused by the contact crew. Many of the Korubo exposed to the 1996 contact group may have died, but to this day, there is no demographic information about the Korubo contact. This is mainly the result of a misguided FUNAI policy that keeps qualified biomedical anthropologists and medical teams out of the Korubo area while allowing a large number of unqualified personnel in. Many of those who were allowed access to the Korubo were journalists whose presence served only to disseminate information about the contact and to increase the chances of spread of diseases that were lethal to the Korubo.

Short life spans and high mortality reflect the high rates of morbidity among natives of South America. The frequencies of low weight for age, anemia, hepatitis, tuberculosis, onchocerciasis, malaria, macroparasitic infestation, and microparasitic infection are not only extremely high, with most over 50 percent, but also concurrent. Natives are infested with multiple pathogens at any one point in time, and the number of these pathogens is higher than among their nonnative neighbors who share the same environments (e.g., chapter 7, this volume).

This summary of mortality and morbidity indicators is a small sample of the wealth of information on native health and biology that anthropologists have accumulated. According to a search in PubMed (National Library of Medicine 2002), approximately 2,000 journal articles have been published since 1960 in this area. Although there is considerable room for improvement in the methods used (see chapter 6, this volume), there is enough information in our sample to conclude that the health of natives is generally marginal, and often, horrific.

Evidently, coevolutionary adaptations between hosts and pathogens over thousands of years are not sufficient protection for natives, as is true for all human populations. Although the response of Yanomamö hosts to disease-nutrition synergistic effects over millennia has probably been to sacrifice body size in favor of immune or reproductive investments (see chapter 7, this volume), disease is still unforgiving (see table 11.2).

Sometimes anthropologists make the incorrect assumption that the absence of many active cases of disease (acute episodes) in spite of massive endemic infection means that the host has "won" the battle against pathogens, and that hosts no longer incur a cost. This is wrong. It often means that the pathogen simply takes longer to kill the host (chronic states). Natives of South America may rarely die of gastrointestinal roundworm infestations, but the worm exacts physiological costs throughout their lives, including a less effective T-helper 1-cell response. Because of this, when exposed to infectious agents, the presence of the parasite increases the risk of premature death.

Causes

To reduce disparities in health between natives and nonnatives, intervention and prevention programs must build on what is known about the causes of these differences. A complex interplay between host, pathogen, and environmental factors is described in this volume.

Black summarizes the hypothesis which suggests that, due to relatively recent bottlenecks, interbreeding, and selection against autoimmunity, South American natives have low human leukocyte antigen (HLA) diversity, which limits the number of pathogenic proteins that their immune systems can recognize. Some native populations have extremely low HLA diversity, like the Awareté, who have only 10 percent of the serotypic alleles found in Western industrialized populations. Even the most genetically diverse populations have only 20 percent of the alleles found in Westerners (chapter 8, this volume).

Black reminds us that pathogens also play an important role in susceptibility to infectious diseases. In order to thrive, pathogens have to find ways to avoid the lethal attacks of immune cells and their products. The more diverse the immune defense, the harder it is for pathogens to avoid death; hosts with more diverse genes display a more diverse immune response. Thus, in genetically diverse hosts, pathogens have a harder time surviving the attacks of the immune system than in less diverse hosts.

The population-level implication of this simple logic is that in communities where genetic diversity is low within hosts and across hosts, pathogens can prosper more quickly than they would be able to in communities with high genetic diversity. In a population with high genetic diversity, more strains have to bypass various responses of the immune system, while in populations with low genetic diversity, fewer strains have to do so. Thus, in populations with low genetic diversity, the pathogen invades the host in a shorter period and is more virulent or deadly (Read 1999).

In addition, native hosts may have evolved immune adaptations that are efficient against health insults that have been prevalent in their ecologies for millennia, mainly macroparasites and trauma. But these adaptations do not allow for an efficient defense against infectious bacteria and viruses (chapter 9, this volume). The Yanomamö, like other South American natives, are less genetically diverse than their neighbors. They are also the only group to have participated in a study that measured the immune response to *Mycobacterium tuberculosis*. Sousa et al. (1997) found that their response is less efficient than the response most nonnatives mount against the mycobacterium. Environmental factors such as exposure to parasites since infancy, wounds caused by biting insects, hunting, collecting, and other work-related accidents, minimal protection from the weather, and conspecifics may favor an immune allocation that is less effective against infectious agents (chapter 9, this volume).

Regardless of what scientific studies will demonstrate about the validity of the various hypotheses presented here, it is clear that, in order to intervene effectively, several phenomena must be considered. These include the biology of hosts and pathogens and the culture, social organization, and behaviors of hosts (Read et al. 1999; Bangham et al. 1999). At present, some implications for prevention and intervention are straightforward: native communities need better sanitation, better nutrition, and greater access to health care. However, over the long term, it will be important to consider the costs and benefits of such changes. Large differences in lipid metabolism, and their genetic correlates (chapter 5, this volume), indicate that native populations of South America are at high risk of developing obesity and diabetes, although the incidence of these conditions is still negligible among them (chapter 6, this volume). With help from outsiders, South American natives need to learn from the experience of North American natives and avoid the wrath of obesity and diabetes through preventative nutritional and exercise programs that are implemented early.

In addition, increases in genetic heterozygosity, while providing some advantages, are also associated with health risks. The higher the genetic diversity, the more likely the onset of autoimmune problems (chapter 8, this volume) and conditions like Fragile X syndrome, which causes mental retardation (chapter 5, this volume).

Moreover, programs based on state-of-the-art work on social and cultural risk factors may introduce undesirable costs. For example, through time, participants in social or cultural intervention programs that increase income-earning options may purchase more Western goods such as blankets. Although they provide important protection, in some environments blankets also serve as breeding grounds for dust mites, an important contributing factor to the onset of asthma (Turner et al. 1988). As asthma rates increase, natives may be given treatments that involve the blockage of Th2 cytokine receptors; unfortunately, such interventions compromise immune responses to macroparasites that are highly prevalent in native communities (see chapter 9, this volume). Thus, these programs, while providing some benefits, also introduce risk factors that can be avoided if biological factors are taken into account from the outset.

Lack of Funding and Networks

If native populations are so important to science, why are the benefits that they receive from Western civilization so meager?

In 1987, the native population of South America was composed of 472 ethnic groups that speak 422 languages, with a total population size of 9,750,561 individuals (Lizarralde 1988). Based on cost data gathered in Aché communities from 1997 to 2002, the per capita annual cost of medications and health care workers' salaries was $9 per year ($733 per month for a population of 1,000 individuals). If we multiply $9 times 9,750,561 individuals, we obtain an estimated cost of $78,044,488 for minimal public health infrastructure and medications for all South American natives, or 9 percent of the annual budget of the World Health Organization ($842,654,000 in 1998–1999; World Health Organization 1999).

In contrast, if we assume that each year an average of 300 scholars from the United States and Europe do research on natives, and that each scholar earns on average $32,000 per year and obtains $1,000 to pay informant fees, the total funds that these scholars generate in one year will be $990,000. This is only 1.3 percent of our estimate of funds that natives would need to start making significant improvements in their health. Even if surveys show that the number of scholars who work with South American natives is much higher, there would have to be 2,363 scholars for their total earnings to match those funds required to make improvements in native health. Even then, researchers would be willing to donate only a small portion of their income after taxes, which is, after all, low for American standards. The contribution would be welcome but insufficient.

Thus, what seems to be an unfair exchange is so primarily because, for decades, anthropological institutions have not addressed the problem of dismal native health, and therefore have failed to find ways to generate funds through agencies and institutions. Neel could not have solved the numerous health problems that the Yanomamö faced at the time of his study. If the population of the Yanomamö of Venezuela had been close to 10,000 individuals in 1968, as it was in 1987 (Lizarralde 1988), he would have had to generate $90,000 per year to provide adequate help.

The problem we face as anthropologists is where to go with this information. If a group of anthropologists today decided to act on the research findings and cost data presented here, they would face a monumental task. Through numerous telephone calls, interviews, and contacts over the past five years, one of us (Hurtado) has determined that the international agencies concerned (World Health Organization, Pan American Health Organization [PAHO], Centers for Disease Control, National Science Foundation, and National Institutes of Health, Fogarty International) do not have, and do not plan to develop, any programs that would allow anthropologists to channel requests for help. Thus, it is not surprising that only 10 out of a sample of 1,824 journal articles on native biology focus on public health solutions.

The few attempts to help improve native health at the international level are frustratingly bureaucratic. Although the United Nations Economic and Social Council's Commission on Human Rights has made a start, the real impact of these efforts to date seems to be negligible. In 1996, the commission gave native peoples an opportunity to share descriptions of their health problems with an international audience (United Nations 1996a,b,c). A total of 244 indigenous peoples' organizations and nations, as well as other interested groups, attended the meeting.

At this fourteenth session of the United Nations meeting on Health and Indigenous Peoples, a representative from PAHO stated that in 1995, the agency had developed a plan of action designed to address native health needs that consisted of four areas: "1) to establish criteria, methodologies and training programs to enable the development of national and local plans, policies and processes to benefit the indigenous peoples of the country; 2) to design and mobilize resources for projects which address priority health problems and vulnerable populations; 3) to develop and strengthen traditional health systems; and 4) to identify and develop efficient mechanisms to coordinate, promote, disseminate and exchange scientific and technical information."

But, by August 2002, very little progress had been made. According to Sandra Land, PAHO's regional adviser in local health services, "health sector reform in the majority of the countries has not responded sufficiently to [native] inequalities in health" (Pan American Health Organization 2002). Unfortunately, PAHO works primarily with government agencies throughout Latin America, which are often corrupt, unstable, and uninterested in native health problems. Thus, even if PAHO's plan is implemented, it is likely that only a fraction of the funds will actually reach native communities.

Academic Battles

Although physicians have dominated the field of public health for decades, greater representation of social scientists in many areas has been achieved. Consequently, multidisciplinary research is no longer the exception. In fact, some of the most influential articles in public health are comprehensive reviews of studies on the relative importance of, and the interaction between, social, psychological, cultural, and biological predictors of adverse health outcomes (Syme and Balfour 1998).

While these originally strictly "scientific" disciplines are reaching out, some anthropologists have become increasingly antiscience. Advocates against science argue that scientific inquiry is mainly political because all knowledge is a political phenomenon (chapter 4, this volume). They generally assume that the results of scientific research are designed to support a political agenda that they find distasteful.

In the introduction to this book, we make a very different argument. We agree that the process of doing science is political in that the actions of researchers have social consequences. And, in the case of natives, these consequences may not be as beneficial as they could be because institutions that fund and support anthropological work are not more responsive to the needs of native communities that participate in research. But science can be an important positive political force because it produces verifiable facts that can be used to improve the fate of native peoples if they are collected responsibly and aimed at discoveries that have lasting and beneficial social consequences. This includes the discovery of many vaccines, antimicrobial therapies, and many other types of medical prevention and interventions, to name just a few.

We *do not* argue that the process of scientific inquiry is intrinsically tied to any particular agenda or more easily employed by one side of a political debate. To the contrary, scientific research has the potential to be the least abused method of inquiry. The process of making theoretical assumptions very explicit, measurable, and subject to change in the face of new evidence is intrinsic to the scientific method. In contrast, alternative methods tend to rely on poorly defined, culturally biased, and difficult-to-corroborate assumptions that usually include the blatant biases of their proponents (Dow 1997). All methods, scientific or otherwise, are at risk of being used deceptively, and in that sense all inquiry is at risk of political manipulation. This, however, is *extrinsic* to the methods themselves. In principle, through political processes such as democratic checks and balances, dialogue, debate, and peer review, the contributions of all inquiries should be kept honest. If we fail to reach this ideal, it is because humans use deceit to get ahead, or to build biases into all their decisions, not because the methods and data generated are flawed.

Antiscience rhetoric is enormously unproductive for anthropologists and destructive to native peoples. Rather than increasing the awareness and skills necessary to evaluate the validity of theoretical or methodological assumptions, and to be explicit about biases, students are encouraged to stay uninformed. In some anthropology departments, students are not encouraged to learn the scientific method, and as a consequence they are unable to critically assess the validity of published scientific findings (this appears to be true of some of supporters of Tierney's views). Perhaps for some questions in anthropology, antiscience debates do not raise ethical dilemmas. If a researcher chooses to interpret the texts of native stories while another prefers to calculate the frequencies of different types of utterances, the differences in the final analyses may be of little consequence to research participants.

But this is not the case in the area of health. There are many ways that one can characterize the context in which health problems arise—qualitatively or quantitatively—but there are a very few, well-established quantitative methods for measuring their rates, and these are all scientific. The validity of the measures and their analyses are constantly under scrutiny. Without this information, interventions are serendipitous, ill conceived, and wasteful. Without these measures, researchers cannot determine what factors of diverse nature—cultural, social, behavioral, and biological—contribute to poor health, to what extent, and under what conditions.

One of Tierney's most serious accusations against medical scientists and anthropologists is that they caused infectious epidemics among the Yanomamö of Venezuela over thirty years ago. Journalists are not trained to decide such things; epidemiologists are. Yet qualified epidemiologists would rarely claim to know what caused an epidemic many years after it took place, as Tierney has done, and if they were attempting to do so, they would require extensive detailed research and analyses. It is difficult enough for epidemiologists to ascertain causality in the midst of an epidemic, because the work is very time-consuming and costly, and their methodologies require experts from multiple public health disciplines who have a great deal of experience collecting and analyzing accurate and reliable quantitative data. We may never know the who, when, and how of the origins of measles and malaria epidemics in the mid-1960s in Yanomamö communities, just as we may never have definitive explanations for why a tuberculosis epidemic broke out among the Aché in the early 1990s (see chapter 9, this volume). What we do know is that the vast majority of epidemics occur when medical scientists and anthropologists are absent from these communities, that it is generally very difficult to determine their source, but that with timely scientific intervention and research, causes can be isolated and effectively addressed. It is unethical to deprive natives of these interventions, particularly when anthropologists do not do so in their own societies.

Anthropologists who promote antiscience sentiment do the greatest harm when they ally themselves with natives. Such alliances deceive natives into believing that research on native biology and health is irrelevant to their well-being. Scientists throughout the developed world promote a balanced approach that combines environmental and biological factors because it provides the "best data to make informed choices about the most effective means to prevent disease" (Willett 2002: 695). Natives should benefit equally from these opportunities.

In summary, in anthropology, several constraints act together to thwart attempts to protect societal welfare in native populations: academic institutions that reward publications and little else, the lack of funding and public health networks, and the battles that divide the field into opposing ideological camps and encourage students and faculty to do less, rather than more, multidisciplinary research.

The Future

The constraints that prevent anthropologists from protecting the societal welfare of native communities can be overcome through three simultaneous initiatives: (1) improvements in existing guidelines for research and publication; (2) implementation of those guidelines by requiring graduate students, faculty, grant reviewers, and project officers to learn and use them; and (3) setting up an Office of Native Health that puts pressure on international agencies to propose, revise, improve, and execute plans of action and funding programs.

In response to the *Darkness in El Dorado* scandal, the American Anthropological Association (AAA) has drafted a series of briefing papers that build on points presented in chapter 10, this volume: (1) on determining what constitutes a health emergency and how to respond in the course of anthropological research with human subjects (Clark and Whiteford 2002); (2) on informed consent (Clark and Kingsolver 2002); (3) on consideration of the potentially negative impact of the publication of factual data on the population studied (Watkins 2002a); (4) on remuneration to subject populations and individuals (Wagner 2002); (5) on the impact of material assistance to the study population (Luong 2002); and (6) for consideration of the ethical implications of sexual relationships between anthropologists and members of the study population (Watkins 2002b). These papers constitute the first step toward improving existing guidelines.

The first briefing paper is particularly relevant to this book. It describes four types of health emergencies addressed in the guidelines: researcher emergencies, research subject emergencies, individual health emergencies (i.e., others that affect individuals present in the community who do not participate in research), and community or population health emergencies. The authors conclude that "for health emergencies of communities or populations, researchers may arrange in advance for consultation on an as-needed basis with a health expert should a disease escalate to epidemic proportions during the course of fieldwork. Researcher interventions for health emergencies experienced by a population in the course of daily life should be undertaken with the guidance of intervention protocols and after consultation with experts."

Ironically, this is exactly what Neel did when the measles epidemic took place among the Yanomamö in 1968. He was an expert in health, and he followed intervention (specifically, immunization) protocols after consultation with experts at the Centers for Disease Control in Atlanta. Yet these behaviors did not protect him from the accusations that Tierney made, and that several anthropologists believed and supported.

Natives may not want to be bothered with research projects when they are suffering from multiple acute and chronic illnesses. They may prefer other types of interventions. For as long as this is the case and these needs are ignored, natives will continue to perceive anthropologists as self-interested, complacent, and neglectful. New guidelines must consider this.

Briefing papers of the AAA Committee on Ethics are currently under extensive revision, and anyone interested is welcome to submit comments to Dr. Joe Watkins, the chair of the committee. Once the guidelines are improved and agreed upon, the process of implementation will be critical.

When and how will this implementation take place? Perhaps the AAA, in collaboration with associations of anthropologists or departments of anthropology in Latin American countries, could set up an office that would coordinate national and international initiatives to ensure the dissemination of guidelines, and the funding necessary to enforce them. The office could summarize information on native biology and health that can serve as justification for requests for funding and training programs from the World Health Organization, the Pan American Health Organization, the Centers for Disease Control, the National Science Foundation, the National Institutes of Health, Fogarty International, and departments of anthropology and public health. These programs, in turn, should involve both native populations and government indigenous affairs agencies in Latin American countries through multidisciplinary collaborations. Partnerships between native communities, academic institutions, government officials, and international agencies will be key to the development of sustainable public health programs in native communities of South America (chapter 6, this volume).

These types of plans may begin to generate hope, optimism, and collaborations and to soften barriers between subfields in anthropology. Through concrete actions, anthropologists will find it easier to leave be-

hind the darkness of Tierney's El Dorado for the sake of future generations of students and natives throughout the world.

REFERENCES

Bangham, C., R. Anderson, F. Baquero, R. Bax, I. Hastings, J. Koella, M.
Lipsitch, A. McLean, T. Smith, F. Taddei, and B. Levin. 1999. Evolution
of infectious diseases: The impact of vaccines, drugs, and social factors.
In *Evolution in Health and Disease*, edited by S. C. Sterna, pp. 152–160.
Oxford University Press, New York.

Castañeda, N., and C. I. Ávila. 2002. Venezuela: Health and Gender. Frente
Continental de Mujeres/CONG of M/CEM-UCV. Caracas, Venezuela.
Available at http://www.socwatch.org.uy/1998/english/reports/
venezuela.htm.

Centers for Disease Control. 2002. National Center for Health Statistics,
Fast Facts from A to Z. Life Expectancy. Available at http://www.cdc.gov/
nchs/fastats/lifexpec.htm.

Clark, L., and A. Kingsolver. 2002. American Anthropological Association.
Ethics Committee Briefing Papers. Available at http://www.aaanet.org/
committees/ethics/bp5.html.

Clark, L., and L. Whiteford. 2002. American Anthropological Association.
Ethics Committee Briefing Papers. Available at http://www.aaanet.org/
committees/ethics/bp1.html.

Cook, N. D. 1998. *Born to Die: Disease and New World Conquest, 1492–1650*.
Cambridge University Press, New York.

Dow, J. W. 1997. How cultural anthropology contributes to culture: the
scientific method in late twentieth century cultural anthropology.
Conference Proceedings. *Science in Anthropology: Late Twentieth Century
Debates*. Seventy-fourth Annual Meeting of the Central States Anthropological Society.

Lizarralde, M. 1988. Indice y mapa de grupos ethnolinguisticos autoctonos
de America del Sur. *Antropologica. Suplemento No. 5*. Instituto Caribe de
Antropología y Sociología, Fundación La Salle de Ciencias Naturales,
Caracas, Venezuela.

Luong, H. 2002. American Anthropological Association. Ethics Committee
Briefing Papers. Available at http://www.aaanet.org/committees/ethics/
bp3.html.

National Geographic Society. 1996. Korubo Expedition Contact. Expedition
Chief Sydney Possuelo meets the Korubo at Last. Available athttp://
www.national geographic.com/features/96/contact.

National Library of Medicine. 2002. Pub Med/Medline. Electronic database of journal articles. National Institutes of Health, Washington, D.C. Available at http://www.ncbi.nlm.nih.gov/entrez/query.fcgi.

Pan American Health Organization. 2002. Health of indigenous people: A challenge for public health. Centennial News and Information. Press information. August 15. Available at http://www.paho.org/English/DPI/100/100feature32.html.

Salzano, F. M., and S. M. Callegari-Jacques. 1988. *South American Indians: A Case Study in Evolution.* Clarendon Press, Oxford.

Sousa, A. O., J. L. Salem, and F. K. Lee. 1997. An epidemic of tuberculosis with a high rate of tuberculin anergy among a population previously unexposed to tuberculosis, the Yanomami Indians of the Brazilian Amazon. *Proceedings of the National Academy of Sciences, USA* 94: 13227–13232.

Syme, L. S., and J. L. Balfour. 1998. Social determinants of disease. In *Maxcy-Rosenau Public Health and Preventative Medicine*, 12th ed., edited by J. M. Last, pp. 795–810. Appleton-Century Crofts, New York.

Thornton, R. 1997. Aboriginal North American population and rates of decline, ca. A.D. 1500–1900. *Current Anthropology* 38: 310–315.

Turner, K. J., G. A. Stewart, A. J. Woolcok, W. Green, and M. P. Alpers. 1988. Relationship between mite densities and the prevalence of asthma: Comparative studies in two populations in the Eastern Highlands of Papua New Guinea. *Clinical Allergy* 18: 331–340.

United Nations. 1996a. Discrimination against Indigenous Peoples. Report of the Working Group on Indigenous Populations on its fourteenth session. United Nations, Economic and Social Council, Fourteenth Session, Document REPORT 14.TXT. Item 14.

———. 1996b. Review of developments pertaining to the promotion and protection of human rights and fundamental freedoms of indigenous peoples: Health and indigenous peoples. Addendum. Indigenous Missionary Council. United Nations, Economic and Social Council, Fourteenth Session, Document IMC-96-TXT. Item 5.

———. 1996c. Review of developments pertaining to the promotion and protection of human rights and fundamental freedoms of indigenous peoples: Health and indigenous peoples. Information received from indigenous peoples and non-governmental organizations. United Nations, Economic and Social Council, Fourteenth Session, Document 96-16746.TXT. Item 5.

Wagner, G. 2002. American Anthropological Association. Ethics Committee Briefing Papers. Available at http://www.aaanet.org/committees/ethics/bp2.html.

Watkins, J. 2002a. American Anthropological Association. Ethics Committee Briefing Papers. Available at http://www.aaanet.org/committees/
ethics/bp4.html.

————. 2002b. American Anthropological Association. Ethics Committee
Briefing Papers. Available at http://www.aaanet.org/committees/ethics/
bp6.html.

Willet, W. C. 2002. Balancing life-style and genomics research for disease
prevention. *Science* 296: 695–698.

World Health Organization. 1999. Proposed budget 2000–2001. Executive
Board 103rd Session. Agenda Item 5. EB103/INF.DOC./5.

Zopf, P. E. 1992. *Mortality Patterns and Trends in the United States.* Green-
wood Press, Westport, Conn.

INDEX